SINNERS? SCROUNGERS?

'...a work that should make readers cheer, fume with rage and on a couple of occasions laugh out loud...a valuable study.'

Mary Evans, *Times Higher Education*

'provides a series of painful snapshots of how difficult life was in this period for many unmarried mothers and their children...Poverty, rather than motherhood per se, emerges as the real social evil here'

Emily Wilson, *Times Literary Supplement*

'This scholarly book will fascinate readers curious both about the lives of unmarried mothers and their children, and about family life and community networks more generally.'

Joanna Bourke, *BBC History Magazine*

'For anyone interested in the history of the phenomenon of unmarried motherhood, the changes to the situation of the families concerned, the expansion of welfare provision and the role of the National Council in providing and lobbying for their welfare, this is an invaluable book.'

Tina Haux, *Journal of Social Policy*

Sinners?
Scroungers? Saints?

*Unmarried Motherhood
in Twentieth-Century England*

PAT THANE AND TANYA EVANS

OXFORD
UNIVERSITY PRESS

OXFORD

UNIVERSITY PRESS

Great Clarendon Street, Oxford OX2 6DP,
United Kingdom

Oxford University Press is a department of the University of Oxford.
It furthers the University's objective of excellence in research, scholarship,
and education by publishing worldwide. Oxford is a registered trade mark of
Oxford University Press in the UK and in certain other countries

First published 2012
First published in paperback 2013

British Library Cataloguing in Publication Data
Data available

Library of Congress Cataloging in Publication Data
Thane, Pat.
Sinners? Scroungers? Saints? : unmarried motherhood in
twentieth-century England / Pat Thane and Tanya Evans.
p.   cm
Includes bibliographical references and index.

ISBN 978–0–19–957850–4 (hardback)

1. Unmarried mothers—England—London—History—18th century.
2. Publication welfare—England—History—20th century.
I. Evans, Tanya, 1972– II. Title.

HQ759.45.T47 2012
306.874'320942—dc23   2012006102

ISBN 978–0–19–957850–4 (Hbk)

ISBN 978–0–19–968198–3 (Pbk)

Contents

Acknowledgements   vi
List of Illustrations   vii
List of Tables   vii

Introduction   1

1. Secrets and Lies: Being and Becoming an Unmarried Mother
   in Early Twentieth-Century England   6

2. Between the Wars   29

3. The Second World War: Another Moral Panic   54

4. Unmarried Motherhood in 'Family Britain': Challenging Bowlby   82

5. Unmarried Mothers in the 'Welfare State'   106

6. The Permissive Society? Unmarried Motherhood in the 1960s   120

7. A Finer Future?   140

8. The Struggle Continues: 1980s–90s   169

9. Into the Twenty-First Century: Progress?   195

Bibliography   209
Index   219

Acknowledgements

We are immensely grateful for the encouragement we received from the staff of One Parent Families (now Gingerbread) to start and continue this project, and for their patience with the length of time it has taken. However, we must stress that the book is entirely the work of the authors and that any opinions expressed concerning issues and events past and present are theirs, and should not be attributed to Gingerbread or its staff.

We are particularly grateful to Kate Green (former CEO of what was then OPF), Fiona Weir (current CEO), Tina Wade, Jane Ahrends, and their colleagues. Also to past staff and trustees of OPF/Gingerbread who provided interviews and information: Frances Cairncross, Catherine Porteous, Angela Richardson, Paul Lewis, Jane Streather, Sue Slipman. To Teresa Doherty, Head of Manuscripts, and Gail Cameron, Head of Exhibitions, at the Women's Library for all their help. To Rodney Bickerstaffe and Wesley Kerr who generously allowed us to write about their life stories; and the late Mary Bennett (daughter of the founder of the National Council for One Parent Families, Lettice Fisher) and Richard Balfe for their willingness to be interviewed. Hera Cook, Jenny Bourne Taylor, Helen Glew, and Kath Sherit helpfully guided us to new sources and gave good advice. Oliver Blaiklock gave invaluable assistance, and Virginia Preston and other colleagues at the Centre for Contemporary British History, now at Kings College, London, were invariably supportive. We are most grateful to the Economic and Social Research Council which funded the research (grant no RES-000-23-0545) and the Faculty of Arts, Macquarie University, New South Wales, Australia, for funding preparation of the manuscript. Mike, William, and Lara deserve special thanks.

List of Illustrations

7.1. 'Campaigning for the Finer Report', National Council of One Parent Families, The Women's Library, Box 120 Envelope 5/OFF/11/5/a.   163

8.1. 'Wedded to Welfare: Do They Want to Marry a Man—or the State?', *Sunday Times*, 11 July 1993.   189

List of Tables

4.1. Illegitimate births per 1000 unmarried women aged 15–44, England and Wales   83

4.2. Ages of unmarried mothers, 1950–7, England and Wales   84

6.1. Extramarital births per 1000 single, divorced, and widowed women, aged 15–44, England and Wales, 1955–2000   121

Introduction

This book tells two intertwined stories: about unmarried motherhood, mainly in England, since the early twentieth century, and about a voluntary organization set up in 1918 to support this unpopular cause, the National Council for the Unmarried Mother and her Child (NC), its sustained activism to the present, and the continuing need for it. Both stories tell us unexpected things about English culture, society, and politics over the century, challenging standard narratives and stereotypes and many of our own expectations. We focus on the mothers, not the children or the fathers, though, obviously, neither can be absent from the mothers' stories, but these are big enough and hard enough to uncover in themselves. The fathers, in particular, all too often are shadowy, their lives even more hidden and little researched. They were by no means always as blameworthy as is sometimes believed. Others are uncovering them and one day the narratives will come together. 'Illegitimate' children also merit more detailed attention to their own lives and experiences than we have space for here.

The conventional narrative about unmarried motherhood is that it was always shameful. Mothers and their 'illegitimate' children were disgraced, abandoned, cast out by society, even by their own families, except possibly among the poorest classes, until the 1960s. It has been suggested that the shame was most intense in the 1950s, at the apogee of 'Family Britain', when the family headed by two parents, married to each other, was dominant, bolstered by influential theories, especially those of the psychologist John Bowlby, whose ideas swept all before them. Then, in the new 'permissive' society of the 1960s, everything changed; open cohabitation and birth out of wedlock became accepted as never before, bringing, in the eyes of some, desirable new freedoms, for others, bearing responsibility for 'broken Britain'.

The stereotypes tell us much about certain influential attitudes through the period, but it is important not to assume that these were widely held or to accept the rhetoric of noisy moralists as generally representative. It became clear to us that the routes into unmarried motherhood, the experiences of the mothers and attitudes to them, were intriguingly diverse at all times. Penetrating beneath the stereotypes and recurrent moral panics, especially before the 1960s, has not been easy, above all because the lives we tried to understand were so often secret, even from close friends and relatives, often not revealed until long after, sometimes by others. We have had to trawl widely through official reports, social surveys, newspaper gossip, oral history, memoirs, and the invaluable archives of the NC, to get a sense—unavoidably incomplete—of the real lives behind the veils of privacy and secrecy. The lives of the middle classes are hardest to penetrate. They were less often than working-class people subject to scrutiny by social researchers and could better protect their secrets from outsiders.

Most unmarried mothers did not become life-long outcasts, but later married, not necessarily the fathers of their 'illegitimate' children. Often, long before the 1960s, unmarried mothers and their children were supported by their families, though sometimes secretly, at the cost of the child believing its grandmother was its mother and its mother an older sister, with possible traumatic impact on the child when the truth came out. This was not confined to the poorest families. Indeed they were often least able to help daughters in trouble due to other stresses in their lives and lack of spare resources.

Unexpected numbers of 'illegitimate' children were born to secretly cohabiting couples, many of whom were in stable partnerships and would willingly have married had divorce not been so difficult before the reform of 1969. Such transgressors of conventional norms were a minority, but they were numerous enough for the law to acknowledge cohabiting couples, for example for payment of benefits such as wartime allowances and unemployment benefits. Respectable neighbours might often know about irregular partnerships and could be remarkably tolerant of them and of children whose parentage was not quite as it seemed, provided that the families behaved discreetly, presented themselves as 'normal' families, and respected the widely accepted code of privacy about sexual matters and other family secrets. Throughout the century, until the 1960s, there seems to have been a widespread, discreet understanding that innocent, well-meaning people could find themselves in difficult situations and should not be rejected, provided that they did not flaunt their transgressions.

It has been suggested that even premarital sex was unusual before the 1960s,[1] though this has been challenged.[2] Official statistics in fact show that it was quite commonplace by the late 1930s, when 30 per cent of 'legitimate' first births were conceived before marriage.[3] But for some unfortunate women, especially in war-time, it could be the route to unmarried motherhood. The gulf between private practice and public morality came more clearly to light in the two world wars, when 'illegitimacy' climbed. For the public moralists this signified the immorality of young people freed from the constraints of family and community by wartime mobility and this has lingered in the popular imagination. More probably in the First World War, and certainly in the Second World War, when official statistics make it clear, couples were behaving as before, enjoying sex before anticipated marriage. But their hopes were more often in wartime disrupted by the man's removal, or death, on war service, leaving another unmarried mother behind.

There have indeed always been desolate women who fit the popular stereotype: often abandoned by a man who deceived them, or carrying the cost of a

---

[1] D. Willetts *The Pinch* (London: Atlantic, 2010), 102, 38–41.
[2] S. Szreter and K. Fisher, *Sex before the Sexual Revolution. Intimate Life in England, 1918–1963* (Cambridge: Cambridge University Press, 2010), 113–64.
[3] See p. 54.

one-off mistake. Their problems were compounded when they were unsupported by a family who might be too censorious or too overburdened with other problems to help, or with no family for whatever reason, perhaps having grown up in an institution. There would have been even more outcast and desperate women had it not been for the support of the NC and other voluntary organizations. The existence of these desperate women was the main reason the NC was founded and why it is still—now named Gingerbread—as active as ever. For almost a century, it has helped women keep and bring up their children, and supported others who lost their children to death or, often unwillingly, to adoption. There has always been a section of society that has treated unmarried mothers and their children as sinful outcasts and the NC has always fought against this.

This is a story of a minority, though it says much about majority culture. The minority rarely deliberately flouted that culture. Many unmarried mothers valued marriage, often expecting to marry a man who turned out to be already married or who just disappeared when the pregnancy was revealed. Quiet understanding of such undeserved horrors was shared by many professional social workers, psychologists, and others in contact with unmarried mothers. In the post-Second World War period, contrary to commonplace interpretations, many of these professionals rejected Bowlby's supposed view that unmarried mothers were too psychologically unstable to rear their own children, though even Bowlby's own views, in reality, were less stark than this.

There were real cultural changes from the 1960s compared with earlier times. Their origins can be detected in the 1950s, sometimes earlier. The changes became dramatic from the later 1960s, and gathered pace through the 1970s and, particularly, the 1980s and 1990s, as divorce, cohabitation, and births out of wedlock reached unprecedented levels in Britain and most higher income countries. The reasons are complex and remain difficult fully to understand. Partly the change was the product of a more confident, better-educated, post-war generation, who also gave birth to student activism, the Women's Liberation and Gay Liberation movements, and benefited from the invention of the birth control pill in the 1960s. But it is hard to judge also how many of this generation were reacting against growing up in marriages less ideal than appeared from the outside. Certainly they were unusually cautious about entering marriage and did so, if at all, at later ages than before. Equally certainly, for whatever reasons, there was a widespread revolt against secrecy into greater openness about matters previously thought shameful—about mental illness and death as well as sex.

These cultural changes owed little to conscious government action. The unprecedented run of liberal legislation of the late 1960s, including divorce law reform, legalization of abortion and of certain homosexual acts, and free provision of the pill, played an important part, but these were at least as much products as triggers of cultural change. Notably, lone motherhood, including unmarried motherhood, grew faster than at any time in history in the 1980s and 1990s, when it was directly contrary to Conservative government policy and spurred on its increasingly strident condemnation as it failed to halt, or even slow, its pace.

An aspect of the general cultural shift was that the experiences of unmarried mothers became less distinct from those of the rising numbers of lone mothers who were divorced or separated. The National Council for the Unmarried Mother and Her Child changed its name, in 1973, to the National Council for One Parent Families (OPF), in recognition of this shift, but its main focus stayed on lone unmarried mothers because they continued to be the most seriously disadvantaged lone parents. Nor, despite increasingly open public tolerance, did intolerance disappear in the supposedly liberated post-1960s culture. If anything, moralistic intolerance became more strident, and certainly received more explicit political support in the 1980s and 1990s, perhaps because the values it expressed seemed under greater threat than before. The attacks were particularly directed at one mythical representation of the unmarried mother: as the unemployed teenager who became pregnant just to qualify for a council home and live on benefits. She was very rarely to be found but the image was pervasive in the moralistic discourse.

OPF, or Gingerbread, as it has been since 2009, after merging with another voluntary organization dedicated to the support of lone mothers, was as determined at its foundation, in 1918, as now to challenge the stereotypes, or to Lose the Labels, as it named a campaign in 2010. It also set out, from the beginning, to change the law in order to bring fathers to account when they were irresponsible, on which there has been some progress; and also to gain legal equality between 'legitimate' and 'illegitimate' children, which was achieved, at last, in 1987.

The story of the National Council/OPF/Gingerbread is important for what it tells us about unmarried mothers, their supporters and detractors, and also because it illustrates important facets of voluntary action through the twentieth century. Voluntary organizations, too, are beset by stereotypes, particularly that they were run by Ladies Bountiful, middle-class busybodies bent on patronizing the poor. This was not so of those who ran the NC at any point in its history. Mostly they have been progressive women and men, opposed to discrimination, intolerance, and prurient moralizing, determined to achieve social and economic equality for unmarried mothers and their children.

Another commonplace assumption is that voluntary action was squeezed to insignificance by the relentless growth of the Welfare State—that the 'Big State' displaced the 'Big Society' in the political rhetoric of 2011. From the beginning the NC worked with the state, at central and local levels, whenever possible, especially during the Second World War when the state depended on voluntary agencies to help pregnant unmarried servicewomen and war workers. After 1945, when the modern Welfare State was established, the NC, like other organizations, had doubts about whether it was still needed or would be displaced by new state services. But by the 1950s it was clear that state welfare was far from comprehensive, that voluntary action had a role in identifying the gaps, filling them where it could and urging the state to do more. On its side, the hard-pressed state needed to delegate certain activities to the voluntary sector, especially specialized services, such as those for unmarried mothers and their children, in which the sector had expertise and experience. Through the past century, the relationship between the two has been complementary and collaborative, not competitive, the boundaries between them continually shifting as needs and policies change. Official statistics show how vibrant voluntary action continues to be in the twenty-first century. British society is unimaginable without it. Reconstructing stories such as that of the National Council, exploring why and how it has survived and how important it still is, helps to make this clear.

That the NC has survived, and is even more active and influential as it approaches its centenary than at its foundation, is in one sense a sign of its success, in another of its failure, for reasons beyond its control despite its massive efforts. For all that has changed, all too much remains the same. Despite greater, more open, social acceptance, condemnation of unmarried mothers, indeed of all lone mothers, holds firm in some quarters. Still, in the twenty-first century, lone parents, especially unmarried mothers bringing up their children, remain one of the poorest groups in Britain. They are still too often labelled and stigmatized as 'welfare scroungers', rearing dysfunctional children programmed to fail at school and become unemployed drug addicts or alcoholics, 'undermining the family' by their very existence.[4] For the morally righteous the term 'family' is reserved for households headed by married parents, ignoring the vast evidence of stable, successful families headed by single, or unmarried, parents, far stronger than the evidence of dysfunctionality.[5]

This book is not a celebratory account of the mothers or of the National Council, nor is it driven by a commitment to any particular family form. It reconstructs the stories of the mothers and of the NC as fully as we can, to help us understand better two important themes of the past century: change and continuity in family life, and the indispensable work of the non-governmental sector.

[4] *Daily Mail*, 'The Collapse of Family Life', 18 April 2011, available at http://www.dailymail.co.uk/news/article-1377940/Half-parents-split-16-births-outside-marriage-hit-highest-level-200-years.html.

[5] Jane Lewis, *The End of Marriage? Individualism and Intimate Relations* (Cheltenham: Edward Elgar, 2001).

1

Secrets and Lies: Being and Becoming an Unmarried Mother in Early Twentieth-Century England[1]

HOW MANY UNMARRIED MOTHERS?

We know roughly how many 'illegitimate' children were born in England and Wales from 1837, when registration of births, marriages, and deaths became compulsory, but we have no clear idea what happened to most mothers and children after the birth. Until as late as the 1970s there are no good national statistics of unmarried women bringing up their children.[2] They have never been a static, easily definable group. Most women married or re-married within a few years. Or they kept their status secret to escape gossip and social stigma. 'Illegitimacy'—and being whispered about or catcalled as a 'bastard'—was a label even harder for the children to escape until the very recent past.

Seven per cent of all births in England and Wales were registered as 'illegitimate' in 1850, followed by a decline to about 4 per cent in 1902. The percentage rose to about 9 during the First World War, falling again to 4 by the eve of the Second, when it rose again. There were regional differences in recorded unmarried motherhood. Until the 1930s it was more prevalent in rural than urban areas. But even the official numbers are approximate. Mothers and fathers might record themselves as married and the child as 'legitimate' so that he or she did not suffer the lifetime shame of 'illegitimacy' evident on the birth certificate, and sometimes also to hide their own irregular cohabitation. We cannot know how often. Censuses are another imperfect source. Family relationships in households recorded in the census could be unclear: an unmarried mother and her child living with her parents—as we will see that many did—would be recorded the daughter and grandchild, respectively, of the head of household, with no reference to their relationship to one another. And people do not always tell the truth about sensitive matters in census returns. Unmarried mothers might describe themselves as widows. It is particularly hard to reconstruct past lives that people strove hard to keep invisible

---

[1] This book focuses mainly upon England, for which more sources are accessible at present than for Wales. Scotland and Ireland are excluded due to major cultural and legal differences that merit detailed analysis but also a much longer book. For some of the differences see Pat Thane, *Happy Families? History and Family Policy* (London: British Academy, 2010), 17–21.

[2] See pp. 145–6.

and, until at least the 1960s, many people tried very hard to keep unmarried motherhood and 'illegitimacy' secret.

This is sadly illustrated in the life of the popular novelist Catherine Cookson. She was born in South Shields, County Durham, in 1906, daughter of an unmarried domestic servant. Cookson discovered only in her late twenties, when she first saw her birth certificate, that when registering her birth her mother had falsely claimed to be married and gave her daughter the surname, Davies, of the handsome, gambling bigamist who was her father, trying to protect her child from the stigma of 'illegitimacy'. Catherine had been called McMullen all her life, the name of her Irish Catholic grandparents who brought her up. Like many other 'illegitimate' children, in her early years she believed that her grandparents were her parents and her mother her older sister. Then, when she was seven years old, she learned the truth from children in the street, where the family had lived for years. During a quarrel, her then best friend, Belle, shouted: 'She's not your ma. If you want to know she's your grandma...your Kate's your ma and she drinks and [shouting] YOU haven't GOT NO DA, me ma says so.'[3] It was hard to keep secrets in close communities and there were, as Catherine later wrote, many 'tragic secrets' in her very poor family, including sexual and physical abuse. Young Catherine felt shattered and deeply confused. The news gave her a 'lost feeling, the feeling of aloneness' that never left her for the rest of her life.[4] She was almost thirty before her mother told her what had happened, and then only the barest details, including her tormented feelings during her lonely pregnancy. When Kate told her family, her stepfather had to be restrained from beating her as he had beaten other family members for lesser offences. She gave birth in her mother's crowded two-room home. She returned to work as soon as possible, in a bakery in another town, returning once a fortnight with groceries and her wages for her mother, who looked after Catherine lovingly. Kate later married and her relationship with Catherine remained tense.

Catherine wrote her autobiography in her fifties, while recovering from a severe breakdown, redrafting it several times. She admitted that she had gradually excluded much of the bitterness she felt in order to write a readable story. The truth would have been unbearable. In reality, at times she hated her alcoholic, abused, and abusing mother, but did her best to maintain a relationship. They lived together and she looked after her before she died.[5] The two were not alone in suffering such pain in early twentieth-century England.

Other than their families, these mothers and children had few sources of help. In late nineteenth-century London a number of 'rescue' organizations worked with unmarried mothers, the largest being the Salvation Army. The Army regarded the mothers as more often innocent victims of male lust than sinners, and believed

---

[3] Kathleen Jones, *Catherine Cookson* (London: Time Warner, 1999), 50–1.

[4] Catherine Cookson's unpublished autobiography, quoted in Jones, *Catherine Cookson*, 52.

[5] Kathleen Jones, 'Dame Catherine Cookson, 1906–1998', *Oxford Dictionary of National Biography* (hereafter *ODNB*) (Oxford: Oxford University Press, 2004–9).

they should not be, as they often were, treated as prostitutes and placed in institutions, but helped to return to their previous, generally respectable, lives. The Army found that about 20 per cent of the mothers who came to them had indeed been prostitutes or had more than one 'illegitimate' child, but most 'got into trouble', like Catherine Cookson's mother, while working as domestic servants and as a result of failed courtships with men of their own class. Most had expected to marry the father.[6] Some discovered, too late, that their lover was married and not proposing to leave his wife.[7]

COHABITATION

Not all unmarried mothers were lonely outcasts. Some lived with their children in stable relationships with the father, but in circumstances no less secret than those pervading Catherine Cookson's family. A major reason for unmarried cohabitation was the problematic state of the divorce law. Divorce became legally possible in England and Wales in 1857 (quite different laws applied in Scotland and Ireland[8]) but the sexual double standard applied. A man could divorce his wife for adultery alone; a woman had to prove additional aggravation, such as desertion, cruelty, incest, rape, sodomy, or bestiality. Neither could gain a divorce simply for desertion or incompatibility. Gaining gender equality in the divorce law in England and Wales, as had applied in Scotland since 1643, was an important campaign of the women's movement from the late nineteenth century. Divorce was also very expensive, beyond the means of many people. Apart from lawyers' costs, the only divorce court was in London, which further increased the cost for those who lived elsewhere.

Couples cohabited because one or both partners was unable to obtain, or could not afford, a divorce after a failed marriage, or was anxious to avoid the public stigma of divorce.[9] People who had been married could, of course, only re-marry legally if they were divorced or their legal partner died, though bigamy was by no means unknown. Between 1857 and 1904 bigamy trials averaged 98 per year.[10] An unknown number of bigamists may have remained hidden. The extent of cohabitation is unknown and can only be guessed at from contemporary commentaries, official policies, and anecdotes.

Charles Booth commented in his survey of the London poor in the 1890s:

---

[6] Anne R. Higginbotham, 'Respectable Sinners: Salvation Army Rescue Work with Unmarried Mothers, 1884–1914', in Gail Malmgreen (ed.), *Religion in the Lives of English Women, 1760–1930* (London: Croom Helm, 1986).

[7] National Council for the Unmarried Mother and Her Child (hereafter NC) Annual Report 1923, 11.

[8] Stephen Cretney, *Family Law in the Twentieth Century: A History* (Oxford: Oxford University Press, 2003), 4–19.

[9] V. Wimperis, *The Unmarried Mother and Her Child* (London: George Allen and Unwin, 1960), 29.

[10] Ginger Frost, *Living in Sin: Cohabiting as Husband and Wife in Nineteenth Century England* (Manchester: Manchester University Press, 2008), 72.

It is noted by the clergy who marry them, how often both the addresses given are from the same house.... More licence is granted by public opinion to the evasion of the bonds of marriage by those who have found it a failure, than is allowed to those whose relations to each other have not yet assumed a permanent form. This peculiar code of morality is independent of recognized law, and an embarrassment to religion, but... those teachers of religion who come in closest contact with the people are the most forward in recognizing that the word 'vice' is inapplicable to the irregular relations that result, whether it be before or after the legal marriage; though they would probably cling (in religious desperation) to the appellation of 'sin'.[11]

The striking thing about this observation is not only that unmarried couples lived together, but that those who might have been expected to be their sternest critics—the clergy—could accept such relationships. Ross confirms that in poor districts of East London between 1870 and 1918 'a great many marrying couples were actually cohabiting when they set out for the church.'[12]

Robert Roberts, describing the poor neighbourhood of Salford (Lancashire) where he grew up at the beginning of the twentieth century, commented:

Strangely enough, those who dwelt together unmarried—'livin' tally' or 'over t' brush', as the sayings went—came in for little criticism, though naturally everyone knew who was or was not legitimate.[13]

Similarly, Robert Moore, who worked as a volunteer poor man's lawyer at the Cambridge House Settlement in Camberwell, told the Royal Commission on Divorce of 1910–12 that his clients had 'no sense of shame in acknowledging their irregular sexualr elationships'.[14] A distinguished legal historian has concluded: 'At the beginning of the twentieth century there were certainly unmarried couples—no doubt a significant number—who lived together in a factual relationship impossible to distinguish from matrimony.'[15] The actual number is impossible to assess.

Nineteenth- and early twentieth-century legislators were aware of these irregular relationships. The Prevention of Cruelty [Amendment] Act, 1894, provided that rules designed to protect children against abusive parents should apply also to step-parents and 'to any person cohabiting with the parent of the child'.[16] The Workman's Compensation Act, 1906, recognized the unmarried family as a unit for the purpose of compensation. An 'illegitimate' child, and the parent of an 'illegitimate' child who was dependent on his or her earnings, could receive compensation (e.g., in case of death

[11] C. Booth, *Life and Labour of the People of London: Final Volume: Notes on Social Influences* (London,: Macmillan, 1903), 41–2.

[12] E. Ross, *Love and Toil: Motherhood in Outcast London, 1870–1918* (Oxford: Oxford University Press, 1993), 64.

[13] Robert Roberts, *The Classic Slum: Salford Life in the First Quarter of the Century* (Manchester: Manchester University Press, 1971), 30.

[14] Royal Commission on Divorce and Matrimonial Causes, *Parliamentary Papers* 1912–13, vol. 18, Q. 4813, quoted in Ross, *Love and Toil*, 64.

[15] Cretney, *Family Law*, 516; Frost, *Living in Sin*.

[16] R. Probert, 'Cohabitation in Twentieth Century England and Wales: Law and Policy', *Law and Policy*, 26:1 (Jan. 2004), 14.

in an industrial accident) although an unmarried partner could not. It was noted in Parliament that 'for the first time...illegitimates are to claim compensation on the same footing as legitimates...this is a most important change in the law.'[17] In early twentieth-century law courts, differing attitudes towards cohabitation were expressed, but the rights of cohabitees in wills, trusts, and contracts could be upheld if this was judged to be the intention of the person responsible for the will, deed, or contract.[18]

The couples involved were not necessarily opposed to marriage and might willingly have married had it been legally possible.[19] The highly restrictive divorce legislation, which made marriage impossible for many, was an increasing cause of concern for this reason. Critics argued that the system discriminated against poor people because proceedings were costly, and against women because of the gender inequality in the law. Under the Matrimonial Causes Act, 1878, women could obtain from magistrates' courts separation orders, with maintenance, on grounds of cruelty by their husbands, but this did not amount to divorce. This was partly an outcome of a campaign by the feminist Frances Power Cobbe against the high rate of domestic violence, 'wife-torture' as she called it, a secret and much under-reported abuse that injured and killed thousands of women each year.[20] Cobbe argued that women were trapped in abusive marriages because they could not support themselves and their children if they escaped and she campaigned to help them. Between 1897 and 1906, 87,000 separation and maintenance orders, granted mainly to poorer women, were issued by magistrates' courts. During the first decade of the twentieth century, an annual average of 7,500 separation orders were granted and only 800 divorces.[21]

Some separated partners, though of course not all, later cohabited with another partner. A strong argument for reform of the divorce law was to enable cohabiting couples to regularize their partnerships, as many evidently wished to do.[22] The Divorce Law Reform Union (DLRU), founded in 1906, described the situation of all too many people as

A Nation's Tragedy. Separated, but bound irretrievably by a lengthened chain; unable to fulfil their rightful functions in the interests of national happiness and prosperity. Forced, many of them, into illicit and irregular unions, and, as a result, bringing into the world children who are branded almost as Cain was branded.[23]

---

[17] Probert, 'Cohabitation', 15.

[18] Ibid. 16.

[19] Frost, *Living in Sin*.

[20] O. R. McGregor, *Divorce in England* (London: Heinemann, 1957), 22–3. F. P. Cobbe, 'Wife-Torture in England', *Contemporary Review*,. 32 (Apr.–July 1878), 55–87.

[21] Roderick Phillips, *Putting Asunder: A History of Divorce In Western Society* (Cambridge: Cambridge University Press, 1988).

[22] CD. 6478 (1912), para. 234.

[23] Pamphlet, *The Divorce Law Reform Union's Objects and Aims*, Papers of Helena Normanton, The Women's Library/7HLN/B/01. The Divorce Law Reform Union was formed initially to campaign for the appointment of a royal commission to study the divorce law. After achieving this they continued to campaign for extension of the grounds for divorce. Following their efforts, bills were introduced in Parliament in 1914, 1917, 1919, 1920, and 1923. Gail Savage, 'Erotic Stories and Public Decency: Newspaper Reporting of Divorce Proceedings in England', *Historical Journal*, 41:2 (1998), 511–28; Cordelia Moyse, 'Reform of Marriage and Divorce Law in England and Wales 1909–1937', PhD thesis, University of Cambridge (1996); Cretney, *Family Law*, 206–15.

Growing criticism of this kind led to the appointment of the Royal Commission on Divorce and Matrimonial Causes in 1909.[24] It was chaired by Lord Gorell, former president of the Divorce Court, an experience that had convinced him that the law needed radical change, in particular because it discriminated against poorer people.[25] The majority report of the Commission, published in 1912, concluded, based on extensive evidence, that 'beyond all doubt' divorce was 'beyond the reach of the poor'. It referred to the extent of cohabitation, de facto marriages and 'irregular and illicit unions' which resulted, which were publicized in contemporary press reports and were, in the Commission's view, a major reason reform was needed.[26] It recommended equality of the sexes in the divorce law and extending the grounds for divorce to include desertion, cruelty, incurable insanity, habitual drunkenness, and penal servitude for life.[27]

The main outcome, in the short term, was reform in 1914 of the ancient 'Poor Persons' Procedure, which, since 1495, had allowed waiver of court fees for poorer people. But it had never exempted them from lawyers' fees or the costs of residence in London while the case was heard. Conditions for gaining the waiver were stringent and few benefited. From 1914, the conditions were relaxed and lawyers were forbidden to accept fees in such cases. This did not eliminate all costs or benefit everyone in need, but in 1918 1,014 divorce petitions, from a total of 2,323, were brought under the scheme, though almost as many cases were dropped for reasons of cost or inability to find a lawyer willing to act unpaid. Following relaxation of the divorce laws in 1937,[28] in 1939 there were more than 10,000 applications under the procedure, of which 5,760 were granted. The Second World War put the system under still greater strain, due partly to the absence of lawyers at war. More accessible legal aid, and so more accessible divorce, was introduced in 1949.[29]

The 1912 Report led to no other immediate change in the divorce law, due partly to the onset of the First World War but also to strong opposition to its recommendations, on the grounds that they would undermine the institution of marriage. The death of Gorell in 1913 deprived the cause of a strong advocate, as did that of his son, Henry, who acted as secretary to the Royal Commission, inherited his father's title and in July 1914 introduced a bill into the House of Lords to give effect to its recommendations. He was killed in action in 1917.[30]

Covert cohabitation continued. This became evident early during the First World War, when the government for the first time introduced tax-funded allow-

---

[24] McGregor, *Divorce*, 26 ff.

[25] J. E. G. De Montmorency, rev. Hugh Mooney, 'Barnes, John Gorell, first Baron Gorell (1848–1913)', *ODNB* (2004–9); Cretney, *Family Law*, 275.

[26] *The Times*, 12 Nov. 1912 and 10 June 1920. Thanks to Adrian Bingham for the following references: *News of the World*, 27 Feb. 1916; *Daily Mirror*, 1 Dec. 1936; *Sunday Pictorial*, 19 June 1938; *Star*, 20 Jan. 1948.

[27] *Report of the Royal Commission on Divorce and Matrimonial Causes*, 1912, Cd 6478.

[28] See p. 34.

[29] Cretney, *Family Law*, 306–18; R. I. Morgan, 'The Introduction of Civil Legal Aid in England and Wales', *Twentieth Century British History*, 5 (1994), 38–86.

[30] Cretney, *Family Law*, 788–9.

ances for the 'dependents' of servicemen. It soon became clear that many service-men had long-term unmarried partners with whom they had children. It was agreed that allowances should be paid to these 'unmarried wives', 'where there was evidence that a real home had been maintained'.[31] They had to satisfy more stringent criteria than other family members, such as dependent parents, who had only to prove that the serviceman had 'helped to keep them'. An unmarried partner had to prove that he was her sole support and she 'would otherwise be destitute', and the relationship must have preceded the man's enlistment by at least six months.[32] The allowance would be paid even if the soldier had a legal wife, if the conditions were satisfied.

It appears impossible to establish how many such allowances were paid because the official statistics do not distinguish unmarried partners from 'widows and other dependents' other than wives and children. However, from February 1916 'unmarried wives' were permitted to receive pensions if their partners died or were injured and statistics exist of the numbers of pensions paid subsequently. By 31 March 1919, 2,645 'unmarried wives' of servicemen received pensions, together with 3,909 'children of unmarried wives' and 3,493 other 'illegitimate children'. This compared with pensions paid from the beginning of the war to 191,317 widows, with and without children, and 338 to 'separated wives'.[33] We have no way of knowing how many irregular partnerships were hidden from the authorities or what difficulties women had in proving their status. However, most servicemen were relatively young and broken marriages leading to cohabitation were more common among rather older people, after some years of marriage.

The legally separated wife of a serviceman could claim a pension if her husband contributed to her support. The amount of the pension should equal that due to her under a separation order or paid voluntarily by the husband, but should not be less than 3s. 6d. per week or exceed 13s. 9d. per week (compared with 21s. maximum, dependent upon the husband's rank, for wives and widows of non-commissioned servicemen who were not legally separated at the time of his death or injury), plus allowances for the children if maintained by her. An 'unmarried wife', who 'had been wholly or substantially dependent on the soldier, and has been drawing separation allowance as for a wife or was eligible for such allowance' qualified for a lower pension of only 10s. a week plus allowances for the children, 'if and so long as she has children of the soldier in her charge'. If she had no children in her charge she might receive 10s. p.w. just 'for the period of the war and 12 months afterwards, or for 12 months after ceasing to have any child of the deceased soldier in her charge...and for any subsequent period during which, from infirmity or age, she is wholly or partially incapable of supporting herself'. A pension could be paid

[31] *Report on the Administration of the National Relief Fund up to 31st March 1915. Cd 7756 Parliamentary Papers*, 1914–16, 5.
[32] Departments of State and Official Bodies, *Separation Allowances for Dependants of Unmarried Soldiers (or Widowers) during the War*, 17 Nov. 1914, quoted in Probert, 'Cohabitation', 29 n. 8.
[33] *Second Annual Report of the Ministry of Pensions, 1918/19*, House of Commons Paper 39 (1920), 79, 82.

to an 'illegitimate' child 'where an affiliation order was in force on account of the child' at the time of the serviceman's death; 'or in the case of a child of a woman who was not married to or supported by the father where there is satisfactory proof that he was its father'.[34] Allowances for the unmarried partners of servicemen and their children were reintroduced during the Second World War.

Recognition of cohabitation continued in post-war unemployment relief regulations, which were designed to support servicemen and their families in their transition to an uncertain peacetime world. The Unemployed Workers' Dependants' (Temporary Provision) Act 1921 then allowed 5s. per week for a wife or 'where a female person is residing with an unemployed worker who is a widower or unmarried, for the purpose of having care of his dependent children and is being maintained by him or has been and is living as his wife'.[35] The Unemployment Insurance Act, 1927, removed the stipulation that the man must be unmarried or widowed, in practice allowing payment to cohabitants with men living apart from their wives, provided that they had children together. It explicitly removed allowances from cohabitants without children[36] and they were not payable for 'illegitimate' children who did not live with the insured parent.[37]

FIRST WORLD WAR AND THE FOUNDATION OF THE NATIONAL COUNCIL FOR THE UNMARRIED MOTHER AND HER CHILD

Unmarried motherhood became a public issue during the First World War also due to the increase in 'illegitimate' births. This was widely attributed to a 'loosening of morals' in wartime, as more young men and women lived away from the supervision of families and communities. More probably, sexual behaviour changed less than the circumstances arising from the war. For centuries it had been normal for couples to have sexual relationships before marriage and for pregnancy to provide the occasion for the ceremony.[38] In wartime, there was a higher probability that the father would be dead or absent when the pregnancy was discovered, leaving the mother alone and unable to marry, temporarily or permanently. And, at all times, women were deserted by the father before marriage, or chose not to marry, and unknown numbers were victims of rape or incest. Women could not apply for affiliation orders and hence support for the child in respect of men about to be, or already, drafted overseas, lest it disrupt the war effort.[39] For some, this made a hard situation even harder.

---

[34] Ibid. 54, 67–8.
[35] Probert, 'Cohabitation', 18.
[36] Ibid. 18.
[37] Sue Graham-Dixon, *Never Darken My Doorstep: Working for Single Parents and Their Children, 1918–1978* (London: National Council for One Parent Families, 1981), 20.
[38] Peter Laslett, *Family Life and Illicit Love in Earlier Generations* (Cambridge: Cambridge University Press, 1978); Tanya Evans, *'Unfortunate Objects': Lone Mothers in Eighteenth Century London* (London: Palgrave, 2005); John Gillis, *For Better for Worse: British Marriages, 1600 to the Present* (Oxford: Oxford University Press, 1988); Frost, *Living in Sin*.
[39] *National Relief Fund*, 14.

Immediately after the war, the National Council for the Unmarried Mother and Her Child (NC) was founded as a voluntary association dedicated to supporting what its founders believed was an unhappy and neglected group of people whose numbers had grown during the war. It was the first organization solely concerned with the needs of unmarried mothers and their children. Its founder, Lettice Fisher, described it as

a product of the energy released by the losses, agonies, and strain of the Great War. We were desperately anxious, wretchedly unhappy, worn, harassed and hard pressed. There was always far more to do than could be done...But there was also an increased clearness of vision, a determination not only to rebuild, but to amend.[40]

Before the war, much of the energy of Fisher and others like her—many of them suffrage campaigners, as she was[41]—was devoted to reducing the high infant mortality rate. This, combined with a falling birth rate and panic in the government and armed services about the apparent 'physical deterioration' of an increasingly urbanized population, led voluntary organizations, often led by and mainly composed of women, to campaign for state action to support mothers and infants at a time when fear of national decline made politicians unusually receptive. Women also established voluntary welfare centres to help mothers and infants.[42] These campaigns intensified during the First World War, amid further official concern about a 'lost generation' of young men, which, it was feared, would weaken Britain militarily and economically in the future.

Death rates were highest among 'illegitimate' infants and they increased relative to deaths of 'legitimate' babies during the war. In 1916, the Registrar General reported that 'the ratio of illegitimate to legitimate mortality in the first week of life has increased from 170 per cent in 1907 to 201 per cent in 1916...These facts suggest that infant welfare organizations might well devote special attention to the first few days of the life of illegitimate children.'[43] Also in 1916, the voluntary Commission on the National Birth-Rate, chaired by the Bishop of Birmingham (later a Vice-President of the NC), presented its first report, arguing that support for unmarried mothers and their children would help to decrease 'illegitimate' births and deaths.[44]

Fisher and her associates were convinced that wartime conditions made it harder than ever for unmarried mothers to keep and care for their children. Among other difficulties, it was hard to find foster-mothers at a time when women could find

---

[40] Mrs H. A. L. Fisher, *Twenty-One Years* (London: National Council for the Unmarried Mother and Her Child, 1939), 3.

[41] Fisher chaired the national executive of the National Union of Suffrage Societies, 1916–18. Cordelia Moyse, 'Lettice Fisher, 1875–1956', *ODNB* (2004).

[42] G. Searle, *The Quest for National Efficiency* (Oxford: Blackwell, 1971); D. Pick, *Faces of Degeneration: A European Disorder, c.1848–c.1918* (Cambridge: Cambridge University Press, 1998); D. Dwork, *War is Good for Babies and Other Young Children: A History of the Infant and Child Welfare Movement in England, 1898–1918* (London: Routledge, 1987).

[43] Quoted in Fisher, *Twenty-One Years*, 3.

[44] *The Declining Birth-Rate: Its Causes and Effects: Being the Report and the Chief Evidence Taken by the National Birth-Rate Commission* (London: Chapman and Hall, 1916).

better paid work. At the beginning of the war, the Child Welfare Council of the Social Welfare Association for London (CWC; which represented 70 voluntary societies concerned with children) established a child welfare office, which was soon overwhelmed by appeals from unmarried mothers for help and advice. In 1917 it set up a special committee to deal with this issue, chaired by Sybil Neville-Rolfe. Her experience as a 'rescue worker' in a 'shelter for fallen girls' in London before the war convinced her that young people, and voluntary workers, needed more education about sex and contraception. It also aroused her interest in the emerging eugenics movement.[45] In 1907 she was a founder of the Eugenics Society, with which she remained associated until her death. During the war she became increasingly concerned to help unmarried mothers and their children. Unlike some eugenicists, she did not interpret unmarried motherhood as necessarily due to mental or moral 'defect', but often to young women being led astray by men. She believed that unmarried mothers should be supported to bring up their children and educated about sex and contraception so that they did not make further mistakes. Her biographer describes her as a feminist.[46] Eugenics and feminism were less incompatible than is sometimes thought; they shared the desire to make motherhood safe for all women.[47]

The work of the CWC committee led directly to the foundation of the NC in April 1918, chaired by Mrs Fisher, with Mrs Neville Rolfe as a Deputy Chair. A Vice-President was Sir Francis Champneys, an eminent obstetrician and campaigner for improved midwife training, which he felt was a key to reducing infant mortality.[48] Men outnumbered women on the committee.[49] The NC's main aims were:

1. To obtain reform of the existing Bastardy Acts and Affiliation Acts;
2. To secure the provision of adequate accommodation to meet the varying needs of mothers and babies throughout the country, with the special aim of keeping mother and child together; and
3. To deal with individual enquiries from, or on behalf of, unmarried mothers.[50]

---

[45] G. Searle, *Eugenics and Politics in Britain, 1900–1914* (Leyden: Noordhoff International, 1976).

[46] Angelique Richardson, 'Sybil Katherine Neville-Rolfe, 1885–1955', *ODNB* (2004). See also Sybil Neville-Rolfe, *Social Biology and Welfare* (London: George Allen and Unwin, 1949). Neville-Rolfe had links to the Racial Hygiene Association in Australia (which later became the Family Planning Association) and was important to this organization's establishment and growth; see Jane Carey, ' "Women's Objective—A Perfect Race": Whiteness, Eugenics and the Articulation of Race', in L. Boucher, J. Carey, and K. Elinnghaus (eds), *Re-Orientating Whiteness: Transnational Perspectives on the History of an Identity* (London: Palgrave, 2009).

[47] Lesley Hall, *Sex, Gender and Social Change in Britain since 1880* (London: Macmillan, 2000), 105–7; Marian Clare Debenham, 'Grassroots Feminism: A Study of the Campaign of the Society for the Provision of Birth Control Clinics, 1934–1938', PhD thesis, University of Manchester (2010), 150–7.

[48] J. S. Fairbairn, revised June Hannam, 'Sir Francis Henry Champneys, 1848–1930', *ODNB* (2004). This entry does not mention his association with the National Council.

[49] Fisher, *Twenty-One Years*, 4.

[50] Ibid. 5.

As Fisher explained, 'There was complete agreement that the separation of any mother from her baby should be regarded as an exceptional and deplorable necessity,' the natural complement to which was that 'the responsibility of fatherhood must be recognized and that any schemes for the welfare of unmarried mothers must include means for bringing home that responsibility more effectively.'[51]

At first the NC aimed to help all lone mothers, including widowed and deserted women, but soon realized that they often had other sources of help, and greater public sympathy, than the unmarried mothers whose need was greatest. Also the NC's own resources were limited. Unmarried mothers were not popular with donors. It decided to focus its limited funds, time, and energy on these neediest people. It sought to encourage provision by public and voluntary bodies of residential homes for expectant unmarried mothers and for babies whose mothers could not keep them. It also campaigned, as we will see,[52] for legal reforms, including simplified affiliation proceedings, increased financial support under affiliation orders, legalization of adoption, and legitimization of children by the subsequent marriage of the parents.

The leaders of the NC believed that 'its first task was to educate public opinion'. They made pioneering use of modern media, publishing newspaper and magazine articles and leaflets and later making some of the first radio appeals,[53] much helped by the press experience of their second full-time paid secretary, Mrs Trounson. They tried to explain to the public in terms they would understand

that the child, whatever the faults and follies of its parents, was not to blame, that far the best method of helping it was to help its mother both before and after its birth, that to keep the mother with her child, to re-educate her for its sake, was the best way of improving her moral standard, that the acceptance of responsibility on the part of both parents was not only the best chance for the child but the course most likely to prevent more illegitimate births.[54]

And, felt Fisher, 'before long we came to feel that we were meeting with sympathy and response.'[55]

The NC was not alone in speaking up for unmarried mothers. During the war, Mrs Layton, a midwife in Bethnal Green, represented the large, mainly working-class, Women's Co-operative Guild before the Executive of the Prince of Wales' Fund, a charity that had decided not to give relief to unmarried mothers. Their explanation was that 'some of the clerics of the Committee were of opinion that, if the unmarried mother was assisted from the fund, the feelings of all the respectable married women would be outraged.'[56] She told them that

As a midwife, I had only the day before attended a respectable married woman and, knowing I had to go the next day to plead the cause of unmarried mothers, my patient, so that I

---

[51] Fisher, *Twenty-One years*, 5.
[52] See pp. 46–53.
[53] See pp. 43–4.
[54] Fisher, *Twenty-One Years*, 6.
[55] Ibid.
[56] Margaret Llewelyn Davies (ed.), *Life as We Have Known It, by Co-operative Working Women* (London: Hogarth Press, 1931; repr. London: Virago, 1977), 51.

would not be late, had sat up in bed to wash herself and was quite willing to let me leave her child unwashed until I could return. I explained that I represented the Women's Co-operative Guild, an organization 30,000 strong, chiefly composed of respectable married women, and that the guild entirely repudiated the statement that married women would be resentful. I…asked them not to forget that every time a woman fell, a man fell also…It was decided before we left the room to treat the unmarried mother with the same consideration as the married mother.[57]

This was another of many indicators that unmarried mothers were not always the pariahs some thought them to be at the time and subsequently.[58] Nevertheless the biggest problem for the NC was fundraising for a cause that was not universally popular.[59] Critics accused the NC of encouraging immorality by helping unmarried mothers. For the first two years they depended on the generosity of their first Treasurer, Sir Charles (later Viscount) Wakefield, a childless, self-made petroleum millionaire from a modest background in Liverpool, Lord Mayor of London 1915–16, and generous philanthropist.[60] He promised to set the NC up financially on condition that they soon learned to stand on their own feet. In the first year he donated £200 and loaned another £200. In the same year £630 was raised from annual subscriptions and individual donations. Regular subscribers included the successful actress Gladys Cooper, herself a single mother of two children after her divorce in 1921, and three after her short-lived second marriage in 1928, until her third marriage in 1937.[61] Another was Margery Corbett Ashby, the Liberal peace campaigner and feminist leader of the National Union of Societies for Equal Citizenship (NUSEC), the successor body to the National Union of Women's Suffrage Societies (NUWSS).[62] Public authorities contributed a meagre £10, and voluntary organizations, including the Lanarkshire Miners' Union and the National Railway Women's Guild, £350. A postal appeal brought in around £70. The main expenses were £426 for staff salaries, £73 rent, and £374 to help individual mothers and children.[63]

In 1920, Wakefield resigned as Treasurer, feeling that he had fulfilled his promises, but causing a 'desperate crisis'.[64] To keep going, the NC 'dunned their private friends',[65] until the newly formed voluntary National Council for Maternity and Child Welfare came to their rescue with a generous grant and offices on favourable terms. This organization's cause aroused more immediate public sympathy and larger donations, but its members recognized the particular needs of unmarried mothers and their children. This, plus donations, remained the NC's main source

[57] Ibid. 51–2.
[58] See pp. 170 ff.
[59] NC Committee of Management Minutes (hereafter CMM), 13 June 1923, 5/OPF/2/1/1/1c.
[60] T. A. B. Corley, 'Wakefield, Charles Cheers, first Viscount Wakefield (1869–1941)', *ODNB* (2004). This does not mention his involvement with the National Council.
[61] Sheridan Morley, 'Cooper, Dame Gladys Constance, 1888–1971', *ODNB* (2004–10).
[62] Jenifer Hart, 'Ashby, Dame Margery Irene Corbett, 1882–1981', *ODNB* (2004–10).
[63] Graham-Dixon, *Never Darken*, 28.
[64] Fisher, *Twenty-One Years*, 7.
[65] Ibid.

of support until the Second World War. Finance remained a constant anxiety, all the more as demand for its services grew. It had hoped for regular donations by statutory authorities, individuals, and voluntary organizations, but was not helped by the economic crisis of the interwar years which constrained public expenditure. A few public bodies and individuals gave regular contributions but not enough to meet the demand from needy mothers and children.

THE LEADERS OF THE NATIONAL COUNCIL

Active members of the NC had to work hard to persuade the public that unmarried mothers and their children were a worthy cause at a time when there were many competing voluntary organizations supporting other good causes. Who were they and what motivated them? The cause seems to have appealed more to some of the 'great and good' of the time than to the general public, especially to medical specialists in public health and obstetrics, feminists and campaigners for improved child welfare, who had encountered unmarried mothers and children in difficulties. It is easy to caricature these philanthropists as patronizing 'do-gooders', but their words and actions suggest a genuine sympathy and capacity to communicate with desperate women of all social backgrounds.

The work of the NC was part of a general expansion of voluntary action between the wars from its strong nineteenth-century base. Though state responsibility for social welfare was growing from the beginning of the twentieth century, voluntary agencies remained important providers of services to groups neglected by the state, such as unmarried mothers, while campaigning for further state action and often working closely with, and subsidized by, statutory agencies. Interwar governments believed that cooperation between the state and the voluntary sector was the desirable way forward for state welfare and many in the voluntary sector agreed.

Lettice Fisher chaired the NC from 1918 to 1950. She was a daughter of a clerk of the House of Commons, Sir Courtney Ilbert, from whom she gained a useful grasp of parliamentary proceedings, in a family strongly interested in politics. She graduated in modern history from Oxford and became a research student at the London School of Economics. She married her former Oxford tutor, H. A. L. Fisher, in 1899 and returned to Oxford where she also became a tutor. She became involved with voluntary work in housing, public health, and child welfare, possibly, her daughter suggested, because she had difficulty conceiving (her only child was born after 14 years of marriage) and would have liked more children of her own.[66] She was a fine public speaker and became an active suffragist. In 1913 her husband became Vice-Chancellor of Sheffield University and through the war she undertook welfare work among women munitions workers in Sheffield. This

---

[66] Tanya Evans, interview with Mary Bennett, only daughter of H. A. L. and Lettice Fisher, Principal of St Hilda's College, Oxford, 1965–80, 5 Feb. 2005.

experience made her increasingly concerned about the scale of 'illegitimacy' and the associated infant death rate.

Her husband, a Liberal, became a very effective, reforming, President of the Board of Education following Lloyd George's coup in December 1916. He appears to have been drawn into politics by his wife and her family.[67] He remained in the office until the defeat of the coalition government in 1922, providing Lettice and the NC with useful contacts. At the time of his appointment, the Board had an important role in promoting child health and was engaged in sometimes tense negotiations with the Local Government Board (LGB) over the uneasy division of responsibility between them for maternal and child welfare. From 1914, both could make grants to different organizations concerned with infant welfare: the LGB to infant welfare clinics, the Board of Education to schools training women in mother-craft, in addition to its existing responsibility for school meals and medical inspection and care of schoolchildren. The two Boards finally agreed that the LGB should take responsibility for preschool children and mothers (taken over by the Ministry of Health when it replaced the LGB in 1918), the Board of Education keeping responsibility for schoolchildren, including nursery schools. This arrangement was embodied in the Maternity and Child Welfare Act, 1918. Fisher remained an MP until 1926 before returning to academic life as Warden of New College, Oxford.[68] There Lettice held an annual Christmas Sale in support of NC, which usually raised the substantial sum of £50.

Lettice Fisher, like many other former suffrage campaigners, was dedicated to fostering 'citizenship'—a key word in interwar political discourse—that is, to enable voters, in her case especially women, to use their votes and their political voices effectively and become involved in politics. She published *The Citizen. A Simple Account of How We Manage our National and Local Affairs* (1927) and, in 1934, in association with the National Association of Women's Institutes (also founded by suffragists in 1915, for the political education of countrywomen[69]), *The Housewife and the Town Hall: A Brief Description of What Is Done by Our Local Councils and Public Services*. This grew out of a series of radio broadcasts aimed at teaching women about government and urging them to participate actively as voters or representatives. Also, as an historian Fisher believed strongly that knowledge of the past could assist understanding of the present, a view she promoted in another book, *Then and Now* (1925).[70]

As already described, other founding members included distinguished lawyers, medics, feminists, and voluntary activists. Another was C. W. Saleeby, the physician and journalist. Like Sybil Neville-Rolfe, Saleeby was a founder-member of the Eugenics Society, but he soon fell out with what he called the 'better-dead' school of eugenicists, who, he believed, were prejudiced against the poor. He came to

[67] Evans, Interview with Mary Bennett; Alan Ryan, 'Fisher, Herbert Albert Laurens (1865–1940)', *ODNB* (2004).

[68] Evans, Interview with Mary Bennett.

[69] Maggie Andrews, *The Acceptable Face of Feminism: The Women's Institute as a Social Movement* (London: Lawrence and Wishart, 1997).

[70] Moyse, 'Reform'.

believe in 'reform eugenics': that, with improved care before and after birth and an improved diet and environment, the physical condition of the mass of the population could improve; people were not doomed by their genes as some eugenicists believed. The eugenics movement was more complex and divided than is always realized.[71] Saleeby worked unpaid for an antenatal clinic, chaired the National Birth-Rate Commission,[72] was a strong advocate of a Ministry of Health dedicated to improving the national health, and of clean air, exercise, and temperance, a Vice-President of the Divorce Law Reform Union (having been divorced and remarried himself), a Fabian, and supporter of women's rights.[73]

Another founder-member was Sir John Robertson, a leading figure in public health with a particular interest in eradicating childhood diseases, Medical Officer of Health for Birmingham, Professor of Hygiene and Public Health at Birmingham University, and adviser to the Ministry of Health.[74] Chrystal Macmillan, suffragist, peace campaigner, and internationalist, one of the first women barristers in Britain and executive member of NUSEC, was a member of the Legal Subcommittee of the NC from the beginning and gave expert evidence to a number of parliamentary committees.[75] Another suffragist among the founders, Mary Phillips, worked for the National Council of Social Service and was a lifelong member of the feminist Six-Point Group.[76] She represented the YWCA on the NC committee from 1918. A former militant suffragette (which led to a period in Holloway prison) among the founders was the socialist Anne Cobden-Sanderson, daughter of the radical politician Richard Cobden. Before the war, she supported a pioneering clinic for children in East London, campaigned for school meals and medical inspection, and was a poor law guardian.[77]

These were joined by 1920 by, among others, Sir Arthur Newsholme, who became Vice-President on resigning as Chief Medical Officer of Health. He had been a pioneer of public health work and, as Chief Medical Officer at the LGB, produced an important series of reports on infant, childhood, and maternal mortality from 1910 to 1916.[78] Also joining the Council was Mary Scharlieb, the first woman to gain an MD from London University in 1888, a specialist in obstetrics and gynaecology. She supported campaigns for improved child and maternal health and welfare, for humane treatment of unmarried mothers, and sex education for the young, but, as a committed Roman Catholic, was a strong opponent of birth control.[79] She believed it was her Christian duty to advance the cause of women, and that wives and mothers had a right

[71] Searle, *Eugenics*; Hall, *Sex*, 66–9.
[72] See p. 14.
[73] G. R. Searle, 'Caleb Williams Elijah Saleeby (1878–1940)', *ODNB* (2004).
[74] Steve Sturdy, 'Robertson, Sir John (1862–1936)', *ODNB* (2004–10).
[75] Sybil Oldfield, '(Jessie) Chrystal Macmillan (1872–1937)', *ODNB* (2004–10).
[76] Leah Leneman, 'Phillips, Mary Elizabeth (1880–1969)', *ODNB* (2004–10).
[77] A. C. Howe, 'Sanderson, (Julia Sarah) Anne Cobden (1853–1926)', *ODNB* (2004–10).
[78] John M. Eyler, 'Newsholme, Sir Arthur (1857–1943)', *ODNB* (2004).
[79] Debenham, 'Grassroots Feminism', 124.

to professional careers.[80] In 1920 she became one of the first women magistrates.

Another pioneering woman doctor, Florence Barraclough Lambert, was another Vice-President. She was active before the war in voluntary child welfare and an early campaigner for state medicine. In 1919 she became Medical Officer at the Ministry of Health, responsible for inspecting local authority child welfare throughout the country. She resigned in 1921 and was elected an alderman of the London County Council, where she played an important role in developing its public health policies and improving London hospitals especially after it took over poor law responsibilities in 1930.[81]

The future Prime minister Neville Chamberlain was Vice-President and then President, 1922–37, and actively supported the NC's campaigns in Parliament, as we will see. He grew up, as a Unitarian, in an atmosphere that encouraged a sense of the responsibility of the rich to the poor. Like his father, Joseph, he had a life-long commitment to social reform, which, like his father, he expressed first through local government work in Birmingham then in national politics. He shared his father's centrist, unionist politics. He was elected to Parliament in 1918, became Conservative Minister of Health in 1923 and again in 1924–9, after the brief first Labour government of 1924, implementing such important reforms as Widows, Orphans and Old Age Insurance Pensions, 1925, and the Local Government Act, 1929, which transferred Poor Law responsibilities to local authorities. Had he resigned with Baldwin in 1937 he might be remembered very differently, as a reformer rather than as an 'appeaser'.[82]

The Council aimed for equal representation of the political parties on its Executive, though they tended to attract more Conservative than Labour supporters.[83] Also among the founders were representatives of religious faiths, most prominently the Church of England, though, like most other campaigning groups of the time, the NC was strictly non-denominational. Also represented were a variety of voluntary organizations, including the National Union of Women Workers (from 1918 the National Council of Women, NCW), the Women's Local Government Society, the Salvation Army, and the Workers Educational Association.[84] The NC's first manifesto declared:

The National Council seeks the support and help of all Local Health Authorities, Industrial, Social and Religious Associations throughout the country, so that public opinion may be influenced and speedy action be taken—not only by such Voluntary Societies and Local Authorities, but also in conjunction with Government Departments.[85]

---

[80] Mary Scharlieb, *Reminiscences* (London: Williams and Norgate, 1924); Greta Jones, 'Mary Ann Dacomb Scharlieb (1845–1930)', *ODNB* (2004). NC Minutes of AGMs and Extraordinary General Meetings, 14 Nov. 1919, 5/OPF/01/14/1.

[81] Colin J. Parry, 'Lambert, Dame Florence Barraclough (1871–1957)', *ODNB* (2004–10).

[82] Andrew J. Crozier, '(Arthur) Neville Chamberlain (1869–1940)', *ODNB* (2004–10).

[83] NC CMM, 10 July 1930, 5/OPF/02/01/1/1d.

[84] Graham-Dixon, *Never Darken*, 3.

[85] Ibid.

An array of prominent people sympathized with unmarried mothers and their children and did not condemn them as 'sinners'. The founders of the NC offer an intriguing glimpse of the variety of ideas and ideals of social reformers and voluntary activists at this time, far from stereotypes of Lords and Ladies Bountiful, patronizing the poor.

FEMINISTS AND UNMARRIED MOTHERS

As we have seen, several, though not all, the founder members of the NC considered themselves feminists and maintained active contacts with feminist organizations and individuals. Feminists did not agree on everything and definition of the term is contentious, but most opposed the sexual double standard and criticized the conditions that led women into unmarried motherhood and public condemnation while fathers escaped judgement. They wished to help mothers bring up their children as useful citizens rather than as shamed outcasts.

Also, despite widespread public condemnation of 'fallen' women, there was sympathy from highly respectable women who might not necessarily describe themselves as feminists, such as the members of the Women's Co-operative Guild (WCG), with 40,000 members at this time, mostly working-class married women.[86] Before and during the war, the WCG campaigned for improvements in maternal and child welfare and access to birth control information for poor women. It supported the NC and shortly after the war it took

a vote from all their members with regard to the unmarried mother,...unanimously in favour of giving the unmarried mother the same opportunities of medical care and nursing...as a married mother.[87]

From its foundation the NC cooperated with the NCW in drafting parliamentary bills relating to their shared interests and also worked with other organizations for a variety of purposes.[88] Representatives of the NCW, Mrs Bethune-Baker and Eva Hubback of NUSEC, Lady Rhondda and Miss Mayo of the Six Point Group (both feminist organizations), Dr Marion Phillips, first Chief Woman Officer of the Labour Party, representatives of the Standing Joint Committee of Women's Industrial Organisations (which included the Women's Sections of the Labour Party, the Women's Co-operative Guild, and various women's trade unions) and of the Women's Political and Industrial League all joined the NC's Legislative Committee in November 1921 to discuss the formulation of the Bastardy Bill for which they campaigned together, one of many such successful collaborations.[89] The NC sup-

---

[86] Martin Pugh, *Women and the Women's Movement in Britain*, 2nd edn (London: Macmillan, 2000), 232.

[87] Graham-Dixon, *Never Darken*, 3.

[88] NC Legal Sub-Committee (LSC), 22 Nov. 1917, 5/OPF/02/12a.

[89] See below, pp. 47–50. LSC, 11 Nov. 1921, 5/OPF/02/12a. The minutes of this Committee end in 1923 possibly as a result of the successful passage of the Bastardy Bill. It was reconstituted at the end of the 1940s.

ported the Consultative Committee on Women's Organisations, first established by NUWSS, then, from 1921, organized by Nancy Astor to coordinate efforts across parties and organizations to promote the position of women, to encourage women to use their votes, and to organize campaigns against MPs who sought to prevent the progress of the women's cause in Parliament.[90] The NC and NUSEC worked together on a committee established by the Home Office to advise on what became the Age of Marriages Act, 1929, which raised the minimum legal age of marriage to 16 for both sexes, from 12 for girls and 14 for boys.[91]

However, the NC refused to be associated, as an organization, with feminist demands for the equal franchise (achieved 1928) for fear that public association with explicitly feminist political issues would damage their already sensitive cause. It also declined publicly to support the Women's International League for Peace and Freedom because its ambitions were too far removed from its own and would divert its scarce time and resources. It was happy to work with the International Women's Suffrage Alliance because it shared its commitment to helping women to use their votes to promote women's interests.[92] Internationalism was a key feature of feminism and social reform campaigns at this time.

The NC joined forces with the NCW in the late 1930s to draw the government's attention to the extent of illegal abortion, but did not support the Abortion Law Reform Association (ALRA) when it was formed in the late 1930s to demand legalized abortion, because their aims were 'outside the scope of the Council'. The NC judged it wise to avoid public association with another controversial topic, though committee members were convinced that a significant proportion of mothers, married and unmarried, were dying in pregnancy and childbirth due to attempted abortions.[93] Evidence on the issue, collected over several years by the Council, was taken into consideration by an Interdepartmental Committee of enquiry into abortion set up by the Government in 1937.[94]

The NC also steered clear of the equally politically sensitive issue of birth control despite its obvious relevance to their work.[95] They mostly supported birth control for unmarried women, but this was politically wholly unacceptable and certainly not to be discussed in public. The NC existed to promote a cause that was unpopular enough. Association with issues such as abortion and birth control, widely deemed to be immoral, would not have helped. However, supporters of NC could and did, as private individuals, support any cause they chose.[96]

---

[90] NC CMM, 9 Mar. 1921 and 11 May 1921, 5/OPF/2/1/1/1c. On Astor's relationship with the Women's Movement see Barbara Caine, *English Feminism 1780–1980* (Oxford: Oxford University Press, 1997), 205; Pugh, *Women's Movement*, 70.

[91] NC CMM, 1 Dec. 1927, 5/OPF/2/1/1/1c.

[92] NC CMM, 5 Dec. 1918, 5/OPF/2/1/1/1a, and 13 June 1923, 5/OPF/2/1/1/1c.

[93] NC Annual Report 1928, 5/OPF/10/1a, p. 11; 1929, pp. 16–17; 1931, pp. 18–19, and NC CMM, 21 Feb. 1934, 5/OPF/2/1/1/1c.

[94] NC Annual Report 1938, p. 25; NC CMM, 20 Nov. 1935, 5/OPF/2/1/1/1d.

[95] Debenham, 'Grassroots Feminism'.

[96] NC CMM, 11 July 1923, 5/OPF/2/1/1/1c.

The NC was part of the large and growing women's movement in the interwar years[97] and, like other women's organizations, chose its alliances and public statements carefully.

GIVING BIRTH

The severe problems of the mothers and children the NC existed to help started at, indeed before, the birth of the child. Hospital births were uncommon for working-class mothers before the establishment of the National Health Service in 1948. Most unmarried, like married, mothers gave birth in their place of residence, perhaps the family home, shared with a partner if they were cohabiting or with the maternal family or other close relatives or friends. But unmarried women might have trouble finding a midwife to attend them. Some district nursing organizations refused to allow their qualified midwives to attend unmarried mothers.[98]

The mother's family might be desperately poor and unable to provide space or support, or might reject her. Then, the likely resort for unsupported women was the workhouse where conditions were intentionally grim. Deaths of infants born outside marriage were highest of all among births in workhouses. A former workhouse baker in Lancashire described the experiences of women he encountered between the wars:

> some of them were from very good families.... The ladies came into the workhouse and did domestic work, cleaning up and washing and they did that until such time as the baby was due and then they were moved into another section to have the baby. Whilst they were with the baby and providing they were feeding the baby they stayed there looking after the babies in the nursery. They came back again, if they had nowhere to go, back into the workhouse to do ordinary domestic work. The children were taken care of by the Cottage Homes and there they remained until such times as they were leaving school when the Board of Guardians...found them employment.[99]

In January 1920, there were 2,783 unmarried mothers in workhouses in England and Wales.[100]

Some particularly unfortunate mothers found themselves consigned to mental hospitals. The Mental Deficiency Act, 1913, allowed local authorities to certify and institutionalize, generally unmarried, pregnant women who were deemed 'defective', at this time of heightened panic over 'racial degeneration' and eugenic concern about the perpetuation of 'unfit' genes.[101] 'Mental defect' was believed by

[97] Cheryl Law, *Suffrage and Power: The Women's Movement, 1918–28* (London: I. B. Tauris, 1997); Pat Thane, 'What Difference Did the Vote Make?', in Amanda Vickery (ed.), *Women, Privilege and Power: British Politics 1750 to the Present* (Stanford, CA: Stanford University Press, 2001), 253–88.

[98] Graham-Dixon, *Never Darken*, 11.

[99] Elizabeth Roberts, interviews Lancaster and Barrow, 1890–1940, Mr B1B.

[100] *First Annual Report. Ministry of Health, Parliamentary Papers*, 1920, vol. xvii, p. 328.

[101] Matthew Thomson, *The Problem of Mental Deficiency: Eugenics, Democracy and Social Policy in Britain 1870–1959* (Oxford: Oxford University Press, 1998).

some to have caused the women's 'immorality'. Destitute women who entered workhouses were most likely to suffer this fate. The numbers involved are unknown and probably few, but some sad victims were discovered in mental hospitals as late as 1971, having been there since the 1920s.[102]

To save women from this degradation and loss of their children, the Salvation Army and other, mainly faith-based, organizations from the end of the nineteenth century provided alternatives. The Army first found lodgings for some women with a midwife in Chelsea, London, who delivered the child and looked after the mother for a while after the birth. Then, in 1890, it opened a small maternity hospital. Demand was such that in 1909 it opened a larger hospital in Hackney, admitting several hundred unmarried mothers each year.[103] Charitable hospitals like this often had to charge fees to keep going. Though relatively modest (10 to 15s. per week) the fees were more than many mothers could afford. The NC helped them, when it could, to find a hospital place and pay the fees. Better-off mothers, married and unmarried, might give birth in private nursing homes.

AFTERWARDS

Mothers institutionalized in workhouses and mental hospitals were separated from their children after the birth. What happened to other unmarried mothers and their children? Sadly, as we have seen, the child might die. The founders of the NC believed that the main cause of this high death rate was the poverty of many mothers and their lack of support. Time and again they were disturbed by infanticide committed by desperate mothers, such as a tragic, but sadly not unique, case in 1921:

Within a few minutes walk of the office (of NCUMC), alone and untended in the servants' quarters of a Mayfair house, this girl gave birth to her child. According to the evidence of the Police Surgeon, she must have endured a long and terrible physical suffering as a climax to the mental strain she had already undergone.

The child was found dead. The jury acquitted the mother of murder.[104]

Other infants disappeared shortly after birth, the NC feared to unsuitable foster care where they died of neglect, descendents of the 'baby-farms' that had caused scandal in the late nineteenth century.[105] To prevent such tragedies, the Salvation Army and other organizations established homes for mothers and children to stay after the birth. By the beginning of the twentieth century there were at least two dozen homes in London solely for unmarried mothers. In Salvation Army homes

---

[102] Ibid. 299.

[103] Higginbotham, 'Respectable Sinners', 219–20.

[104] On infanticide see Daniel J. R. Grey, 'Women's Policy Networks and the Infanticide Act, 1922', *Twentieth Century British History*, 21:40 (2010), 441–63; and see pp. 51–2.

[105] George K. Behlmer, *Child Abuse and Moral Reform in England, 1870–1908* (Stanford, CA: Stanford University Press, 1982).

some stayed just a few weeks, the average was three and a half months. Almost one-third then returned to live with friends or family; for about half, the Army Women's Social Services section found positions in domestic service, living-in with their child. When it was difficult for the mother to combine work with childcare, the Army might arrange foster care, for which the mother paid. By the time of the First World War they were opening more hostels for mothers and children and had started a home for 'illegitimate' children.[106]

Children whose mothers could not care for them might be taken into orphanages or workhouses, permanently or temporarily, with varied outcomes. Voluntary organizations, including Barnardo's and the Salvation Army, had, since the early nineteenth century, dispatched 'unwanted' children to the colonies, mainly Canada and Australia, often without the knowledge of their parents, while the children were kept ignorant that their parents were alive. Between the 1880s and 1914 Barnardo's arranged for over 24,000 children to go to Canada alone. Transportation to Australia continued to the late 1960s. In these far countries, the children might be adopted into homes where they were well cared for, or indentured for hard labour on remote farms, sometimes suffering exploitation and abuse.[107]

Or they might be fostered or adopted in Britain. Fostering could be done by relatives or caring women who looked after the child well, or by people mainly interested in the fees, who did not. All too many mothers could not afford good foster care with sometimes tragic results. Fostering was not officially regulated until the Public Health Act, 1936, empowered councils to subsidize and inspect foster families, but few did so before the Second World War.

The difference between fostering and adoption was not always obvious in the absence of a formal, legal, adoption process in England and Wales before 1926, when it was introduced, later than in many other countries.[108] It was extended to Scotland in 1930, with the important difference that the Scottish law allowed adopted children to know the identities of their birth parents from age 17. Not until 1975 did adoptees in England and Wales gain the same right, at age 18.

Informal adoption had long existed within families, neighbourhoods, and other networks.[109] Ross found in East London between the 1870s and 1918 that

informal adoptions—some permanent, others temporary—by neighbours was not unusual... in Whitechapel Rd in the 1900s when a German baker and his wife out for a stroll saw a 'parcel in a doorway', a baby girl, that they picked up, took home and raised along with their other children. In a Battersea district in the 1890s, illegitimate children whose mothers were in service were often adopted by their aunts or grandmothers and thus absorbed into existing families.[110]

---

[106] Higginbotham, 'Respectable Sinners', 222–4.

[107] Jenny Keating, *A Child for Keeps: The History of Adoption in England, 1918–45* (London: Palgrave, 2009), 40–1; Joy Parr, *Labouring Children: British Immigrant Apprentices to Canada, 1869–1924* (London: Croom Helm, 1980); Margaret Humphreys, *Empty Cradles* (London: Doubleday, 1994), reissued as *Oranges and Sunshine: Empty Cradles* (2001).

[108] George Behlmer, 'Artificial Families: The Politics of Adoption', in George Behlmer (ed.), *Friends of the Family: The English Home and its Guardians, 1850–1940* (Stanford, CA: Stanford University Press, 1998). Keating, *A Child*; Cretney, *Family Law*, 596–606.

[109] Keating, *A Child*.   [110] Ross, *Love and Toil*, 134.

The Poor Law might assume parental rights over children under legislation of 1889 and 1899, where the parent was dead, had deserted the child, or was unfit to have care of the child by reason of mental deficiency, vicious habits or mode of life, was under sentence of penal servitude or imprisoned in respect of any offence against the child, was permanently bedridden, an inmate of a workhouse and consented to the action.[111] Children could then be put in supervised foster care or an institution. The child's legal parentage remained unchanged. In 1908, 12,417 children were cared for under this law; numbers in other years are uncertain.[112]

An important reason for the introduction of legal adoption procedures in 1926 was evidence of the exploitation and even death of informally 'adopted' children, many of them 'illegitimate'. The Society for the Prevention of Cruelty to Children (later the National Society, NSPCC) was founded in 1883 in response to evidence of child abuse, including 'baby-farmers' taking babies from often desperate mothers for a fee, promising to care for them but putting them to death.[113] In the early 1920s, the NSPCC was still concerned about the extent of child trafficking for financial gain, sometimes to meet the demands of paedophiles, another hidden vice not openly discussed at this time, though it was certainly not new. Campaigning groups made public long-hidden secrets and crimes. The NSPCC revealed one 'terrible story', among others, of a 'little girl of five who when twenty two months old was adopted by a man and woman of no repute living in Wigan. This child was outraged continuously from the age of four, was suffering from acute gonorrhoea and, but for the intelligent observation of a neighbour, would still be living in these appalling conditions.'[114] The NSPCC and the NC worked to avoid these terrible outcomes, the latter by trying to help women keep their children. Where this was impossible, they supported legal adoption processes designed to intensify supervision of carers for children who were not close relatives.

In general the NC was unenthusiastic about adoption. They feared that it was too often forced upon unwilling mothers, sometimes to protect a family from shame, whereas the mothers, with adequate support, could, and would prefer, to bring up their child themselves. But they recognized that sometimes it was the best or only option, for example, for rape and incest victims, children who had been deserted by their mothers, or whose mother had died or was an alcoholic. Also, under the 1926 legislation, unmarried mothers could adopt their own children. This enabled the child born 'illegitimate' to escape the desolate, legal status of *filius nullius*, nobody's child, into which they were born, granting them certain rights, such as that of inheritance from a mother who died intestate. The NC encouraged such adoptions and also, where appropriate, encouraged grandparents to adopt, to increase the child's security.

---

[111] Cretney, *Family Law*, 641.
[112] Ibid. 642.
[113] Behlmer, *Child Abuse*.
[114] R. Parr (Director of NSPCC) to S. W. Harris, Home Office, 31 May 1923, The National Archives (TNA), Home Office (HO) 45/11540. Quoted in Cretney, *Family Law*, 596 n. 4.

CONCLUSION

The experiences of unmarried mothers and their children, and attitudes to them, were more diverse in the nineteenth and early twentieth centuries than is often thought. Unmarried mothers who did not have a stable partner, a supportive family, or a good income, as many did, had a very hard time still in the 1920s. They faced passionate social opprobrium but also strong and influential support that brought some improvements. How did they manage through the interwar years?

2

Between the Wars

MAKING ENDS MEET

The biggest obstacle to mothers keeping their children was lack of resources—income or support from family or friends. How did they get by?

Maintenance and the law

Under the Bastardy Laws Amendment Act, 1872, mothers could apply for maintenance from the father. This allowed a 'single woman' (including any married woman who had lost the common law right to be maintained by her husband by deserting him or committing uncondoned adultery, or who was in fact separated from him) to take out a summons against the man she alleged to be the father of her child. The magistrates, based on the evidence, could judge that the man was the 'putative father' and make an order against him for the child's maintenance and education. The amount could not exceed 5s. weekly, not a large sum even then and providing nothing for the mother.

The mother was required to establish paternity only on the balance of probabilities, not 'beyond reasonable doubt' as required in criminal law. But she had to provide satisfactory corroborating evidence, to 'prevent men being at the mercy of profligate women' making 'wicked or unfounded charges'.[1] Evidence could include letters from the father admitting or implying paternity, his having made financial provision in the past, or proof 'that the two young people concerned were, perhaps, a courting couple or sweethearts or, at any rate were associating together on terms...of intimacy'.[2]

Evidence could be hard to find and even harder to interpret:

In 1917, a 15-year-old-girl, employed to do light jobs at Crew Farm Kenilworth [Warwickshire], claimed that she had been seduced by the farmer's son and that he had frequently made love to her in a barn in the farmyard. She also said that she had never slept with anyone else. The justices held evidence from the girl's mother that she had several times seen the two together in the barn to be sufficient corroboration of her story, and made an order. The Divisional Court held that they had been wrong: all that the mother's evidence did was

---

[1] Stephen Cretney, *Family Law in the Twentieth Century* (Oxford: Oxford University Press, 2003), 530 n.
[2] Ibid.

to show that it was *possible* the couple had had intercourse at the relevant time, whereas corroborative evidence had to show that it was *probable* that they had done so. If (said the Lord Chief Justice) the man and woman were 'seen in the neighbourhood of a wood or other dark place where they had no occasion to be' that might possibly be corroborative evidence. But in the present case the parties' work required them to be in the barn; and they had a reason (other than love-making) to be in the same place. There was thus no corroboration of the applicant's claim and the case was dismissed.[3]

Two years later, Miriam Jones was more successful:

[She] went to work for a 43-year-old bachelor as servant and housekeeper at his farm. On 11 May 1919 (the day before her period of service ended) she was ill and moaning. The farmer made a fire and gave her some brandy and tea. A doctor was called and a baby girl was born. The farmer allowed Miriam and her child to stay at the farm for some five weeks thereafter. On 14 July she wrote to him: 'Dear sir, I just take the priviledge (sic) of writing these few lines to you hoping you are well as it leaves me at present. I should like to know what you intend in regard to the child, Do you intend paying or not.... you know the child is yours..., Your's (sic) truly, Miriam Jones.' The farmer, who denied ever having intercourse with Miriam, did not reply. The magistrates held the farmer's actions on the morning of the birth, coupled with his actions in allowing her to stay on at the farm for a period (said by the Divisional Court to have far exceeded the 'usual period of recovery in such cases') and in not answering the letter were capable of corroborating her evidence. They made an order, and the Divisional Court (by a majority) accepted that the magistrates had been right... The magistrates had believed the woman and that decision had to stand.[4]

Despite the difficulties, the success rate of applications by mothers was high: of 7,895 in 1900/4, almost 80 per cent succeeded; of the 11,862 applications in 1919, 82 per cent.[5] In 1900 an Austrian scientist established that blood tests could show that a man could *not* be the father of a certain child. The first reported use of such a test in a British (divorce) case was not until 1942. It came into widespread use only from 1969.[6]

Court applications were difficult and stressful for unsupported mothers who were often not highly literate or accustomed to legal proceedings and might have good reason to fear confronting a violent former partner. The NC helped mothers contact absent fathers and obtain affiliation orders, supporting and advising them in the courts, but they could not ensure that the fathers paid. This could be most difficult when the fathers were foreigners who left the country. As we will see, they set up networks of overseas advisors to help trace the fathers and ensure enforcement of affiliation orders, including in Ireland to help the numbers of pregnant women who came to England to escape censure and harsh treatment at home.[7]

---

[3] Cretney, *Family Law*, 531–2.
[4] Ibid. 532.
[5] O. R. McGregor, L. Blom-Cooper, and C. Gibson, *Separated Spouses: A Study of the Matrimonial Jurisdiction of Magistrates Courts* (London: Duckworth, 1970).
[6] Cretney, *Family Law*, 536–9.
[7] See p. 45; NC Annual Report 1929 (supplementary document), 1930; M. Luddy, 'Unmarried Mothers in Ireland, 1880–1973', *Women's History Review*, 20:1 (Feb. 2011), 109–26.

From before the First World War there was sustained pressure to increase the liability of fathers to support their children. One outcome was a Select Committee on Bastardy Orders. This recommended in 1909 that there was a 'general and well-founded consensus' that the law should aim 'to secure the adequate care and maintenance of the child until it reaches the age when it can be expected to earn something for itself', and 'to facilitate the process by which mothers...and others can recover from the male parent expenses incurred in the child's birth or maintenance'. But, as a leading legal historian has commented, 'Equally there was little doubt that the law failed in these objectives.'[8]

The maximum amount a father could be required to pay was raised from 5s. to 10s. in 1918 (following rapid wartime inflation), then to £1 as a result of the Bastardy Act, 1923. This was the outcome, as we will see, of campaigning by the NC supported by its future president, the Conservative politician and future Prime Minister Neville Chamberlain, though it was a very limited compromise in a Parliament reluctant to shift the legal balance of responsibility for 'illegitimate' children onto the father.[9] Women were still treated by the law as the guilty parties, bearing the main responsibility for an 'illegitimate' birth. The maximum limit was not raised again until 1952 and the law remained essentially unchanged until 1987.[10]

Poor relief

If a mother could not get support for the child from the father, she could apply for relief under the Poor Law. This was normally the last resort of a desperate woman and might lead to the consignment of mother and child to the workhouse and separation, though some Poor Law Unions would, as they long had, provide minimal 'outdoor relief' to enable them to live, frugally, in their own homes. As we have seen, some unfortunate women were deposited in mental hospitals.[11] The local Union could apply for a court order to recover from the father the amount of relief they paid in respect of the child. In practice, they were more likely to assist the mother to apply for an affiliation order, which would remain in force if she ceased to receive poor relief.[12] The NC pressed Guardians to grant out-relief routinely. One of its founder-members, Mrs Baker, representing the mainly working-class organizations in the Standing Joint Committee of Industrial Women's Organizations, went further and proposed that

where paternity was unproved the State should maintain the child until the age of 16...the organized working women whom she represented were particularly anxious to see the physical welfare of the child and the moral welfare of the mother guaranteed in this way.[13]

---

[8] Cretney, *Family Law*, 557.
[9] See pp. 47–50; Cretney, *Family Law*, 557–9.
[10] Ibid. 559.
[11] See p. 25.
[12] Cretney, *Family Law*, 557.
[13] Sue Graham-Dixon, *Never Darken My Doorstep: Working for Single Parents and Their Children, 1918–1978* (London: National Council for One Parent Families, 1981), 17.

There was no realistic possibility of this and it was not promoted by the NC or others at this time. From 1929 the responsibilities of the Poor Law passed to local councils under the new Local Government Act. The progressive London County Council (LCC) then paid for expectant and nursing unmarried mothers 'of previous good character' to stay in approved voluntary homes and some other authorities followed. The NC urged more to do so.[14] The LCC also greatly improved the care of children who remained in Poor Law institutions.

Charity

So inadequate was public support in the 1920s that the NC encountered some desperate women, including two in 1921. The first was

A nursery governess just over twenty, seduced by a married man, this girl left her situation in terror that her condition might be noticed. Her parents were dead and she had no relatives to whom she could apply for help, so she threw herself on the mercy of a friend who took her in temporarily. The little money left by her father had all gone during the long, severe illness of her mother, and she had only ten pounds saved...

The other was a clerk who

called at the office in a very weak condition, leaving her six-weeks old baby in hospital. Her very respectable parents...were quite unable to support her; on the contrary the loss of her wages had brought the whole household to dire straits, and she was pawning her clothes to buy food.[15]

The NCUMC provided small sums—the most they could afford, often just 5 or 10s. (25p or 50p)—to help unsupported mothers equip their homes, provide for their children, or find work. It reported in 1929 that

Payment has been made for...legal expenses, a railway fare or an advertisement or some uniform when a new job was required...a loan or gift for dental treatment, extra nourishment before or after confinement, woollies for a scantily-clad baby, extra milk, food, convalescence, boots or clothing for a small boy or girl. Most important of all have been entrance fees paid for beds in maternity homes...providing shelter for both mother and child at the most critical time.[16]

But the NC did not see its role primarily as a relief agency; rather it wanted to enable mothers to support their children and themselves, with financial help from the father. In the 1930s the NC was licensed by the LCC to act as an employment agent to help mothers find work.[17] Between the wars this generally meant finding them posts as living-in domestic servants, one of the very few jobs where mother and child could stay together, though this could expose women to exploitation by employers who knew they were desperate. Others were helped to find places in

---

[14] Graham-Dixon , *Never Darken*, 18.   [15] Ibid. 17.   [16] Ibid.
[17] NC Annual Report 1933, 7, 5/OPF/10/1a, p. 31.

hostels that provided childcare while they worked. These were often run by religious foundations, were strictly disciplined, and were unappealing to many women.[18]

Fathers

We have no idea how many fathers supported their children voluntarily since this would not normally be the subject of court proceedings or appear in any public record. Such fathers were likely to be better off and there is no reason to believe that their numbers were few. Similarly, fathers who evaded payment were quite likely to be very young, poor, unemployed, low paid, or already responsible for a family and unable to support another, perhaps the very reasons why they had deserted the mother.

If she was fortunate enough to have an assured income from the father, her family, or her own earnings or inheritance, the mother could move to a new district and claim to be a respectable widow, credible enough following the Great War. She could care for her child at home or pay a servant to do so while she worked.

A place to live

It was hard for unmarried mothers to find lodgings with their children if they were open about their status, even if they could afford to support themselves. Landladies and landlords could be hostile. If she found lodgings, the mother might pay relatives or another woman in the neighbourhood to care for her child while she worked.[19] Or, if she could not, she placed her child with friends, relatives, or foster-parents, in the latter case usually for payment, sometimes happily for the child, sometimes not. Where fostering involved payment, the 1908 Children Act required registration with the local authority, and the number of children under age seven foster parents could care for was limited. The arrangement might end when the mother married or found another way to live with and support her child. Sometimes children and foster parents grew attached to each other and were unwilling to part.[20]

Some working-class women managed to support themselves and their children. Ernest Bevin, later a leading trade unionist and Labour Cabinet Minister, was born in Somerset in 1881, the seventh child of Diana (known as Mercy) Bevin, who was then aged 40. She had married William Bevin, an agricultural labourer in 1864, but in 1867 or 1868 he left her. Thereafter she called herself a widow. Ernest's father is unknown. His mother had the advantage of having her own home. She earned a frugal living as a domestic servant, midwife, and occasional help in a public house, perhaps helped out by her older children as she brought up Ernest. After her early death he lived with an older sister and her husband.[21]

---

[18] See p. 62.
[19] E. Ross, *Love and Toil: Motherhood in Outcast London* (Oxford: Oxford University Press, 1993), 136.
[20] NC Committee of Management Minutes (CMM), 25 Oct. 1938.
[21] Chris Wrigley, 'Bevin, Ernest (1881–1951)', *Oxford Dictionary of National Biography* (hereafter *ODNB*) (Oxford: Oxford University Press, 2004–9).

COHABITATION BETWEEN THE WARS

After the war, following pressure from the Divorce Law Reform Union (DLRU) and women's organizations, the Matrimonial Causes Act, 1923, at last enabled women to divorce men for adultery alone. Further legislation in 1937 equalized the grounds for divorce between the sexes and allowed it on grounds of cruelty or after three years desertion 'without cause'. The 1937 Act explicitly aimed to amend the law 'for the true support of marriage, the protection of children, the removal of hardship, the reduction of illicit unions and unseemly litigation, the relief of conscience among the clergy, and the restoration of due respect for the law.' A. P. Herbert, who led the campaign for the 1937 reform, insisted that the previous law was a 'definite incitement to immorality',[22] implying, again, that irregular relationships were not uncommon.

Joanne Klein's study of 'irregular marriages' among that most respectable section of the working class, policemen, in three major British cities, 1900–39, concludes that 'flexible notions of marriage persisted within the working class...into the interwar era...while only a small minority of policemen lived in unusual situations, their more conventional colleagues had few problems with their choices. Senior officers showed remarkable tolerance for domestic irregularities' and 'their choices did not necessarily meet with disapproval from their respectable neighbours.'[23] Klein comments that by no means all irregular partnerships involving policemen came to official notice.

Male and female workers in a similarly respectable occupation, the Post Office, protested vigorously in 1924 against the Civil Service regulation that unmarried mothers should automatically be dismissed. This, wrote 'A Mere Man', 'attempts to starve the innocent child and force the unfortunate mother to desperation'. There are signs that at least some senior Post Office officials quietly ignored the rule and kept unmarried mothers at work.[24] These are further signs that public opinion did not universally condemn unmarried mothers and cohabitees if their behaviour was acceptable in other respects.

A study by Manchester Health Department in 1938 of all traceable 'illegitimate' children born in the city in 1933 (427) found that 35 per cent of the parents, the largest single group, were cohabiting stably at the time of the birth. The Medical Officer of Health reported:

This largest group were born into households in which there was an irregular union, and therefore a fairly permanent home in which the children had two parents. In some cases the illegitimacy was not known outside the home. A number of parents had postponed their

---

[22] O. R. McGregor, *Divorce in England* (London: Heinemann, 1957), 29; and Jane Lewis, 'Marriage', in Ina Zweiniger-Bargielowska (ed.), *Women in Twentieth-Century Britain* (Harlow: Pearson Education, 2001), 72.

[23] Joanne Klein, 'Irregular Marriages: Unorthodox Working Class Domestic Life in Liverpool, Birmingham and Manchester, 1900–1939', *Journal of Family History*, 2 (2005), 210–29.

[24] Helen Glew, 'Women Workers in the Post Office, 1914–1939', PhD thesis, Institute of Historical Research, University of London (2010).

marriage, others were indifferent to the marriage ceremony, but the largest number were living together in an irregular union because one partner had a husband or wife, and was living apart.[25]

By 1938 some of the parents could not be traced, but 32 per cent were still cohabiting and lived with their children in apparently stable family relationships. A very few had married each other.[26] Roughly 8 per cent of all the unmarried mothers married the child's father within five years of the birth, 7 per cent married another man.

LIVING WITH GRANDPARENTS

Many unmarried mothers and their children vanished from the public record through absorption into the mother's own family. Some children, like Catherine Cookson, grew up thinking that the grandmother was his or her mother and the mother a sister.[27] Some families accepted an unmarried pregnancy more readily than others. A woman interviewed by Elizabeth Roberts in Lancashire reported of her sister:

M'father never spoke to her for a long time...[but] she stayed at home and m'mother brought up the baby as one of her own.... After she was born Nellie was the apple of my mother's eye. She never called any of us aunty....but m'mother was heartbroken.
Was you sister herself very upset about it?
No, I don't think so. I think she just took it quite calmly. I've never thought Edith was upset. She must have misbehaved herself so many times.

Edith later married and her husband adopted the child, but

The child wasn't happy and m'father was vexed. He said that it wasn't right to take her with her...she was about four or five and she was going to school. It was a complete change for the child because she'd always called her Edith and she'd to start to call her mum.[28]

The pregnant sister of another Lancaster woman drowned herself.[29] Another woman, Mrs Chadwick (born 1897), was herself 'illegitimate' and had happy memories of growing up with her grandmother, mother, and aunt:

My mother was one of those good girls who never went out and she had to stay at home and look after ten children...she couldn't hardly read or write...she just brought me up with love...My grandmother she was lovely...That was another love in my life...my auntie she was a rock to lean on. I have been blessed that way. It's never weighed upon me that I am what you would call illegitimate at all...He was married and he didn't tell her.

---

[25] V. Wimperis, *The Unmarried Mother and Her Child* (London: Allen and Unwin, 1960), 68–9.
[26] Ibid.
[27] See p. 7.
[28] Elizabeth Roberts, *A Woman's Place: An Oral History of Working Class Women, 1890–1940* (Oxford: Blackwell, 1995), 76.
[29] Ibid. 77.

She was thirty-six when she had me and I believe she tried to commit suicide...she wouldn't let me call her mother, I had to call her Hannah.[30]

It is impossible to know how many people lived in these situations. Of the 'illegitimate' children born in Manchester in 1933, 90 (21 per cent) lived in the maternal grandparents' family, while 3 lived with other relatives.[31] Twenty-five per cent of all the mothers worked as live-in domestic servants accompanied by their children. About 12 per cent lived with their children alone. This group gave the Health Department most anxiety:

Living rather precariously with mothers who were either widows or single girls living on their own earnings, the child being looked after by a landlady while mother went to work.[32]

The Ministry of Health commented:

On the whole, the circumstances of the children living with two parents or as part of the grandmother's family, did not differ from that of legitimate children...the child living with two parents usually had a brother or sister, and therefore some sort of family life, and the one living as part of the grandmother's family was regarded as the youngest member, with the real mother as an older sister, the child addressing her by her christian name.[33]

Some of Roberts' respondents recalled mothers asking their married siblings to adopt their children.[34] She describes a culture in interwar Lancashire in which a minority were censorious of unmarried motherhood, but most people took it in their stride.

Grandmothers were the most likely carers when possible. One grandmother asked the NC to help her daughter have her child adopted because she had five children of her own to care for and could not cope with another.[35] Grandfathers were often initially less sympathetic, but this did not always last, as one of the above examples suggests. A woman described what happened when her aunt gave birth to an illegitimate child:

My grandfather threw her out. The baby was born as we called it on the other side of the blanket...anyway granny, granny got her back in.[36]

Another who was initially rejected by her parents was later helped by her father to bring an affiliation order against the father of the child and the grandfather took

[30] Roberts, *A Woman's Place*, 77–8.
[31] Wimperis, *Unmarried Mother*, 51.
[32] Ibid. 258.
[33] Ibid. 255.
[34] Roberts interviews (hereafter ER), 'Early Collection' (i.e. covering the period 1890–1940; hereafter EC), Mrs B2P, Mrs W2L.
[35] NC, Case 1916, CCM, 26 Aug. 1920, 5/OPF/2/1/3/1a.
[36] ER, 'Late Collection' (i.e. covering the period 1940–70; hereafter LC), MrT5B, Mrs J1B.

responsibility for her care: 'he practically brought her up, he used to sit and rock her. Because she was so small.'[37]

At least in the working-class Lancashire neighbourhoods in Preston, Barrow, and Lancaster studied by Roberts, unmarried mothers were accepted in the early twentieth century with varying degrees of tolerance. One respondent described how in Preston in the 1930s,

People would talk about it and she would probably know and be ashamed. It was the shame that was the worst part. If they got married I suppose it wasn't looked on as bad, it was when they didn't get married you know. No, they wouldn't shun her or anything, but she would know they had been talking about her. It was quite a thing.[38]

Another said: 'in them days they didn't care; they never seemed to worry,'[39] and neighbours helped out. One 'illegitimate' child born in Preston in 1887 could not remember suffering any discrimination, 'They just accepted me. Perhaps they were more tolerant, but I never suffered from it.'[40] But it was rarely openly discussed. 'This was a respectable area and people kept it very quiet. There was more of it than you ever got to hear.'[41] Neighbours, it was said, could be more hostile to mothers who gave children up for adoption than those who kept them.[42]

The NC worked to persuade sometimes reluctant families to support their daughters and grandchildren. It described in 1920:

another fresh-looking girl of 20, in service in London, who had got into trouble through ignorance and folly. Her parents were highly respected in their district and the father refused to allow her to take the baby home; she might return but the baby must be got rid of. Correspondence was opened, pointing out that the father was probably driving the daughter to further wrong-doing. Persuasion prevailed, and permission was given for the mother and baby to return home.[43]

Such arrangements were less visible in the early twentieth century, when large families were common despite declining fertility, and siblings 20 years apart less surprising than they later became, which does not, of course, mean that neighbours failed to notice. Simple 'nuclear' family households were less dominant when death in youth and middle age as well as poverty were common, and flexible arrangements, with grandparents and other relatives rearing the children of widowed, deserted, or impoverished offspring relatively common in all classes, especially the working class.

Grandparents played a big role and seem often to have felt a strong need to protect their grandchildren from the uncertain and often unwelcoming world

---

[37] ER, LC, Mrs N3L.
[38] Roberts, *A Woman's Place*, 79.
[39] ER, EC, Mrs E1P, Mrs S5P.
[40] ER, EC, Mrs C3P.
[41] ER, EC, Mrs W1B, LC Mrs A4L; MO 1990 Directive Respondent P 1796.
[42] ER, LC, Mr M10L.
[43] NC Annual Report 1921.

their parents had brought them into. For example, the great grandmother of a well-known twenty-first-century television presenter was an elderly widow in a respectable working-class district of South London in the mid-1930s, known for her upright Presbyterianism and strict family discipline. Yet, when her son's girlfriend became pregnant and was thrown out by her parents, she allowed the unmarried couple to live in her house, which the neighbours cannot have failed to notice. They were still unmarried when the child was born and placed in foster care. The grandmother visited her grandchild, until she perhaps despaired of the parents' failure to support her. For whatever reason, she arranged an adoption that was, fortunately, successful. Like many stories of unmarried motherhood at this time this is revealing but frustrating: revealing about the behaviour that could be tolerated in a respectable working-class neighbour-hood, though perhaps not without gossip behind the curtains and over the garden fences; frustrating because we do not know why the couple did not marry. Did the mother not want to lose her independence? She later opened a hairdressing shop, which suggests ambition and resourcefulness, and access to some capital. Perhaps the couple felt unsuited, unready, or too poor to commit? They did later marry and had more children, after the mother had successfully established her business.[44]

Tolerance and gossip coexisted with public and private silence. Many Lancashire people told Elizabeth Roberts how many unmarried mothers were known in their neighbourhoods as they grew up, but 'You never spoke of anything like that.'[45] Nevertheless:

'I find when I look back that people helped one another, if a girl got into trouble they helped her. They would knit for her and make things for the baby and look after her in bed.'

ER: Do you remember many girls having babies when they weren't married?

Oh, yes it was quite common. It's more common today but they get rid of them.... The men want their fun and games and don't want to settle down or they hadn't the money. Money was the big problem, they couldn't afford to get married. A lot of them would prob-ably like to get married.

ER: So who would look after the babies can you remember?

The grandmas had to do it. Then there were baby-minders up and down the streets that took these poor kids in and [the mothers] had to go out to work. They had no choice, people don't realize how poor people were.[46]

They didn't think nothing about it because they nearly always had somebody in their own family in that way, way back...but it always seemed to be hushed up and brought up as one of their own sisters or brothers. The parents thought it was going to spoil that girl's chance of getting married. She didn't say it happened a lot but it happened.[47]

[44] Private information.
[45] ER, Preston 1890–1940, Mrs J1P.
[46] ER, Mrs P2P.
[47] ER, Miss T4T, Preston.

However, tolerance was not universal, as suggested by the playground taunts suffered by 'illegitimate' children, such as Catherine Cookson.[48]

Family arrangements could be short or long term, enabling the mother to work and contribute to the household economy, perhaps ending with her marriage. A high, but again unknown, proportion of unmarried mothers eventually married. Unmarried motherhood was not so shameful as to leave women unmarriageable. She might then take the child into a new family relationship, like one of the examples above. After 1926 the child could be adopted by the married couple and cease to be 'illegitimate'. But a new husband might reject another man's child, who would then stay with the grandparents.

MIDDLE-CLASS SECRETS

Such family arrangements were probably more common in working-class families, but middle- and upper-class experience is even harder to reconstruct. Their lives were more secret and less exposed to intrusive social surveys than those of working people. Secrecy was pervasive in all social classes not only about illegitimacy but about mental illness, crime, rape, divorce, or separation in the family—all believed to be shameful.[49] Certainly some unmarried middle-class couples quietly lived together, with and without children, and successfully hid their irregular relationships.

Where there was no such stable relationship, better-off families could arrange a discreet adoption or abortion for unfortunate daughters, but not all 'middle-class' families were well off, especially among the growing lower middle class of the interwar years; and abortion, even when performed by a doctor, was by no means safe before effective antibiotics were available from the late 1930s. Pressure on a couple to marry may have been the common response, though both the 1911 fertility census and a survey in 1939 concluded that it was relatively rare for middle-class parents to conceive before marriage, compared with working-class people.[50] Whether this was due to greater sexual restraint, fear of the consequences, or greater use of effective birth control is unknown. Yet pregnancy outside marriage did occur to middle-class women. The NC worked hard, and with some successes, to persuade middle-class families to support their pregnant daughters and take them home. Again, they found that some fathers could be especially intransigent.

Middle class, like much working-class experience, can only be reconstructed from scattered and possibly unrepresentative stories. David, interviewed by

[48] Ginger Frost, '"The Black Lamb of the Black Sheep": Illegitimacy in the English Working Class, 1850–1939', *Journal of Social History*, 37 (2003), 293–322. But discourse of this kind requires careful analysis: playground taunts (which can be directed at any child deemed to deviate from the norm—by being fat, wearing spectacles or the wrong clothes, having red hair, etc.) do not necessarily transparently convey the attitudes of the whole community.

[49] L. Davidoff, M. Doolittle, J. Fink, and K. Holden, *The Family Story: Blood Contract and Intimacy, 1830–1960* (London: Longman, 1999), 244–65.

[50] Wimperis, *Unmarried Mother*, 82.

Katherine Holden, was born in 1910, the son of an unmarried male veterinary surgeon and a private secretary/teacher. His mother, Ida, brought him up, but pretended she was his aunt who had adopted him after his parents died. He guessed the truth in his teens but kept quiet until his mother died. He kept in close touch with her and felt lasting regret that they had never shared the secret. He said:

I mean the credit really, if there is any credit, goes to my mother for not . . . hiving me off, because in those days it really wasn't a good thing to have an illegitimate child and her mother, my grandmother, disapproved very strongly of me. It's funny she took it out on me.[51]

Another anonymous respondent, born in the 1920s, 'described the coldness of a grandmother who in old age had felt obliged to bring her up. Like David, she had known her aunt was her mother since her schooldays and told of her sadness that she had never been acknowledged as her daughter.'[52] The victimization experienced by some unmarried mothers in all classes encouraged concealment.[53] On the other hand, some eugenicists, such as the birth control pioneer Marie Stopes, concerned about the falling birth rate, argued that 'suitable' unmarried middle-class women who wished to become mothers should not be discouraged, though they did not expect the numbers to be great or the notion to be popular.[54]

Mothers and their children survived in secrecy in a variety of situations. Frank Underwood reported how

I and my elder brother and sister were the unofficial family of a Church of England clergyman. I was born in 1926 and my mother, who was unmarried, brought us up on our own.

My father had gone as an organist to a parish in Northamptonshire and my recently widowed grandmother set her eyes on him. Eventually they married and moved north. But a close relationship had also developed between her daughter (my mother) and the clergyman. My mother went into a convent near Oxford, he got her out, set her up in London and around 1910 my brother was born.

There was an element of farce. Now and then father would pop down having told his wife that he was attending a theological conference. My mother later told stories of how she would try to keep him out by bolting all the doors and windows. My grandmother probably suspected—at some point she had a breakdown and spent the next 30 years in bed.

My father did write regularly and always enclosed a pound or two—not an inconsiderable sum then. My mother managed well in that we never went short of clothes or food and even developed a social life herself—going to dances at the Speedway Motorcycling Club in Crystal Palace.

I guess unmarried motherhood went on quite a bit then, though I still don't know how my mother—or I—managed. But it was all so hidden. Later, when my sister and I

---

[51] Katherine Holden, *The Shadow of Marriage: Singleness in England, 1914–60* (Manchester: Manchester University Press, 2007), 117–18.
[52] Ibid. 118.
[53] Ibid. 118.
[54] Ibid. 123.

attended father's funeral as adults, all we could say was that we were friends of the family.[55]

By contrast, the unmarried writer Rebecca West's decade-long liaison with the married H. G. Wells was no secret in their circles. In 1914, the day after war was declared, aged 21, she gave birth to their son, Anthony Panther West. Wells assured her during her pregnancy that, in due course, she would have a central role in his life, while simultaneously giving the same assurance to his wife. West gave birth in furnished lodgings Wells found in a quiet seaside town. She lived with her son through the war in discreet places, easily accessible to Wells, then from 1919 in a flat in London. Anthony was told that he was their nephew.[56] She broke with Wells in 1923 and married a banker in 1936. She and Wells wrangled over Anthony's education, his visits to Wells, finances, and Anthony's inheritance, which was less than that of Wells' two sons of his marriage. West adopted Anthony after her marriage, but even this outspoken, radical woman demanded privacy over this aspect of her life. She was hostile to biographies of Wells that referred to it, including that written by her son, which was very critical of her.[57] In 1947 she suppressed an article in *Time* magazine describing Anthony's parentage.[58] Anthony, despite, or because of, living with his mother, 'grew up to revere his father and to blame much of his unhappiness on his mother', often very bitterly.[59]

Another unmarried writer, Dorothy L. Sayers, was even more secretive about her son, John Anthony, when she gave birth in 1924. She did not love the father. She was just establishing herself as an author and the child went to live with her unmarried cousin and lifelong friend, Ivy Shrimpton. Dorothy did not tell her parents about his birth, but kept in touch and provided for him at a distance. She was evidently concerned about her own reputation and the effect on her career and social life and that of her son, if he was known to be 'illegitimate'.[60] In 1926 she married a journalist, Atherton Fleming, and hoped to take her son into their home. It never happened, though he took the name Fleming and was publicly represented as their adopted son. He was well cared for by Ivy Shrimpton and the full story, like many others, was only revealed by biographers in the less secretive, perhaps more intrusive, later twentieth century.[61]

The suffragette and socialist Sylvia Pankhurst was more open when, in 1927, at age 45, she gave birth to her only child, Richard Keir Pethick Pankhurst. She had lived for some years with his father, Silvio Corio, an Italian libertarian socialist exiled from fascist Italy, and continued to do so, in Woodford Green, Essex. She

[55] Hilary Macaskill, *From the Workhouse to the Workplace: 75 Years of One-Parent Family Life, 1918–1993* (London: NCOPF, 1993), 21.

[56] Patrick Parrinder, 'Wells, Herbert George', *ODNB* (2008).

[57] Anthony West, *H. G. Wells: Aspects of a Life* (New York: Random House, 1984).

[58] Bonnie Kime Scott Andrews, 'Dame Cicily Isabel [Rebecca West] (1892–1983)', *ODNB* (2008).

[59] Parrinder, 'Wells'. Anthony West, Introduction, in *Heritage*, 2nd edn (London: Coronet, 1984).

[60] Barbara Reynolds, *Dorothy Sayers: Her Life and Soul* (London: Hodder & Stoughton, 1993).

[61] Catherine Kenney, 'Sayers, Dorothy Leigh (1893–1957)', *ODNB* (2004).

was open about the relationship and about her son and refused to marry, in keeping with her and Corio's beliefs in sexual freedom and women's emancipation, despite pressure from her far more conservative sister, Christabel.[62] She and Christabel never spoke again. Richard had a close relationship with his parents and wrote a loving biography of his mother, focusing particularly upon her less well-known skills as an artist, though he shared her unflagging political commitments.[63]

Less famous now is the actress Rachel (Ray) Litvin, a rising star at the Old Vic Theatre in London during and after the First World War. Unmarried, in 1920 she gave birth to Natasha, who later married the poet Stephen Spender. The father was Edwin Evans, a married music critic. While her mother earned a living on the stage, Natasha was sent to a foster mother in Sussex, 'the awful Mrs James' as Natasha later described her, who left her in a high chair all day. When Natasha was two-and-a-half, a friend of Ray's intervened and Natasha was transferred to the care of Mrs Busby, a 'wonderful, steady working class woman' in Maidenhead. Natasha said later, 'I really owe all the stability I have in my temperament, such as I have, to Mrs Busby.' She grew up calling Mrs Busby, 'Mother'; Ray was 'Mummy'. She spent happy holidays on the Sussex Downs with friends of her mother, learning to move easily between the working-class environment in which she lived every day and her mother's smart friends, adjusting her accent as required. Her mother paid 'rather alarming' visits every three months, instructing Natasha that she was not to play with other children in the street, which Natasha ignored.

When Natasha was 12, her mother contracted typhoid, became deaf and could no longer perform on the stage. Natasha went to live with her for the first time, in a one-room flat in Primrose Hill, North London, occasionally returning to visit the Busbys and their two children. Ray was now short of money and unexpectedly told Natasha that she must visit her father to ask for help. As she later described it: 'Not the best beginning to a relationship. Somehow we got over it.' She was emerging as a talented pianist and became a musician, which was a bond between them. She described him as 'the fattest man in London'. He wore a huge opera hat and she found him rather frightening, but he seems to have paid up. When she met Spender in 1940, one of the family servants warmed to her because 'she's illegitimate, and don't care who knows it'.[64]

The fact that unmarried women, and men, generally middle class, could and did adopt children, with legal sanction after 1926, setting themselves up publicly as unmarried parents, suggests a certain flexibility about social norms and family arrangements at this time, as well as sometimes providing a socially acceptable cover for unmarried parenthood.[65] Single men were not allowed to adopt young girls without special permission from the court, which was occasionally granted.

---

[62] June Hannam, 'Pankhurst, (Estelle) Sylvia (1882–1960)', *ODNB* (2007).

[63] Richard Pankhurst, *Sylvia Pankhurst, Artist and Crusader: An Intimate Portrait* (London/New York: Paddington Press, Virago, 1979).

[64] Harriet Lane, 'I Was Never in the Faintest Doubt of His Devotion to Me'. Interview with Lady Spender, *Observer*, 9 May 2004.

[65] Holden, *Shadow*, 140 ff.

Adoption statistics are patchy before the 1970s but a Home Office survey of the first year of the 1926 Adoption Act showed that 3,548 adoption orders had been made, of which about 450 were to men and 150 to women adopting singly. About two-thirds of the children were illegitimate; an unknown number, probably small, were adopted by one or both of their parents.

Where we can penetrate the veil of secrecy, among the middle classes, attitudes to and the experiences of unmarried mothers and their children were as diverse as those of working people, if still more hidden.

FIGHTING FOR MOTHERS

Whatever flexibility of attitudes to lone motherhood may have existed in some quarters of society, all too many mothers were desperate and looked to the NC for help.

It stressed the variety of backgrounds of women who appealed to it, refusing 'to accept the theory that unmarried mothers are of any one particular type or class',[66] reporting:

Applications have come from clerical and domestic workers, from women and girls in factories, shops or other business houses, from companion-helps and from women engaged in various professions.[67]

But, tragically, still some women killed themselves when they found they were pregnant with no hope of marriage.[68]

As awareness of the NC's work spread and the need did not diminish, it faced an endless problem of fundraising. The organization rose to the challenge in imaginative ways and was quick to use new media to promote its cause and raise donations. The BBC was formed in 1922 and Lettice Fisher, helped by one of her former Oxford students, Hilda Mathieson, the first talks director of the BBC, made an early radio appeal in 1925 on behalf of the 'innocent and helpless children' and their mothers who, 'if only they can be given the chance…become splendid mothers and self-respecting citizens'. The audience was not persuaded. The NC received only one donation of 5s., three applications for support, and two offers of help from voluntary workers.[69]

Their then president, Neville Chamberlain, was more successful in 1930. He went for a more personal approach, highlighting success stories such as that of Freddy who

spent his childhood in a London garden whilst his mother learned to cook. He now takes her out to tea in holidays, their mutual affection and pride a joy to see.

---

[66] NC Annual Report 1936, 5/OPF/10/1a, p. 27.
[67] NC Annual Report 1937, p. 30.
[68] Roberts, *A Woman's Place*, 75–80.
[69] NC CMM, 12 Mar. 1925, 5/OPF/2/1/1/1c.

...Then there is Jackie, whose mother had been obliged to leave him in Italy. With our help and a cheque, he was brought all the way back to England and sent to his grandparents in a northern city.

He concluded: 'I would remind my fellow-men that these women and children are often the victims of some man's utter selfishness—it is our job to do what we can to alleviate their sufferings.'[70] This talk raised £460. The actor Cyril Maude raised a record £1,500 from over 3,500 contributors from three dramatic appeals in 1936, 1940, and 1943, declaiming:

If we do not all help in this as well as subscribe liberally we are through our apathy and our ignorance <u>helping</u> to <u>murder</u> thousands of absolutely blameless children.

...drop your prejudices some of you, lower your elevated eyebrows, give up your sniffs of disgust at such a subject having to be discussed on this Sunday night, and for heavens sake turn a deaf ear to the Goebbels-like lies of those who urge that we are encouraging immorality. WE ARE NOT! Come down to earth now and realize how terribly needful it is that we should help these poor little ones and their unfortunate mothers.[71]

As well as arranging further radio appeals, the NC made pioneering use of film. A documentary, *Unmarried*, was made by a production company with the Council's help and released in 1921. It publicized the work of the NC by showing the hardship of unmarried mothers and their children but also, subversively, suggested that the lot of the respectably married was not necessarily better.[72]

More conventionally, Lady Astor and Mrs Neville Chamberlain arranged fundraising 'drawing room meetings'. The NC gained the patronage of Queen Mary, who visited the offices in 1924, and they were among the charities benefiting from the sale of seats at the wedding of Princess Marina and the Duke of Kent in 1924 and the Royal Jubilee in 1935. The Royal Family clearly did not find it problematic to be associated with a body sympathetic to unmarried mothers and their children. The Hector Sassoon Trust provided £500 a year for several years from 1926. Otherwise, the NC relied on proceeds from sales, garden fetes, flag days, postal appeals, annual dinner dances, concerts, a dog show, and legacies. For some years a London cinema donated a proportion of their Sunday takings.[73] It was a condition of cinemas opening on the Sabbath that a donation be made to charity.

The Council raised enough funding to keep going and expanding. It established a Case Committee with a dedicated worker who interviewed and helped individual mothers. It handled 600–800 new cases a year, rising to over 1,000 in the 1930s, coordinating its work with other organizations, including the Salvation Army, Barnardo's, the Foundling Hospital in central London, and Jewish, Roman Catholic, Anglican, and Non-Conformist organizations, referring clients when and where

---

[70] NC Radio Broadcast Appeals (RBA), 1930, 5/OPF/2/2/7/1.

[71] NC RBA, 1940, 5/OPF/2/2/7/1.

[72] NC CMM, 13 May 1919, 5/OPF/2/1/1/1a; NC Annual Report, 1919–20, 5/OPF/10/1a, p. 6. No copy seems to survive. Technically, it was criticized in the film press. Popular papers were impressed by the stat cast (including Gerald du Maurier); society papers by the celebrity supporters of the NC. Eve Colpus 'Landscapes of welfare: concepts and cultures of British women's philanthropy, 1918–39'. Oxford University D.Phil 2011, 158–9.

[73] Mrs H. A. L. Fisher, *Twenty-One Years* (London: National Council for the Unmarried Mother and Her Child, 1939), 10.

appropriate. It advised on the establishment of residential homes and ran conferences on ways to help mothers and children. In consultation with the new Ministry of Health it drew up plans for homes and hostels and lobbied local authorities and voluntary agencies to fund them.

The NC continued to help mothers, including victims of rape, to bring the fathers to account, and gave what support it could to women pregnant due to incest.[74] It also further developed its international contacts, partly to trace men from overseas who fathered children in Britain then returned home. One man was pursued through the German courts until he agreed to pay 90 Reichsmarks each quarter to his daughter.[75] And they supported foreign women made pregnant by British men, helping them return home since they were not entitled to apply to the British courts to enforce payment from the father. Unmarried pregnant Irish women who fled to Britain from the puritan moral code at home regularly needed help, on which the NC worked with sympathetic Roman Catholic organizations.[76] Male Indian students in Britain posed particular problems in the 1930s. The NC worked closely with the Indian High Commission and held meetings with the Joint Council to Promote Understanding between White and Coloured People in Great Britain about how best to pursue fathers who fled and their mixed-race children who were left behind in an often intolerant society.[77] Representatives of the NC met fellow-workers from the colonies and Dominions at the British Empire Exhibition held in London in 1924 to discuss common issues. In 1926 they sent a representative to the Congress of the International Woman Suffrage Alliance in Paris, which urged that every effort should be made to keep unmarried mothers and their children together and 'that the father should not be allowed to escape his responsibilities' no matter where he tried to go.[78] The NC gave evidence to the League of Nations on these and other issues related to the needs of unmarried mothers and their children and the difficulties caused by nationality and other laws.

Mothers learned about the Council from friends, advertisements, other voluntary organizations, nurseries, public health departments, hostels, and, increasingly, women's magazines.[79] The Council was committed to listening with respect and confidentiality. It encouraged mothers to be as honest as possible with family, friends, and employers, though they recognized that this might encourage exploitation by some employers who knew how hard it was for the women to find another post.[80] Mothers were also advised to be truthful with their children as they grew up:

the child should be told the truth and should not be brought up on lies. It should know who is its mother and should gradually be helped to understand that 'Daddy' went away.

[74] NC Grants Committee Minutes (GCM), 1 July 1930, 5/OPF/2/1/3/1a; CMM, 11 June 1937.
[75] NC Annual Report 1932, 5/OPF/10/1a, p. 18.
[76] Luddy, 'Ireland'.
[77] NC Annual Report 1930, 5/OPF/10/1a, pp. 14–15; CMM 18 June 1931, 5/OPF/02/1/1/1d.
[78] NC Annual Report 1926, quoted in Graham-Dixon, *Never Darken*, 4.
[79] NC GCM 1942–5, 5/OPF/02/01/3/1h, p. 6.
[80] NC Annual Report 1922, 5/OPF/10/1a, p. 9.

Sooner or later the mother must tell her child the whole truth, but she should be urged not to be emotional about it.[81]

The death rate of 'illegitimate' babies continued to be disproportionately high and some babies died because their mothers neglected their own health in pregnancy from fear of revealing their condition. The NC worked with Women's Citizens Associations in particular to persuade mothers to use local authority ante- and post-natal services.[82] Sometimes they helped unmarried fathers, such as one in 1923 who needed

A Home for his twin girls of 15 years, who had been with a foster-mother since birth. The father had made payments but felt unable to continue... The Case Committee managed to secure vacancies in a very suitable Home where the training of the children for the future could begin.[83]

They paid for tired mothers and their children to take seaside holidays, funded by the Sassoon donation, and for others to take work training such as in shorthand and typing.[84]

Grateful mothers who had been helped in the past kept in touch. One, whom the NC had helped to emigrate to Australia, wrote in 1929 describing how she had 'furnished my home and just sent £30 to bring my mother out to keep house for the boy and myself... my little boy is now five and really well and healthy.'[85] She was one of many women the NC assisted to emigrate to a new life.[86] Other past beneficiaries sent gifts to help less fortunate mothers.

CHANGING THE LAW

Changing the law to help unmarried mothers and their children was a central purpose of the NC from the beginning. Campaigning and negotiating for legal changes to promote social, including gender, equality was an important aspect of the work of many voluntary associations, including women's organizations, at this time.[87] These associations, including the NC, collaborated and learned from one another in these campaigns, particularly the women who were getting accustomed to their new political rights and legitimacy after gaining the vote.[88] The activities of

---

[81] NC Homes and Hostels Committee Minutes (HHMC), 28 Mar. 1949, 5/OPF/02/10a and b.
[82] NC CMM, 27 Sept. 1933, 10 May 1938, 5/OPF/02/01/1/1d. NC Annual Report 1935, 5/OPF/10/1a, p. 20.
[83] Graham-Dixon, *Never Darken*, 12.
[84] NC GCM, 10 May 1932, 5/OPF/2/1/3/1e.
[85] NC Annual Report 1929 (supplementary document), 5/OPF/10/1a.
[86] NC GCM, 6 May 1920 5/OPF/2/1/3/1a; 18 Feb. 1930, 5/OPF/2/1/1/1d. Annual Report 1931, p. 26.
[87] Pat Thane, 'What Difference Did the Vote Make?', in Amanda Vickery (ed.), *Women, Privilege and Power: British Politics, 1750 to the Present* (Stanford, CA: Stanford University Press, 2001), 253–88.
[88] Stephen Cretney, '"What Will the Women Want Next?" The Struggle for Power within the Family, 1925–1975', in Cretney (ed.), *Law, Law Reform and the Family* (Oxford: Oxford University Press, 1998), 155–83; Thane, 'What Difference Did the Vote Make?'

the NC provide a case study of a wider theme in interwar politics. Like other organizations, they drafted parliamentary bills, formed deputations to Ministers, held public meetings, gave evidence to official committees, and propagandized for them, placing articles in the press promoting their aims and seeking to educate the public.[89] Lettice Fisher was central to the NC's campaigning.[90]

The NC's first targets were to increase the sums payable to mothers under affiliation orders and to improve the payment process; also to enable the legitimation of children whose parents subsequently married. In most European countries, including Scotland, this had been possible for some time, in some for centuries. The NC started by organizing deputations to inform and persuade the government,[91] supported by press publicity and letters to MPs, Party whips, and to other voluntary organizations to build support.[92] They worked particularly closely on these issues with the National Society for the Prevention of Cruelty to Children and the Reformatory and Refuge Union.

The Home Office, which was responsible for affiliation orders, refused to meet them. The NC then used personal contacts, in this case Lady Margery Greenwood, soon to be a Vice-President of the NC and wife of Sir Hamar Greenwood, Under-secretary for Home Affairs. She reported in March 1919 that her husband had told her 'unofficially' 'that if the application were made to him direct a little later, when the industrial situation was less acute [i.e. when the strike wave subsided] there might be a chance of success'.[93] But in April he became Chief Secretary for Ireland and the chance was lost.

Since the Government was evidently unwilling to address these issues directly because they feared that they were unpopular with voters, the NC took the conventional route of extra-parliamentary organizations seeking to change the law: they found sympathetic MPs to put forward Private Members' Bills. These MPs were mainly male, since there were few women in Parliament and the few there were not all sympathetic to the aims of the NC.[94] The legal subcommittee of the NC, composed of lawyers including Chrystal Macmillan and Mr Warden Gowing, Hon Solicitor to the NC, drafted and advised on legislation.

In August 1919, the NC and its allies organized a conference at the House of Commons, to which MPs of all parties were invited, to discuss a draft Bastardy Bill.[95] A wide-ranging Bill was introduced in the Commons by Neville Chamberlain in May 1920,[96] but it tried to do too much and attracted an equally wide range of opponents. It aimed, firstly, to increase and enforce the financial responsibilities of fathers. It wanted fathers, for the first time, to be identified and required to

[89] Helen McCarthy and Pat Thane, 'The Politics of Association in Industrial Society', *Twentieth Century British History*, 22:2 (2011), 217–29.
[90] NC CMM, 14 Oct. 1919, 5/OPF/02/1/1a; 17 Mar. 1920, 5/OPF/02/01/1/1c.
[91] NC CMM, 11 Mar. 1919, 5/OPF/02/01/1/1a.
[92] NC CMM, 5 Dec. 1918, 28 Feb. 1919, 5/OPF/02/01/1/1a.
[93] NC GCM, 11 Mar. 1919, letter from Lady Greenwood.
[94] NC CMM, 4 June 1919, 5/OPF/02/1/1a.
[95] NC CMM, 9 Sept. 1919, 5/OPF/02/01/1/1a.
[96] NC CMM, 11 Nov. 1919, 5/OPF/02/01/1/1a.

make payments before the birth. The mother would be required to name the alleged father, who, even if he denied paternity, would have to submit to affiliation proceedings in court. This was more stringent than previous legislation. So was the provision that no agreement could be made for the support of an 'illegitimate' child without the approval of the court. This would put an end to voluntary, private agreements and bring unwelcome publicity to some secret fathers. Not surprisingly, it aroused particular opposition. Fathers would also face stronger compulsion to pay, under binding, court-approved maintenance agreements. Magistrates' courts would appoint collecting officers, to remove the burden of collecting the payment from the mother. This had been permitted since 1914 but many districts had not taken it up. The Bill further proposed that every 'bastard' under age 16 should become a ward of the Juvenile Court, which would be empowered to appoint guardians and otherwise safeguard the young person's welfare. Finally, it provided that children should be legitimated by the subsequent marriage of their parents.

Chamberlain found much support in the House of Commons, largely due to the belief that the burden of shame fell unfairly on the mother of an illegitimate child, and the Bill passed its second reading by 117 votes to 9, but there were many abstentions and strong opposition. The Home Secretary, Edward Shortt (Liberal), committed the Government to supporting the principle of legitimation by subsequent marriage in some form, and to raising the top limit for affiliation orders to 15s. a week,[97] but opposed the other provisions. The Home Office believed, not unreasonably, that the Bill was too complex and raised too many tricky legal issues.[98] The parliamentary procedure exposed the limits of what would be publicly tolerated.

Some opponents feared the threat of blackmail to men of property, and that legitimated children would acquire rights to inherit property and titles, displacing the children of previous marriages, though legitimation following marriage had been legal for centuries in Scotland apparently without such ill-effects.[99] Previously in England and Wales, children born 'illegitimate' had no right to inheritance if their parents died intestate. Fears were expressed about bogus claims by children whose mothers subsequently married someone who was not, in fact, his or her father. Resistance on these grounds was particularly strong in the House of Lords, and was shared by Lady Astor (Conservative), the first woman to take her seat in the Commons, though she and her husband (whose seat she had inherited on his elevation to the Lords) supported the NC in other respects. There were frequent claims that the proposed legislation was biased against men. As one Home Office civil servant commented, 'we must guard against the assumption that every woman is a saint and every man a sinner in this connection. Still, the woman, in most of these cases, is under a decided inherent disadvantage as compared with the

---

[97] *Official Report* (House of Commons), 7 May 1920, vol. 128, col. 2397.
[98] Cretney, *Family Law*, 558 n. 93.
[99] *Official Report* (House of Commons), 7 May 1920, cols. 2395–452. See also Charles Oman's contribution to the debate in *Official Report* (House of Commons), 27 June 1924, cols. 848–9.

man.'[100] Another serious difficulty was establishing fatherhood while the courts remained reluctant to use blood tests.[101]

Legitimation following the marriage of the parents aroused at least as much opposition, including from Anglican bishops and the Archbishop of Canterbury,[102] mainly on the grounds that it condoned and could encourage adultery. Fears were expressed that the Bill might cause pressure on the 'innocent' party in a broken marriage to agree to divorce in order to allow legitimation of the child. Of the six women MPs in 1920, three opposed this clause: Lady Astor, again, the Duchess of Atholl, and Mrs Hilton Phillipson, both Conservatives and opposed to most issues supported by feminists including the equal franchise.[103] But feminists, including supporters of the National Union of Societies for Equal Citizenship (NUSEC), also opposed it. Lady Rhondda, leader of the feminist Six Point Group, wrote to *The Times* in 1924 arguing that to legitimize children born in adultery 'must weaken the marriage tie and encourage a state of affairs that practically amounts to bigamy'.[104] Three female MPs supported the change: the Liberals Mrs Wintringham and Lady Terrington, and Susan Lawrence (Labour). The latter argued that women on the whole were not opposed to the proposal and working-class women in particular would benefit. The Home Office Legal Adviser, Sir Ernley Blackwell, noted that legislation to allow subsequent legitimation was 'desired by all parties and especially by women'.[105] Many opponents argued that the issue was better dealt with by reforming the divorce law to reduce the number of couples living and having children 'in sin' by enabling them to dissolve previous marriages. Legalized adoption was also proposed as a preferable way forward. Chamberlain referred to countries, mostly in Scandinavia, that had introduced similar legislation allowing legitimation, without destroying marriage.[106]

The Labour Party supported the principles behind the Bill but objected to the requirement to disclose the identity of the father and the consequent danger to mutually agreed private financial arrangements. They also opposed the state interference in family lives implicit in the compulsory wardship proposal. This was widely unpopular and quickly dropped, though the NC continued to favour it in order to safeguard vulnerable children. Labour also opposed the continued use of the term 'bastard' in the title of the Bill.[107]

Faced with so much opposition at the committee stage, the promoters of the Bill withdrew everything but the legitimation provision and some minor amendments to the Bastardy Acts, but it made no further progress in Parliament. The Bill was reintroduced in modified form in 1921, focusing just on legitimation following

[100] The National Archives, HO 45/19015, 24 Mar. 1924. Note 'Illegitimacy Bill, 1924' signed RJD.

[101] See p. 30.

[102] *Offical Report* (House of Lords), 21 Feb. 1924, vol. 56, col. 256.

[103] Martin Pugh, *Women and the Women's Movement in Britain*, 2nd edn (London: Macmillan, 2000), 53–4.

[104] Cretney, *Family Law*, 550–1 n. 29.

[105] Ibid. 548.

[106] *Official Report* (House of Commons), 27 June 1924, cols. 857, 862–3.

[107] Cretney, *Family Law*, 547 n. 13.

the parents' marriage. It was introduced this time by Captain Bowyer (Conservative), another supporter of the NC. H. A. L. Fisher, Lettice Fisher's husband, chaired the Cabinet meetings that discussed this and related bills. This time it was approved in the Commons, but defeated in the Lords, due mainly to fears that legitimated children would threaten the inheritance rights of children of a previous marriage, and of condoning adultery, which were expressed especially strongly by the bishops.

The NC then reverted to the less contentious issue of the sums payable under affiliation orders. In 1923 a modified Bastardy Bill was put forward, again by Captain Bowyer, minus the clauses enforcing disclosure of parentage and voluntary payments. This time it had stronger support from the new Conservative Government, in which Chamberlain was a Minister, and it became law.[108] It doubled to 20s. a week the maximum sum payable under an affiliation order.

The legitimacy issue continued to be promoted unsuccessfully: eleven bills on aspects of legitimation were brought before Parliament between 1918 and 1926. On other occasions supportive MPs were unsuccessful in the ballot for Private Members' Bills.[109] The NC and their allies in both Houses worked tirelessly on the issue, lobbying and sending letters to Ministers including the Prime Minister. The arguments hardly changed and emotions remained strong. Legislation was promised in the King's speech in 1924 by another Conservative Government,[110] but took until 1926 for the Legitimacy Act to result from a bill promoted by the Government. This allowed a child to be legitimated by the subsequent marriage of the parents, provided that neither had been married to another partner at the time of the birth, an amendment on which a majority of MPs insisted.[111] The new law enabled legitimated children to inherit property and land, including from an intestate parent, but not titles. A legitimated person's seniority among his or her siblings was to date from legitimation, not from birth, to prevent their displacing the inheritance rights of siblings who had been born legitimate.[112] At the time of the marriage, the father had to be resident in England or Wales and of British nationality. If the mother was not British at the time of the marriage, she would acquire British nationality on marriage, but a child born before the marriage could not, even after the Act was passed. This left some children stateless because some national laws denied nationality to children born of foreign fathers.[113]

---

[108] NC CMM, 14 Feb. 1923, 5/OPF/2/1/1/1c.

[109] Cretney, *Family Law*, 548 n. 20.

[110] Ibid.

[111] NC Annual Report 1926, 5/OPF/10/1a, p. 11; CMM, 9 July 1925, 12 Jan. 1926, 5/OPF/2/1/1/1c and Legal Sub-Committee Papers (hereafter LSC), 26 Nov. 1920, 6 Apr. 1921, 5/OPF/02/12a. Chamberlain and Bowyer both represented the Council's interests within Parliament during the twenties. Following Bowyer's appointment as a Government Whip in Jan. 1926 Victor Cazalet agreed to act on the Council's behalf in the Commons. See NC CMM, 9 Mar. 1926, 5/OPF/2/1/1/1c.

[112] Cretney, *Family Law*, 550 n. 27.

[113] Ginger Frost, '"Revolting to Humanity": Oversights, Limitations and Complications of the English Legitimacy Act of 1926', *Women's History Review*, 20:1 (Feb. 2011), 31–46.

This was the most Parliament would accept.[114] By 1936 over 31,000 children had been registered as legitimate under the new law,[115] many fewer than acquired legitimacy by adoption following the Adoption Act, 1926.[116] Between 5 and 9 per cent of children born 'illegitimate' between 1921 and 1959, when the law was next revised, were legitimated by their parents' subsequent marriage. Legitimation was automatic on the parents' marriage, but if parents or children wanted birth certificates and other documents amended to record this, the procedure was slow and costly.[117] The NC was glad to achieve some change, but the problem remained of children born to cohabiting parents who were married to others due to the limitations of the divorce law. The NC decided not to seek to amend the new law by drafting further legislation, but kept lobbying ministers and backbenchers,[118] with the support of women's and welfare organizations, including NUSEC, the Salvation Army, National Council of Women (NCW), and Six Point Group, for improved security for mothers and children and changes in the divorce law.[119]

With other organizations, it also carried on a fight started in the nineteenth century to stop desperate mothers who killed their newborn in the shock and shame of a secret birth being charged with murder, with the possible penalty of death by hanging.[120] The campaign took off with renewed vigour following a tragic case in Leicester, in June 1921. Edith Roberts, an unmarried 21-year-old factory worker, was charged with murder. A newborn girl had been found strangled in a wooden chest in the bedroom Edith shared with her sister in their parents' home. The family had not suspected she was pregnant. She was believed to have been a victim of rape. Edith pleaded not guilty to killing her child, but was found guilty of wilful murder. The all-male jury made a strong recommendation for mercy, but the judge pronounced the death sentence.

The local Board of Poor Law Guardians, among others, called for a change in the law to prevent the death sentence in such cases. Edith's sentence was commuted to penal servitude for life. She appealed, unsuccessfully. The case featured in the local press and 500 people attended a protest in Leicester, demanding a change in the law. Such cases of infanticide were believed to be most common among unmarried mothers, due to shame and poverty, and were regarded by many as tragic rather than criminal. A committee of local branches of the NCW, Women's Co-operative Guild (WCG), Women's Sections of the Labour, Liberal, and Independent Labour Parties, the National Union of Women Teachers, NUSEC, and the Leicester Board of Guardians wrote to Nancy Astor, as the only female MP, asking her to raise the case in Parliament. The Women's Freedom League took up

---

[114] E.g., House of Commons, 15 June 1923, col. 87; 27 June 1924, cols. 823–84; *The Times*, 28 June 1924, 16 June 1923.

[115] NC Annual Report 1936, 5/OPF/10/1a, p. 18.

[116] See p. 26. McGregor, Blom-Cooper, and Gibson, *Separated Spouses*, 174.

[117] Frost, "Revolting to Humanity".

[118] NC CMM, 22 July 1926, 5/OPF/2/1/1/1c.

[119] *The Times*, 16 June 1923. 2nd Reading of Bill, 15 June 1923.

[120] Graham-Dixon, *Never Darken*, 16.

the case, pointing out that the child's father had got off scot-free and that everyone involved in the case, except Edith, had been male—judge, jury, lawyers, police—despite the fact that following the Sex Disqualification (Removal) Act, 1919, women were allowed to serve on juries and become lawyers and police. The NC supported the campaign but was not prominent for fear of giving its critics further ammunition, this time the accusation of condoning child-murder.

Male MPs, including the Liberal MP for Leicestershire, petitioned the Home Office for a change in the law. The Home Secretary said that he feared a change would encourage immorality, but his civil servants were aware that women convicted in circumstances such as Edith's were normally released after three years, which contradicted the severity of the verdicts pronounced in court, and they were prepared to accept a change in the law to bring it closer to the practice. In fact, following the campaign, Edith was quietly released on permanent licence after a year. The Home Office regarded her as a generally virtuous, hard-working young woman from a respectable background: 'She has good parents and a home to go to when the time comes.'

The campaign continued, promoted by the Magistrates Association (newly formed by some of the first women magistrates[121]) and the Howard League for Penal Reform, headed by Margery Fry, a magistrate affiliated to the Labour Party. In February 1922, Arthur Henderson, Labour Party Chief Whip, introduced the bill, which, following amendments in Parliament, became the Infanticide Act in July 1922. This introduced the new charge of 'infanticide', which allowed women such as Edith an alternative plea to murder and the prospect of a lighter sentence. The first charge brought under the case was that in October 1922 at Lincoln Assizes against Emma Temple, a 19-year-old domestic servant. She had strangled her daughter shortly after giving birth in the privy at her employer's home. She was charged with wilful murder, but confessed to the new offence of infanticide and sentenced to four months' imprisonment.[122]

The NC had a role in other important changes in the law between the wars. It supported the Adoption Act 1926 and gave evidence to the official investigations that led up to it.[123] Despite regarding adoption as a last resort for unmarried mothers, the NC believed that it was sometimes necessary and should be better regulated. Neville Chamberlain consulted the NC when drafting the 1929 Local Government Act, the most far-reaching reform of the Poor Law administration since 1834. The NC was anxious that local authorities should improve the numbers and standard of homes for unmarried mothers and their children. The new law permitted authorities to inspect them but it was not mandatory.

As Fisher put it, during the interwar years the NC came into 'close and friendly relations with Government offices, and are solidly established as the recognized central organization for dealing with unmarried mothers and illegitimate children'.[124]

---

[121] Anne Logan, *Feminism and Criminal Justice: A Historical Perspective* (London: Palgrave, 2008).

[122] Daniel J. R. Grey, 'Women's Policy Networks and the Infanticide Act, 1922', *Twentieth Century British History*, 21:40 (2010), 441–63.

[123] Jenny Keating, *A Child for Keeps: The History of Adoption in England, 1918–45* (London: Palgrave, 2009), 67–113.

[124] Fisher, *Twenty-One Years*, 10.

She believed that by 1939 much had been achieved. There were now more and better residential homes:

The old 'penitentiary' has changed into the modern home, full of air and sunlight, where wretched, unhappy and often half-starved expectant mothers in the course of time develop into not only healthy mothers of healthy and well-cared for babies, but into more or less competent workers with a changed moral standard, a new self-respect and a new view of citizenship.

This was optimistic. She continued, more realistically, that:

Homes, of course, vary enormously and some are still behind the times, but that there has been a very great improvement as well as an increase in numbers is quite clear.[125]

And more hostels were needed, especially for working mothers.

Also optimistically, she pointed out that there were fewer illegitimate births and the death rate had fallen, but she qualified this by admitting that the general birth rate had also fallen and the proportion of 'illegitimate' births had changed little. The relative death rate of 'illegitimate' babies had shown a welcome decline over the interwar years but it remained 'far too high'. This was due sometimes, she suggested, to the efforts of a desperate mother 'to get rid of it before its birth', which could result in its 'coming into life terribly handicapped and through no fault of its own'.[126] The lack of support and feeling of shame, isolation, and hopelessness that forced some unmarried mothers into such behaviour had changed all too little, despite all the efforts of the National Council.

---

[125] Ibid. 14.
[126] Ibid. 14–15.

3

The Second World War: Another Moral Panic

During the Second World War, as during the First, 'illegitimacy' increased from 4.19 per cent of total live births in England and Wales in 1939 to 9.18 per cent in 1945.[1] A bright spot was that in this war, unlike the previous one, the infant death rate fell, from 90 per 1,000 illegitimate births in 1939 to 69 per 1,000 in 1944, due to the general wartime improvement in child and maternal welfare services.[2]

However, again, the numbers of births outside marriage looked alarming. As in the previous war, there was panic in the press and elsewhere about the 'immorality' especially of young women freed from the constraints of home and especially those in the armed forces, complaints that may often have been expressions of distaste for women experiencing such new freedoms at all. But in this war there was clear official evidence that the fears and gossip had little substance. The war brought into the open much of the reality of sexual practice and the experience of unmarried motherhood that had previously been secret. It also revealed the serious inadequacy of support services for unmarried mothers and their children and influenced post-war improvements.

SOBER STATISTICS

In 1939 the Registrar General published the first *Statistical Review of England and Wales*. This estimated, to widespread surprise, that almost 30 per cent of first children born in 1938–9 had been conceived out of wedlock. This was based on the number of births within eight-and-a- half months of the parents' marriage, as recorded on birth certificates. Information about the date of marriage was not required before 1938.[3] Some births might have been premature and still, in practice, parents did not always record a date of marriage, often precisely to hide a pre-marital conception.[4] But, on balance, the Registrar General felt confident about his estimates. He calculated that among mothers under 20 at least 42 per

---

[1] Mrs H. A. L. Fisher, *Twenty-One Years* (London: National Council for the Unmarried Mother and Her Child, 1939), 19.
[2] S. M. Ferguson and H. Fitzgerald, *History of the Second World War*, Studies in the Social Services (London: HMSO and Longmans, 1954), 171–5. Fisher, *Twenty-One Years*, 19.
[3] It was required by the Population (Statistics) Act, 1938, 1 & 2 Geo. 6, ch. 12.
[4] *Papers of the Royal Commission on Population*, vol. 11, *Reports and Selected Papers of the Statistics Committee* (1950), 136.

cent of first births had been conceived before marriage; 31 per cent for those aged 21, 22 per cent at 22, 10 per cent at 25–29, 8 per cent at 30–34.[5] Later *Statistical Reviews* showed that the total number of babies conceived out of wedlock (both 'illegitimate' and 'legitimate') *fell* from 14.6 per cent of all births in 1938, to 11.8 per cent in 1943, before rising to 14.9 in 1945.[6] The number of pre-marital pregnancies fell between 1939 and 1945 from 60,346 to 38,176, while 'illegitimate' births rose from 26,569 to 64,743. There is no means of knowing how many of these children were legitimated when their parents were reunited after the war and able to marry.[7]

So, strikingly, in view of public panic—and self-righteousness—over the supposed sexual irregularities of unmarried younger people in wartime, the official statistics showed that the total number of pre-marital conceptions plus unmarried deliveries among mothers under 25 actually declined throughout the war. Among women aged 25–30 it rose by 24 per cent, at ages 30–35 by 41 per cent, at 35–40 by 19 per cent, at 40–45 by 20 per cent.[8] The reasons are unclear, though the trend was paralleled by a rise in the number of first babies born to older women within established marriages, signalling perhaps the beginning of the sustained rise in both the marriage rate and the birth rate, which began during the war and continued to the late 1960s.[9]

The Registrar General concluded that the explanation for the wartime rise in illegitimate births

is almost unquestionably to be found in the enforced degree of physical separation of the sexes imposed by the progressive recruitment of young males into the Armed Forces and their transfers to war stations at home and abroad, rendering immediate marriage with their home brides increasingly difficult—and, in the case of many quite impossible...

...To the extent to which this is the explanation, the lapse will often have been of a temporary character only, since it is to be presumed that in many, probably a large proportion, of the cases where the parents were reunited after the war they will have married and thereby legitimated many of the children registered as illegitimate and secured to them the normality of home life and upbringing of which they might otherwise have been deprived.

...Taking the six war years as a whole the average increase of 6% in the total number of irregularly conceived births will hardly be regarded as inordinate, having regard to the wholesale disturbance to customary habits and living conditions in conjunction with the temporary accession to the population of large numbers of young and virile men in the Armed Forces of our Dominions and Allies.[10]

---

[5] Ibid.
[6] Ferguson and Fitzgerald, *History*, 91–2. *Registrar General's Statistical Review of England and Wales for the Six Years 1940–1945, Text*, vol. II, *Civil*, 110. Gail Braybon and Penny Summerfield, *Out of the Cage: Women's Experiences of Two World Wars* (London: Pandora, 1987), 215–16.
[7] Ferguson and Fitzgerald, *History*, 92.
[8] Ibid. 93–4.
[9] Ibid.
[10] *Registrar General's Statistical Review of England and Wales for the Six Years 1940–1945, Text*, vol. II, *Civil*, 144.

A notably more sober—and convincing—assessment than some lurid contemporary accounts of teenage girls 'running wild' and'going out for a good time', especially with American servicemen.[11] The Bishop of Norwich chastised 'women and
especially young girls in town and village alike' for their casual acquaintanceships
with soldiers, warning

we are in danger of our national character rotting at the root...nothing is more alarming
than the decay of personal standards of sexual morality...nothing threatens more the
future of our race. When men and women grow loose in personal morality they endanger
their own eternal salvation and they endanger too the England of to-morrow.[12]

As ever, women received most of the blame for perceived moral laxity, though men
were unavoidably involved and despite evidence that wartime blackout put them
at still greater risk of harassment and sexual assault than in normal times.[13] As ever,
some unmarried motherhood was due to rape. Some at the time contested this
castigation of the younger generation[14] and historians have agreed with the Registrar General (whose views had the merit of being based on firm evidence) that
there was no dramatic change in young women's sexual behaviour. Rather war
conditions 'made visible what might have occurred with much less comment had
there not been a war'.[15]

WHO WERE THE UNMARRIED MOTHERS?

As ever, there was much speculation and generalization about the characteristics of
wartime unmarried mothers. For this war we have firmer evidence about the realities of unmarried motherhood from the careful researches of the two, largely
unsung, female official historians of wartime social services, Sheila Ferguson and
Hilda Fitzgerald.[16] They challenged the more lurid speculations about wartime
female sexuality, which long outlived the war:

---

[11] Sonya O. Rose, *Which People's War? National Identity and Citizenship in Wartime Britain, 1939–
1945* (Oxford: Oxford University Press, 2003), 74.
[12] *Norfolk News and Weekly Press*, 9 Oct. 1943, 4. Quoted in Rose, *People's War*, 79–80.
[13] Braybon and Summerfield, *Out of the Cage*, 206–7.
[14] Rose, *People's War*, 91.
[15] Ibid. 74; Derek Thompson, 'Courtship and Marriage between the Wars', *Oral History*, 3:2
(1975), 42–3; David Reynolds, *Rich Relation: The American Occupation of Britain, 1942–1945* (New
York: Random House, 1995), 276.
[16] The volume was originally to be written by Richard Titmuss, with the assistance of Sheila Ferguson and Hilde Fitzgerald as a successor to his *Problems of Social Policy* (London: HMSO, 1950), on
which Hilde Ferguson also worked as a research assistant. Due to ill-health and university duties he
withdrew but continued to work with the authors on the volume. W. K. Hancock (General Editor of
the official *History of the Second World War* volumes), 'Preface' to Ferguson and Fitzgerald, *History*,
p. ix; Richard M. Titmuss, 'Preface' to *Problems of Social Policy*, p. xi. This chapter draws extensively
on the work of Ferguson and Fitzgerald because it was comprehensive, has been relatively little used
by historians, and drew upon sources, including official documents, that are no longer available. Their
book is a valuable primary source in itself.

From all the reports and case histories that have been studied, it would appear that the women who bore illegitimate children during the war belonged to all classes, types and age groups. Some were adolescent girls who had drifted away from homes which offered neither guidance nor warmth and security. Still others were married women with husbands on war service who were unable to bear the loneliness of separation. There were decent and serious, superficial and flighty, irresponsible and incorrigible girls among them. There were some who had formed serious attachments and had hoped to marry. There were others who had had a single lapse, often under the influence of drink. There were, too, the 'good time girls' who thrived on the presence of well-paid servicemen from overseas and the semi-prostitutes with little moral restraint.[17]

Furthermore,

Some of the unmarried mothers of the war were of a 'new type' and surprised the moral welfare workers to whom they were referred. Their spirit of independence was considerable and there was little of the sinner or penitent among them.[18]

These women resented the punitive atmosphere of some of the voluntary homes and the very term 'moral welfare', which to them implied undeserved moral censure. A Ministry of Health official commented sympathetically:

I do not think it is entirely the 'unthankful and the forward' who object. It is also that a more independent type of young woman is coming to be dealt with and one who, I think, even the old-fashioned among us sometimes feel is not suitably dealt with by the old methods…The modern girl, accustomed to keep herself, will not lightly give up her liberty and submit to rules.[19]

These 'modern' women wanted to regain their independence as soon as possible after childbirth, not to be kept in a 'home'. They could find work and earn good enough incomes to support themselves and their babies. The historians went on:

These were not women of low mentality, amoral and without self-respect. They were of normal intelligence and their ideas of right and wrong were not very different from those of other girls. … They could not usually master their problems without assistance but most of them were not of the type to take that assistance for granted. The lowest mental group among the unmarried mothers appears to have been comparatively small.[20]

A substantial new group among mothers of 'illegitimate' children were the married women who became pregnant while their husbands were away at war. Birmingham, where the public health department had taken especial care for unmarried mothers for some years and kept in touch with most of them in the district, found that the percentage of married women needing support trebled between 1940 and 1945. In the last two years of the war, one-third of all 'illegitimate' children in the city were born to married women. Other districts reported up to 50 per cent. In

---

[17] Ferguson and Fitzgerald, *History*, 95.
[18] Ibid. 95.   [19] Ibid. 96.   [20] Ibid. 96.

Birmingham not all remained married: of the 520 reported in 1945, 283 regarded themselves as still married to husbands in the services (5 of them prisoners of war), the rest were divorced, separated, or widowed. It is not clear how many had long-term relationships with the father of the child.[21]

A probation officer in London reported:

Many excellent young mothers have been unable to stand the loneliness at home, particularly when their husbands are abroad, with not even a spasmodic leave to break the monotony...Hasty war marriages, on embarkation leave, sometimes between comparative strangers, with a few days or weeks of married life, have left both parties with little sense of responsibility or obligation towards one another.[22]

Such women could be particularly desperate. They could not disguise the fact that their absent husband was not the father. They could not have the child adopted without the husband's permission, because any child born to a married woman was legally the child of her husband and his permission was required. Some husbands were unforgiving; others relented if the child was adopted; others accepted the child as their own. The Forces' Welfare Services appear to have given sympathetic help to husbands and wives.[23] The NC helped many such women and reported: 'all present heart-breaking features: all too few show any sign of happiness for the child, whether it remains with its mother or not.'[24]

The support mothers received varied according to their role in the war effort, whether civilians, war workers, or servicewomen.

CIVILIAN MOTHERS

Wartime conditions made life harder for all unmarried mothers who did not have family support or an adequate income. Childcare was even harder to find. Nurseries—few enough before the war—were closed due to shortage of staff and, increasingly, destruction by bombing. There were fewer foster mothers, as women could find better paid war work, and fewer voluntary welfare workers, who were diverted to urgent war work.[25]

The evacuation scheme made life easier for single mothers of school-age children in big cities when the children were removed to homes and schools in the country; but not for mothers of younger children unless they wanted to move with their children, often to places where they had few prospects of finding work or support from local public or voluntary services.[26] Pregnant unmarried women were accepted for evacuation to maternity homes in the country in the ninth month of pregnancy, like other mothers, under the wartime Emergency Medical Service. Many

[21] Ferguson and Fitzgerald, *History*, 98.   [22] Ibid. 99.   [23] Ibid.
[24] Fisher, *Twenty-One Years*, 19.
[25] Ferguson and Fitzgerald, *History*, 104.   [26] Ibid. 106.

would have preferred to stay at home but there was a shortage of maternity beds in London and other large cities. By the beginning of 1943, eight or nine unmarried expectant mothers were evacuated from London weekly. By early 1945, fifteen were evacuated in an average week. They were discharged from the maternity home two weeks after the birth, then, in theory, billeted in the country with their babies unless they preferred to return home. But it was hard to find billets for unmarried mothers who could not return home or afford the return journey. Landladies did not want them. Many stayed longer in the homes or had to move to poor law institutions, many of which filled up. Rural local authorities felt overwhelmed by the unaccustomed numbers and the costs imposed by evacuees on public assistance and other services for which they received no compensation from the Government. The evacuees' home authorities were expected to pay, under the ancient poor law 'settlement' regulations, which were still in force, but the rural authorities feared they would not do so.[27] Some responded by putting the women and their children on trains and sending them home.[28] Also, war conditions led, as, the founder of the NC put it, to a 'fever of adoptions' by desperate women, unable to care for their children, 'often arranged with the minimum of care and the maximum of irresponsibility'.[29]

At first, the Government refused to help unmarried mothers and their children, arguing that illegitimacy was not a new problem specific to wartime, overlooking the unprecedented problems caused by bombing and evacuation. The Ministry of Health insisted on the principle of equal rights for all mothers, allowing no overt discrimination against unmarried mothers but also no favours. Hence their particular difficulties were ignored at first.

Increasingly, the Ministry received bitter complaints from rural authorities about the burden of unmarried mothers and their children. It called for help from the NC and the Church of England Moral Welfare Council, the leading voluntary organizations in the field. In December 1939 it encouraged regional medical officers to contact local welfare agencies and tried to secure the admission of unmarried mothers and their babies to voluntary homes.[30] But there were few places and the homes would not take mothers just for short periods, seeing their role as long-term rehabilitation and training, requiring at least three months residence; and, as we have seen, some mothers were hostile to the often punitive rigours of these institutions. In reality, cooperation between local medical officers and voluntary organizations was, at best, patchy.

The evacuation authorities tried to send unmarried mothers to areas where voluntary welfare organizations were particularly active, such as Oxford, where the Moral Welfare Association sought to help mothers become self-supporting. They asked the Ministry to fund a hostel where working mothers could live with their

---

[27] Ibid. 104.   [28] Ibid. 106.

[29] Fisher, *Twenty-One Years*, 19. For discussion of adoption see pp. 79–81 below.

[30] The National Archives (TNA), Ministry of Health (MH)/55/1653–4, 1943–5; MH/52/423, 1936–44; MH/52/551.

children, but by summer 1942 Oxford was paying the price: it was overwhelmed with unmarried mothers and could not accommodate more.[31] Public sympathy for the plight of the mothers and children grew. The Bishop of Derby wrote to the Minister of Health in 1943 urging the state to take responsibility because local services could not cope: there were no hostels or mother and baby homes in the whole of Derbyshire.[32] In letters to *The Times*, public figures, including MPs, demanded more hostels and residential nurseries.[33]

In 1943, unmarried mothers and their children were mentioned in the Ministry's annual report for the first time since its first report in 1919 and then became a regular feature.[34] In spring 1943, the Ministry asked its Advisory Committee on the Welfare of Mothers and Young Children to look into the issues. Its members included representatives of the NC and the Church of England Moral Welfare Society. The Committee strongly recommended that the Ministry should act and that action 'must not be merely expedient, but such as will be conducive to the welfare of the child now and in the future'. It proposed that the care of unmarried mothers and their children should be a special duty of welfare authorities and treated by them as of paramount importance. Carefully selected social workers should be appointed to support and advise mothers. Where possible they should cooperate with voluntary organizations, but the Committee recognized that these had limited resources and that 'many unmarried mothers were not in sympathy with their objects'.[35]

These recommendations were embodied in Circular 2866 issued by the Ministry in October 1943, which formed the basis of subsequent government policy. It was warmly welcomed by the NC because it 'embodied so many of our own views',[36] not surprisingly since they had advised on it,[37] though they objected to the proposed appointment of social workers specifically for illegitimate children because it singled them out. Zoe Puxley, a senior official in the Ministry, signed the circular and had a large role in drafting it. She worked closely with the NC during and after the war, chaired it from 1953 to 1958 and served as a Vice-President between 1949 and 1967. She played an important role in guiding wartime Ministry policy in this area.

The Circular urged local authorities to cooperate with voluntary organizations and to do their best to keep mother and child together, advising on adoption only 'in special cases e.g., where the mother is very young, or is the wife of a man not the father of the child'. They should appoint trained social workers to cooperate with health visitors, though the circular recognized that such workers were not easy

---

[31] Ferguson and Fitzgerald, *History*, 104–8.

[32] Ibid. 126.

[33] Letters to *The Times* by Lady Caldecote, 7 July 1943; Viscountess Davidson, Irene Ward, Ralph Glyn, and Quintin Hogg, all MPs, 16 July 1943.

[34] *Summary Report of the Ministry of Health for the year ended 31st March 1943.* Cmd 6468, 31. Ferguson and Fitzgerald, *History*, 125 n. 2.

[35] Ibid. 127.

[36] Fisher, *Twenty-One Years*, 20.

[37] TNA/MH/55/1653–4, 1943–5.

to find. Where possible, the social workers should 'persuade the girl to make known her circumstances to her parents and, if the home is likely to be a satisfactory one, to persuade the grandparents to make a home for the little one'. They should advise the mother on finding a home, if she could not live with her parents, on finding work and, if necessary, a foster mother or nursery place, and on obtaining an affiliation order. There was no reference to the Poor Law, now known as Public Assistance, which, for the first time since its foundation, was no longer automatically assumed to be the appropriate public service for unmarried mothers and their children.[38]

By March 1945, 339 authorities in England and Wales had introduced schemes based on these principles, 210 in collaboration with voluntary organizations. Fifty had appointed qualified social workers and others had placed a health visitor in charge of the work. Some had introduced subsidized fostering schemes as recommended by the Ministry, whereby they guaranteed payment to the foster mother and recovered what they could from the mother according to her means. A few opened hostels or residential nurseries. Local authorities and voluntary organizations worked more closely together. In some areas health visitors and other employees learned from the experience of voluntary workers; in others the local authority contributed to the salary of moral welfare workers. Voluntary organizations received grants from local authorities to admit mothers to their homes.[39]

However, under wartime conditions, with trained personnel in short supply, practice was locally highly variable. Among the leaders were Kent and, above all, Birmingham. Birmingham was the first authority, in 1930, to appoint social workers to support 'illegitimate' children. It had opened a fostering scheme and a mother and baby home and operated a 'selected lodgings' scheme, whereby the authority found landladies/lords willing to take unmarried mothers, and paid the rent for approved lodgings, repaid by the mother once she was earning. The landlady looked after the child while the mother worked. Birmingham regarded this as the best system for mothers who could not return to their families. Between 1926–30 and 1936–40 the death rate for 'illegitimate' infants in Birmingham fell by 30 per cent compared with 10 per cent for all infants in the city; in 1940 and 1943 it was below that of 'legitimate' babies.[40] But few authorities followed Birmingham's lead. There was a close relationship between the NC and Birmingham. Apart from Neville Chamberlain's close connection with both Birmingham and the NC, the Bishop of Birmingham was a Vice-President from its foundation and the MOH of Birmingham, Dr John Robertson, was a founding member.[41]

In 1945 the Ministry surveyed areas with particularly high 'illegitimate' birth rates to review the effect of Circular 2866. MOHs in 11 counties and 16 boroughs were asked for detailed reports and their views on future policy. The survey revealed great differences in approach and achievement. During the first six months of

---

[38] Ferguson and Fitzgerald, *History*, 128.   [39] TNA/MH/1653, 1943–5.
[40] Ferguson and Fitzgerald, *History*, 129–30.   [41] See p. 20.

1945, 7,500 illegitimate children were born in these areas. Four per cent were stillborn or died shortly after birth. Eighty-one per cent stayed with their mothers, 59 per cent of whom lived with grandparents or other close relatives, 9 per cent stayed in a mother and baby home, 7 per cent in lodgings; the remaining 25 per cent returned to the home of its cohabiting mother and father, or to the mother's own home. Sixteen per cent of all the babies were separated from their mothers: 12 per cent were adopted, 4 per cent were with foster mothers or in residential nurseries.[42] Both of the latter were still in short supply. The Ministry concluded that services fell short of needs. Only 10 per cent of mothers in the survey (571) had been admitted to mother and baby homes. Just a few local authorities, including Leeds and Essex, had long-stay hostels for mothers and children. Mothers were still being forced into adoption by inadequate services.[43]

Encouraging cooperation between local authorities and voluntary organizations was not easy. There was much mutual mistrust. Not all voluntary organizations welcomed state 'intrusion' in their work. Public funding exposed voluntary organizations to public criticism, as local authorities scrutinized the quality of services and methods of work. In particular, conditions in some moral welfare homes were regarded as unsatisfactory and excessively penal. A retired Senior MOH from Birmingham commented that

Some of these homes for mothers are much too rigorous and impose unreasonable discipline and too heavy work, while the diet, heating and sanitary arrangements may be of too low a standard for a woman in advanced pregnancy...In some homes floor polish is more noticeable than cheerfulness.[44]

Mother and baby homes in fact varied considerably. The Church of England Moral Welfare Association did not favour strict rules and informed its affiliated bodies of its views, but it could not control them. The Salvation Army maintained strict regulations in all its homes. Most Army homes required the mothers to wear uniforms, attendance at prayers was expected, and help with household duties was required. 'Girls', as they were called, regardless of age, were not allowed out alone and their 'comings and goings' were restricted; correspondence was supervised and sometimes withheld; writing materials, stamps and money were confiscated. Boredom was rife. The rules of homes affiliated to the Catholic Moral Welfare Council were comparably strict. They expected the worst of unmarried mothers and treated them accordingly. The Ministry of Health had no power to intervene in the running of voluntary homes, other than to ensure adequate sanitary and medical provision.[45]

The Ministry and the NC were eager to encourage cooperation between public and private sectors to improve standards and increase places in both and they

---

[42] *Homes and Hostels of the Future: Report of a Conference arranged by the NCUMC* (London: NCUMC, 1945), 5–6.
[43] Ferguson and Fitzgerald, *History*, 130.
[44] Ethel Cassie, 'The Care of Illegitimate Children', *Public Health*, 57 (Feb. 1944), 54.
[45] Ferguson and Fitzgerald, *History*, 132–3.

worked increasingly closely together to achieve this. From 1943 the NC received an annual grant of £500 from the Ministry in recognition of its indispensable contribution to the support of mothers and children during the war, which greatly relieved its perennial financial problems. This owed much to the support of Zoe Puxley. The annual grant continued for many years after the war.[46]

Despite the positive impact of Circular 2866 in some areas, it was published late in the war and, nationally, the situation for civilian unmarried mothers and their children did not ease substantially during the war. As Ferguson and Fitzgerald put it: 'All through the war these mothers and their babies remained an embarrassment to local authorities and voluntary workers up and down the country.'[47]

WAR WORKERS

After a while, women recruited for essential war work received a little more support. Munitions work was often located in quiet places away from potential bombing and unaccustomed to extensive social problems, such as Hereford, where the Royal Ordnance Factory was located.[48] Most of the women were away from home and sometimes worked close to the dangers and temptations of large military camps. Regional medical officers strongly opposed siting female war workers' hostels close to these camps, for fear of the outcome.[49] By summer 1941, seven illegitimate children had been born to war workers in Hereford.

Pregnant war workers had to give up work two months before confinement and could not return until one month after. Meanwhile they were unpaid. They were expected to return to their family home and many did so. But others could not or would not and, again, it was hard for them to find places to live and care for the child. They faced the same problems as other unmarried civilian mothers. Some hid their condition for as long as possible, occasionally giving birth in the hostel.

The Ministry of Health initially argued that the mothers were the responsibility of local authorities, who would be reimbursed for war-related expenditure on them. As we have seen, the authorities often could not cope with these new problems, nor could the voluntary organizations. As demands increased, staff became harder to recruit, under wartime restrictions it was impossible to build or extend institutions, and the voluntary organizations were short of funds. In wartime, donation to charity was not a priority for many people.

By summer 1941, the problem of providing for pregnant unmarried war workers was widespread enough for the Ministry, under pressure from the Ministry of Labour and the Ministry of Supply, to acknowledge responsibility, despite Treasury resistance to the anticipated cost. The Ministry of Health agreed that if the 'girls'

---

[46] TNA/MH/55/1509, 1942; TNA/MH/55/2346; TNA/MH/55/1534, 1943–58; TNA/MH/1535, 1949–61.
[47] Ferguson and Fitzgerald, *History*, 109.
[48] Ibid. 109.   [49] Ibid. 109–10.

could return home, their fares would be paid, plus a sickness allowance of 3s. 6d. per day for three weeks. If they were unable or unwilling to go home and local authorities could not help, they should be admitted to voluntary homes two months before confinement, until they could return to work. The usual charge in the homes was 25s. per week. Each mother was expected to contribute at least £5, the Exchequer would pay the balance. There was no provision for clothes or pocket money or other needs, except in cases of extreme hardship. The scheme was primarily designed, as the Ministry put it, 'to maintain the usefulness of the factory worker',[50] rather than to provide for her long-term welfare and that of her child. No thought was given to the care of the child after the mother returned to work. Voluntary societies were expected to be the primary sources of support, unrealistically, as we have seen.

Again the Ministry called in the NC to help. It undertook to find vacancies in homes, but there were few to be found. Florence Horsbrugh, Conservative MP and Parliamentary Secretary to the Ministry of Health, acted as intermediary between the Ministry and the NC throughout the war. She was sympathetic to the problems of unmarried mothers and had chaired the departmental committee leading to the 1939 Adoption Act, which tightened up the regulation of adoption and steered it through Parliament.[51] But she could not persuade the Ministry or the Treasury to be more generous to pregnant war workers.

To make matters worse, the war workers scheme was deliberately not widely advertised and few mothers, local authorities, or social workers even knew of it. Factory welfare officers, often the first to know of a woman's condition and to try to help, were also kept in ignorance. In Swynnerton (Staffordshire), where up to forty babies were born annually to workers at the local Royal Ordnance Factory, voluntary workers tried to raise funds for an ante-natal hospital but no one knew about the government scheme.[52] At the end of the first six months of the scheme only ten applications had been received: four were granted, five refused and one was under consideration. By the time it was wound up in 1948, only 36 mothers had been helped, only 11 of them receiving the maximum £20 that the Exchequer agreed to contribute to the cost of residence in a home. The scheme did very little to help women, some of whom were in real distress. At least one health region reported breakdowns and attempted suicides among mothers. The number of illegal abortions, successful or otherwise, is unknown. Lack of residential nurseries compelled some to give their babies up for adoption or place them in unsatisfactory foster care. The failures of the scheme were criticized within the Ministries of Health and Labour, but nothing changed.[53]

---

[50] Ferguson and Fitzgerald, *History*, 112.
[51] This was not implemented until 1943. See pp. 79–80. Jenny Keating, *A Child for Keeps: The History of Adoption in England, 1918–45* (London: Palgrave, 2009), 154–67.
[52] Ferguson and Fitzgerald, *History*, 113.
[53] Ibid. 112–15.

SERVICEWOMEN

Pregnant servicewomen were treated very differently—eventually. In August 1941, the Ministry of Health raised the question of unmarried mothers in the armed services, but was assured by the services that 'military discipline and an emphasis on the prestige of the Services were encouraging good standards of behaviour and the number of illegitimate pregnancies was negligible.'[54] It was, above all, concern about the 'prestige of the services' and the damaging effects of rumours of immorality, including on recruitment, that in the end drove change. In 1942, the army's Auxiliary Territorial Service (ATS) for women and the Women's Auxiliary Air Force (WAAF) both asked for the war workers scheme to be extended to servicewomen. The Ministry refused, arguing that the services themselves should deal with the problem they had described as 'negligible'.

Unmarried mothers in the services faced even greater problems than civilians. They were discharged after the third month of pregnancy, if they could not keep it hidden, and could not re-enrol until six months after the confinement and then only if the baby was adopted, or other care was available, and their record of previous service was good. If they kept the child, they were not eligible for dependants' allowances, unlike fathers of illegitimate children. They were left for at least nine months without pay.

Women who could not return home looked for help to local authorities and welfare agencies, with the same uneven results as other women, placing particular burdens on authorities with large numbers of service bases. The services would commit no funds to help the mothers, but some tried to help them with some sensitivity. WAAF officers were instructed to 'bear in mind that the single airwoman "may be under great mental strain...and will need sympathetic handling. It is essential to gain the woman's confidence." '[55] They were advised on sources of help for the women and the support they might themselves give. For example, they should not ask the name of the father, but advise on obtaining an affiliation order after the birth, if marriage was unlikely. They should ensure the women knew their rights to National Insurance and other benefits, and how to find a day nursery, and that they received their discharge certificate, outstanding pay, emergency ration card, travel warrant, and cash allowance of 21s. 6d. for civilian clothing. They should provide a list of possible adoption agencies 'but the woman should not be persuaded to take this course of action against her will'.[56] They should try to persuade airwomen to take relatives into their confidence in the hope that they would help.

ATS officers were instructed to cooperate with voluntary organizations and inform local employment exchanges if a mother needed work between discharge and her confinement. A discharge depot was established where women could stay

[54] Ibid. 115.
[55] WAAF Pamphlet no. 1, 'Notes for the guidance of WAAF officers in dealing with pregnant airwomen' (Apr. 1942), 1. We are very grateful to Kath Sherit for this reference.
[56] Ibid. 5.

between announcing the pregnancy and completion of discharge arrangements. After discharge, the services accepted no responsibility, though the mothers might keep in touch and officers were asked to note complaints about the voluntary services. But, again, overstretched voluntary services and local authorities could not always help and some women were forced into poor law institutions. This particularly disturbed the service authorities, not least for its impact on their reputation. Prostitutes were exempted from conscription further to protect the reputation of the services. Predictably, it was alleged that some women claimed to be prostitutes to evade conscription.[57]

An official report in 1942 on 'Amenities and welfare conditions in the women's services' by a committee chaired by Violet Markham helped persuade the Government to change its stance. Markham had a long history of voluntary and government work and close connections with the political elite. In the First World War she was secretary of an official investigation into suggestions of 'immorality' among the Women's Auxiliary Army Corps (WAACS) stationed in France, which were found to have no foundation.[58] The new committee investigated rumours of widespread immorality among servicewomen in this war and rejected them equally firmly:

Rumours that illegitimate pregnancy was both common and on the increase in the Services have been rife. This is the kind of rumour that starts in every war. The facts are otherwise. We can...with certainty say that the illegitimate birth-rate in the services is lower than the illegitimate birth-rate among the comparable civilian population.[59]

The committee urged the Ministry of Health to give urgent attention to the needs of servicewomen who became unmarried mothers, pointing out that extending the unsuccessful war workers scheme was unlikely to meet this challenge.

From May 1943, the Ministry finally began to work with the voluntary and armed services and created a special maternity scheme for servicewomen. They were still urged to return home, or helped to enter voluntary moral welfare homes, where possible. Many of the 'girls', again, resisted the discipline of these homes. If both sources of refuge failed, they could be admitted to the under-used government hostels for evacuated mothers for two months before and after confinement, contributing to the cost if they could. Again, the NC played a key role, together with the Soldiers', Sailors' and Airmen's Help Society (SSAHS). Pregnant servicewomen were referred to them for assessment. They took responsibility for them, giving help to find work, lodgings, or mother and baby homes after the birth and ensuring that they received ante-natal care and advice on their future plans. The Treasury agreed to provide £25,000 for the scheme, assuming that up to 1,000

---

[57] G. B. Stern, *Trumpet Voluntary* (London: Cassell, 1944), 121.

[58] Helen Jones, 'Markham, Violet Rosa (1872–1959)', *Oxford Dictionary of National Biography* (Oxford: Oxford University Press, 2004–9).

[59] *Report of the Committee on Amenities and Welfare Conditions in the Three Women's Services* (1942), Cmd 6384, 31, 50.

women would need help, considerably more generous than its response to the war workers' scheme.[60]

Three hundred and thirty-eight women were supported in the first year, 17 of them married, 22 widowed, divorced, or separated, 44 expecting a second or subsequent illegitimate child, none of whom would have been admitted to moral welfare institutions. Most were admitted to one of seven units established solely for unmarried servicewomen or with beds reserved for them. Two had small maternity units; others gave birth in nearby homes run by the wartime Emergency Medical Service, the integrated national service that foreshadowed the post-war National Health Service.

Servicewomen who became pregnant overseas were brought back immediately, if possible by air, to safeguard their health and to avoid the complication that a child born abroad would not qualify for British nationality. By 1944 the Home Office knew of only 18 cases of children born abroad to servicewomen. The official view was that the mothers and children should be brought home and the nationality issue quietly ignored for fear of the wider implications concerning the nationality of putatively British children born abroad.[61] But the NC made the issue public and Conservative MP Irene Ward, a member of its executive committee for some years, introduced in Parliament (with support from the War Office and in the press) an amendment to the nationality law ensuring that the children of servicewomen born abroad automatically gained British nationality. She succeeded in persuading the reluctant Home Office to issue these children with a certificate of British nationality, to be followed 'when the child is of suitable age', by the taking of the oath of allegiance.[62]

By 1945, senior officers in the RAF were very concerned about the rising rates of unmarried pregnancy in the WAAF, which, they believed, had 'reached an inexcusable level'. They did not blame this only on the women. It was, wrote an Air Marshal, 'a bad show primarily on the part of the RAF, a reflection . . . on individual decency . . . on the discipline of the Service . . . and the powers of command of our officers. . . . There is bound to be a certain amount of illicit intercourse and some unfortunate women are bound to become pregnant.' But the result for the woman was 'far more drastic and enduring . . . the man often gets clean away with it.' He noted that 'the highest incidence is among those trades which do not require a high standard of intelligence or education.' Commanding officers were advised to:

Make a confidant of your senior WAAF officer. Encourage RAF personnel to regard WAAF personnel as daughters of comrades and as potential wives.

Post one party or the other if a normal healthy relationship is developing in an 'undesirable direction'—rely on chaplain, senior WAAF officer and senior RAF colleagues to keep you informed.

[60] Ferguson and Fitzgerald, *History*, 117.

[61] TNA 213/179, 'Illegitimate Children Born Abroad to British Women: Discussion of Methods of Conferring British Nationality' (1944).

[62] NC Annual Report 1943–4.

strict supervision of WAAFs going to entertainments.
younger WAAFs are not induced to drink too much.[63]

ıs to the ex-servicewomen's scheme rose steadily, reaching an average 16
ın early 1945, requiring at least 240 ante-natal beds at any one time.
Admissivns peaked at 23 per week in January 1946 when 260 beds were available.
The rise was partly due to welfare societies and local authorities leaving servicewomen to the government scheme, so that they could help other mothers. Some
ex-service mothers had family support but could not find another place to give
birth. Under pressure of numbers, admissions of married mothers of illegitimate
children and of those expecting a second or subsequent illegitimate child were cut
back. Through 1946 applications declined and hostels began to close.

The service authorities would never reveal the 'illegitimate' birth rate among
servicewomen. In the three years of the scheme, there were 2,118 applications,
1,019 from ATS, 918 from WAAF, and 181 from the Women's Royal Naval Service (WRNS); of which, 22 were refused. Twenty-five per cent of applicants were
homeless, having grown up in institutions or with foster parents or step-parents,
were from unhappy homes, or rejected by their families. In the first year, one-third
of applicants were rejected by their parents. Thirty per cent were 'made welcome
with their babies by their families or by friends and could rebuild their lives among
their own people'.[64] An unknown number went straight to their families and did
not apply to the scheme. Others had parents who were sympathetic but unable to
help. One-fifth refused to contact their relatives. The service authorities would not
do so without their permission unless they were minors under age 21. Some women
refused even to apply for national insurance benefits if that required applying close
to their home, lest their predicament became known in their local community.
Initially most mothers could not afford to contribute, though the proportion who
did so increased over time.

The servicewomen's mother and baby hostels were run economically but without the severity of poor law or many moral welfare institutions. Efforts were made
to admit each woman to a hostel suited to her psychological and well as physical
needs. The mothers shared household tasks and could attend classes in sewing,
baby care, and household duties. The central purpose of the hostels was to help
them train for work and to resettle with their children. The NC and SSAHS filled
the gaps in official services. The hostel matrons were often helpful and supportive,
and were encouraged and advised by the Ministry and the voluntary organizations
to help mothers find legal advice when needed, seek financial support from the
father, arrange adoption if it was unavoidable, find work and a home, and perhaps
become reconciled with their families.

The work of the hostels was described in unusually human terms in a Ministry
of Health report on the first three years of the scheme. Most matrons, it reported,

---

[63] TNA: AIR 75/47, draft letter from Air member for Personnel (Air Marshal Slessor) to Com-
manders in Chief, May 1945. Again we are grateful to Kath Sherit for this reference.
[64] Ferguson and Fitzgerald, *History*, 126.

have known how to turn depressingly bare and shabby premises into a temporary haven for large numbers of utterly friendless girls who may never in their lives have known a home, or whose parents set their own petty respectability above the ordinary decencies of human relationships... Some day it may be possible to describe the life in the hostels, from the day in each week when an uneasy collection of newcomers waits to be met at the railway station, to the day, several weeks later, when they return to play their parts in civilian life. In between times they may have learned how to cook and sew and look after a baby. They may have realized that, thanks to the persevering devotion of matrons and social workers, parents may relent or baby's father may be fetched home on compassionate leave for a wedding. Those who are not so fortunate will, however, leave the hostel with a great deal more confidence than they had when they arrived.[65]

This report was never published.

Officials and workers involved in the scheme made every effort to help mothers keep their babies and find work. Adoption was the last resort and many mothers initially determined to adopt changed their minds while in the hostel. But, if they insisted, arrangements were made through the National Children Adoption Association. About one-third of mothers in the hostels had their children adopted, often because their parents insisted and they did not want to break with them or they felt they had no choice, given the shortage of nurseries and foster parents. The proportion of adoptions was relatively high in government hostels because moral welfare homes would not admit women who were determined on adoption. Senior women officers, the Ministry of Labour, and hostel matrons helped mothers return to their former occupations when possible, or to join the government scheme of training for a trade or as a teacher, secretary, or nurse. Nine per cent of babies went to residential nurseries run by the Government when their mother took up essential war work.

Other mothers, as before the war, had no choice but residential work if they wanted to keep their children. It was rarely easy:

We have the mother who goes into domestic service with, let us hope, a quiet baby who lies contentedly in his pram all day and gives no trouble. But in a few months that same baby will be teething and fretful and will take up more of his mother's time. Before long he will begin to crawl, then to toddle. He will fall, tweak the cat's ears and the dog's tail, clutch everything that comes his way and howl when the damage is done. The employer will not always be long-suffering or a child-lover, and mother and baby may end up travelling from pillar to post.[66]

Sixteen per cent of the ex-service mothers became resident domestic servants.[67] There was a shortage of servants now that women could find other work and some employers approached the hostels for staff.

When the war ended, the nurseries established under the servicewomen's scheme closed and the old problems returned. The armed services protested, but the

[65] Ferguson and Fitzgerald, *History*, 123.
[66] Ibid. 125 n. 2.   [67] Ibid. 125.

Ministry of Health argued that service charities or other welfare organizations should take over. While it lasted, the scheme to help pregnant unmarried service-women, by contrast with the war workers scheme, was humanely administered and apparently successful. Ferguson and Fitzgerald concluded that

Most mothers were deeply grateful for the help they received and anxious to contribute to the cost if they possibly could. Troublemakers were few and there was no evidence that second confinement cases were more difficult to handle than others. The social value of the scheme was demonstrated again and again.[68]

For the first time, a government department had been closely involved with help-ing unmarried mothers and their children, providing more than the bare necessi-ties of food, shelter, and maternity care in a punitive environment. The Ministry of Health, voluntary organizations, the armed services, and local authorities coop-erated more closely than ever before. For many of those involved in its administra-tion, the scheme dispelled stereotypes of unmarried mothers as feckless young women or prostitutes.

But all of this was kept secret during the war, beyond those who needed to know, and all the records of unmarried motherhood among servicewomen were destroyed after the war. The first public mention of the scheme was in November 1945, by a Senior Medical Officer at the Ministry of Health at a conference arranged by the NC. Press reports of her comments led many expectant unmarried mothers or their relatives to write to the Ministry or to the press appealing for help, since they were still suffering from the inadequacy of the public assistance and local authority services. One factory worker wrote:

I can assure you I have regretted it most bitterly and deeply, and life to me has since been just torture. I beg of you to believe me, when I tell you I am not a bad girl...My home is a long way from here, as soon as I knew I was going to have this baby I came up here, as I dare not let my mother know, she has had such a hard life herself, still has, there are eleven of us in the family...I am the first to fall, if my mother knew, I feel she would never forget or forgive me and it hurts me terrible...Please I am pleading with you for some advice and help.[69]

The Ministry put her and other women in touch with local services and the NC, which did its best to help.

For those forced to resort to public assistance, the pioneering geriatrician Dr Marjorie Warren described conditions she observed in a public assistance infirmary in 1946:

In the same ward were to be found senile dements, restless and noisy patients, who required cot beds, incontinent patients, senile bedridden patients, elderly sick patients who were treatable, patients up and about all day, and unmarried mothers and infants.[70]

---

[68] Ferguson and Fitzgerald, *History*, 120.   [69] Ibid. 138 n. 2.
[70] Marjorie Warren, 'Care of the Chronic Aged Sick', *The Lancet*, 1 (1946), 841.

Lessons were learned from the wartime experience which contributed to the post-war reform of services whose inadequacy had been clearly revealed. It was obvious that the voluntary services could not cope without more state support, and that, in their present state, they were not always acceptable to those in need. Nor were poor law services, which, like local authority public health services, were inadequate to the task and ill-coordinated.

WARTIME LIVES

Glimpses of the personal experiences of unmarried mothers in wartime as in peace are rare and not necessarily representative, and those of the middle class rarest of all because they were least likely to encounter the scrutiny of welfare services. An exception is the wartime diary written by Doreen Bates for Mass Observation.[71] She was quite a senior civil servant, a tax inspector, born in 1908. It describes her personal experiences in detail because, as she explained to Mass Observation, she believed that 'they would be of general interest at the moment. I believe I am the first woman civil servant of my rank to challenge the marriage bar[72] by pushing it to its logical conclusion—dispensing with the ceremony and starting a baby.' She also believed, rightly, that 'the attitude of my department is of some general interest as it is exceedingly difficult to gain any precise information of this kind except through individuals.'[73] One reason for writing the diary appears to have been her desire to challenge discrimination against women, including unmarried mothers, in the civil service, while making clear that such discrimination was by no means universal in the service.

The father of what turned out—to everyone's surprise including Doreen Bates' doctor—to be twins, a boy and a girl, born in early October 1941, was a married colleague, referred to as 'E', of whom the diarist was very fond. When the diaries begin, in early 1940, they spent a lot of time together, eating meals, walking in London and in the country, attending plays, exhibitions, the opera. Nothing is said about E's personal circumstances. One day at the beginning of February 1941 she 'had the morning off with E in Elsie's room'.[74] When her pregnancy was confirmed, she 'was thrilled'. She gives no sign that it was a shock or a source of shame; indeed, it appears to have been planned. She appears as one of the intelligent, independent 'modern women . . . (with) . . . little of the sinner or penitent' described by Fitzgerald and Ferguson.[75]

'E' was supportive, as was her sister who was on good terms with him. Doreen's mother was very upset and as the pregnancy advanced would allow her to visit her

---

[71] Mass Observation (MO) diarist 5245, Mass Observation Diaries 1939–45.

[72] The rule whereby women were required to leave the service on marriage. For the debate about this in the civil service, see Helen Glew, 'Women Workers in the Post Office, 1914–1939', PhD thesis, Institute of Historical Research, University of London (2010).

[73] MO diarist 5245, 30 June 1940.

[74] Ibid. 1 Feb. 1941.

[75] See p. 57.

suburban home only after dark. She softened as the pregnancy went on and even more after the children were born, though the first time she visited after the birth, 'It was an ordeal for her and upset her so that I had to give brandy.'[76] 'Tho' the more she sympathizes with me the more bitter she is to E.'[77]

Her civil service colleagues were supportive also, while the Director of Establishment, in charge of personnel,

was surprisingly broadminded and said if I could avoid a scandal inside or outside the office a broad view would be taken of medical certificates and I should get a long period of paid sick leave. If there was a scandal [presumably if E's wife sued for divorce] it would have to be unpaid.

He, wrote the diarist, 'apparently insisted on treating it as an unfortunate accident. It is odd that people find it easier to condone this than a deliberate decision.'[78]

But she did not get paid sick leave. This decision lay with the Treasury who were under pressure from a woman official who was determined to refuse sick pay to another unmarried woman clerk who, Bates reported, 'is having a baby (unwillingly)'.[79] It was decided to deny sick pay to both women. E, in response, was 'inclined to advise agitation outside', which suggests that he thought there would be sympathy for the women, though they did not pursue this. Her immediate colleagues continued to sympathize. They arranged for her to return from a period working in Belfast to be with E and her family and to work from home late in pregnancy, in order to shorten her period of unpaid leave.[80]

During the pregnancy, she experienced some stereotyping and prejudice but not, it seems, a lot. The almoner at Queen Charlotte's Hospital, which had no room for her, 'talked unnecessarily about the welfare officer with whom they usually put "unmarried girls" in touch—and seemed quite balked because I didn't need that'.[81] The doctor she saw at Queen Charlotte's asked 'if I was having the baby adopted! When I said No, I wanted it, he said, oh I see. Planned for was it?'[82] St Mary's Paddington 'weren't admitting unmarried women apparently because they were limited in numbers and so discriminated'.[83]

The twins were born in a nursing home in Stanmore, north London, where she stayed for four weeks. She then moved to a house in suburban London, chosen by E and her devoted sister who also found a living-in childminder. A friend informed her of the procedure for an unmarried mother to adopt her own children, as she later did.[84] 'E' was a regular visitor, gave financial support, and 'was far more doting than I expected'.[85] He kept promising to tell 'K', presumably his

---

[76] MO diarist 5245, 6 Nov. 1941.   [77] Ibid. 26 Sept. 1941.   [78] Ibid. 29 May 1941.
[79] Ibid. 17 Aug. 1941.   [80] Ibid. 2 Sept. 1941.   [81] Ibid. 22 Aug. 1941.
[82] Ibid. 1 Sept. 1941.   [83] Ibid.   [84] Ibid. 20 Nov. 1941.   [85] Ibid. 25 Oct. 1941.

wife, but not getting around to it:[86] 'E did not talk to K at the weekend as he had a cold at the time';[87] 'E says he will tell K this weekend, but I have no expectation. It would be lovely if he could live here. I love to see him with the twins. They begin to like him and he is practiced at holding them.' He never did live with them.[88]

When she went to register the birth of the twins, 'A well-made-up young married woman was the Registrar—no comment when I was not married.'[89] She returned to work six weeks after the births. The Director of Establishment sent a message that 'if I repeated my performance I would be sacked'. But her immediate superior—a long-time socialist, who brought the message—said that their professional association (of very respectable Tax Inspectors) would protest 'against such unduly harsh treatment', though 'he felt B himself would not go so far if the occasion arose'.[90] She found it hard combining care for her beloved twins and a full-time job, even with a live-in childminder, but she had no alternative: she had to earn a living.

Not all civil servants were so fortunate. Another, older, woman civil servant told Mass Observation in 1945:

I know of one case of a girl having to resign from our office because she had 'got into trouble'. Other girls talked about her and the occasion quite freely, and the general attitude seemed to be that it was a great pity that she had been so foolish—but she always was a queer sort of girl—and there were sympathetic conjectures about how she would get another job. Years ago, when a similar thing happened, the girl concerned simply dropped out of office life—no-one even said openly why she left—she just went home on sick leave and never returned. I can remember one of her best office friends saying very seriously, 'Oh, she was a *bad* girl', but apart from that her name was never mentioned.[91]

There were signs that the veil of secrecy around illegitimacy was gradually becoming more transparent, and attitudes were shifting. Doreen Bates benefited from this and probably also from her relatively senior position in the civil service and a good income. Hers was an unusually detailed account of the experiences of a middle-class unmarried mother. Another woman, Pauline Long, who chose to be an unmarried mother during the war for different reasons, gave a briefer account of her experience. She was 18 when war broke out, a member of the Communist Party, and influenced by reading 'free love' feminists, such as Dora Russell. She wrote in later life, evidently without regret:

During the war I was conscripted in to the Services, first in the ATS and then changed when I became pregnant and had a child to becoming a cook in the Land Army. In this way I was able to get a roof over our heads and earn a living for us both. There was no other relevant way: 'service' was still more than a memory and it was the only thing a 'bad girl' could do. My 'badness' at the time was based on left-wing politics, and I did

---

[86] Ibid. 13 Nov. 1941.   [87] Ibid. 20 Nov. 1941.   [88] Ibid. 2 Dec. 1941.
[89] Ibid. 29 Oct. 1941.   [90] Ibid. 6 Nov. 1941.
[91] MO File Report 2205, Jan. 1945, quoted in Braybon and Summerfield, *Out of the Cage*, 217.

not want to be dependent on a man, believed marriage was Bourgeois, and that women were equal (but different). We relied on the sheath as contraception since there was no way I knew then of getting as an unmarried woman, anything different. The idea of an abortion arose, but the backstreet stories were so horrific that I discounted the idea immediately. Anyhow, even backstreet abortions required cash and I had none. The child's father was also a revolutionary and also believed in all my ideals so therefore he saw no reason to do anything for me, and indeed would not have known what he could have done.

She believed that wartime changes made unmarried motherhood easier:

Suddenly it was possible to have a baby and get a second ration book: to find quite easily a place in the nurseries and to have lunch at the 'British Restaurants' for (I think) 1/6d.[92]

Another Mass Observation diarist told a sadder story, as an observer wholly lacking condemnation of an unmarried mother. Nella Last, married to a joiner and fitter in Barrow-in-Furness (Lancashire) was an active worker for the Women's Voluntary Service (WVS) during the war. She wrote on 3 April 1941:

One of our members is in bitter trouble. Her adored daughter has had a baby and the young soldier father went East nearly eight months ago and they could not marry. We have tried to make her happy, and the daughter went to stay with an aunt in the Lakes. We never mentioned it at all to the mother, beyond a passing enquiry as to her health. It seems, though, that the poor girl has fretted badly, both for her own sake—that her sweetheart could not come home so they could marry—and for the 'disgrace' she had brought on her mother. The baby, by its snapshot, is such a wistful-eyed, solemn mite, but there is no hope at all for the mother's recovery. From apathy and fretting she has drifted into TB and it's a matter only of a few weeks' more life for her. She has no interest in her baby, or its father's frantic letters that the girl's mother says would 'melt stone'— such that she cannot bear him hatred for the 'ruin of her daughter's life' in a way that might seem indicated. Just another of Hitler's crimes. There was so little we could say and nothing we could do.[93]

Elizabeth Roberts heard another desolate story from Lancashire, from Mrs Needham who became pregnant in 1940. Her partner was from a different social background. He was under 21 and unable to marry without his parents' consent:

Well I met him at a dance. I was going with him and he knew I was having this child and we went to face down his mother and father. And his mother's words were that she didn't want her son to marry a labourer's daughter. They were high up in society. They moved away to Plymouth and he went with them.

Her family tried to find him, without success, so she was left to face poverty and the anger of her mother:'My mother put me in the workhouse because she thought

---

it was wrong what I had done. When you were put in there, while the time came to have your baby you had to work. But I couldn't work because I was ill.' Her mother's hostility continued after she returned home with the baby and she eventually 'arranged' a marriage between her daughter and the son of one of her friends.[94]

Eric Clapton, the rock and blues musician, was born in Surrey in 1945. His mother was an unmarried 16 year old, his father a 24-year-old Canadian serviceman who turned out to be married. His father moved abroad on war service before Eric's birth and later returned to Canada. His mother returned to her parents and he was born at their house. Within two years she left and later married another Canadian serviceman and moved to Canada. Eric remained with his loving grandparents, whom he believed were his parents, in

a house full of secrets... in the smallness of this house there were always conversations being carried on in front of me as if I didn't exist... But, bit by bit, by carefully listening to these exchanges, I slowly began to put together a picture of what was going on and to understand that the secrets were usually to do with me. One day I heard one of my aunties ask, 'Have you heard from his mum?' and the truth dawned on me that when [uncle] Adrian jokingly called me a 'little bastard' he was telling the truth.[95]

The effect on him was 'traumatic', aware that, despite his love for his family, he might be an embarrassment, given the stigma attached to illegitimacy, 'particularly so amongst working class families such as ours who, living in a small village community, knew little of the luxury of privacy'. His life was 'soured' and he 'withdrew into himself', and 'attached himself to the family dog' and later to music, but 'observed the code of secrecy which existed in the house—"We don't talk about what went on"'.[96] When he was nine, and knew the truth, his mother returned for a visit with her two children by her marriage. He suddenly asked '"Can I call you Mummy now?" There was an awful moment of embarrassment and the tension in the room was unbearable. The unspoken truth was finally out. Then she said in a very kindly way, "I think it's best, after all they've done for you, that you go on calling your grandparents Mum and Dad." In that moment I felt totally rejected... I had expected she would sweep me up in her arms and take me away to wherever she had come from. My disappointment was unbearable and almost immediately turned into hatred and anger... I became surly and withdrawn rejecting everyone's affection.'[97] Like Catherine Cookson, his relationship with his mother remained tense for the rest of his life, though he too helped her as his earnings grew. He continued to suffer psychological stress, aware how this experience had conditioned his life and his relationships.

---

[94] Elizabeth Roberts, *Women and Families: An Oral History 1940–1970* (Oxford: Blackwell, 1995), 70.
[95] Eric Clapton, *The Autobiography* (London: Broadway Books, 2007), 2.
[96] Ibid. 5.   [97] Ibid. 17.

THE NATIONAL COUNCIL AT WAR

The NC, like the Government, learned lessons from the war. As we have seen, they worked closely with the Ministry of Health. Their president reported in 1946 that the war had greatly increased their workload: 'we have been chronically short-handed and consequently overworked.' But 'as the years wore on, it became, we believe, increasingly clear that our previous experience was of real value.'[98] The Council gave up campaigning for new legislation because Parliament was preoccupied with other matters, but they kept a close eye on policy discussions and proposals.

In 1939 it handled an average of 90 cases each month; by mid-1943, 200; by early 1946, 400: a total of 16,360 from September 1939 to April 1946.[99] In 1943 an independent Scottish Council was formed to share the work and deal with the different systems of law and administration in Scotland. Towards the end of the war, the NC became a clearing house for particularly difficult cases, especially those involving overseas servicemen who fathered children in England and Wales. In 1945, 25 per cent of all their cases concerned US servicemen. If these men denied paternity or had left the country there was little hope. Those who admitted paternity could claim a dependant's allowance for an illegitimate child and some did so.

When the children were 'coloured' there was a particular problem, especially in the large areas of Britain unaccustomed to people of a different skin colour. In 1945, the League of Coloured Peoples reported to the Ministry that it knew of 554 'illegitimate' children born to 'coloured' US servicemen, apart from those who were being well supported. The Ministry of Health was officially firmly opposed to discrimination, or to singling out mixed-race children for special attention, for fear of increasing prejudice against them. They wanted them to be treated as other British children, but, without positive discrimination, this was hard to achieve.[100] The NC also tried to ensure that 'these children should be brought up among other children, and in no way segregated, so that they may take their place among the other British subjects with whom they will live.'[101] But problems remained. Foster mothers and adoptive parents generally would not take them and if the mother was married, her marriage rarely survived, though the NC observed that

Many of the mothers, however, did not want to part with their babies and did not seem in the least perturbed about their colour. The fathers moreover, rarely tried to back out of their responsibility and often offered to marry the mothers and adopt the child.[102]

The presence of 'coloured' servicemen and their relationships with British women created another moral panic, complicated by resistance to the even greater

---

[98] Fisher, *Twenty-One Years*, 17.   [99] Ibid.
[100] Ferguson and Fitzgerald, *History*, 131 n. 4.   [101] NC Annual Report, 1943–4.
[102] Ferguson and Fitzgerald, *History*, 131–2.

discrimination US servicemen experienced from their 'white' compatriots.[103] A Lady in Waiting to Queen Mary, the Queen Mother, wrote to Violet Markham, while her committee was in session, about this 'difficult but important issue', summing up the tensions surrounding it, giving a fascinating glimpse into an unusually socially elevated perspective:

Her Majesty has been gravely concerned to hear of the unfortunate results, in many places, of association between American coloured men and English girls... They are friendly, generous and have a great deal of money to spend; and there is no reason to believe that they are particularly ill-behaved, though I fear that there is very little doubt but that many English girls—often about fifteen years of age—do run after these men (and their money!) most persistently... This is not chiefly a question of morals—however important that aspect may be—but of international complications. American men refuse to allow negroes to associate with white girls, and they are ready (unpunished by their own authorities) to 'beat up', first, the offending blacks, and subsequently the white girls who encourage them. Thus—apart from the fact that ultimate marriage would in any case be the rarest possibility (it is unlikely that the Government would welcome an invasion of negro workers after the war, or that they themselves would wish to settle down here, whilst they would certainly not be allowed to return to the USA with white wives!)—Apart from all this, there is a serious risk of grave ill-feeling between English and Americans, of possible lynchings, with all the disastrous consequences, not to mention the problem of half-caste births on a much bigger scale than heretofore.

The Queen feels strongly that wardens of hostels, factory welfare workers and others who are concerned with social conditions affecting girls, should give them definite instruction and enlightenment in this matter, and that it is an urgent one.

At the same time it is important that colour should *not* be stressed in writing, and that no written or printed word on this subject ever fall into the hands of those who are, after all, our country's guests. These black soldiers have come over with a tremendous sense of patriotism and determination to show that they are proud to work and fight for the U.S.A. The American authorities... are determined to crush all association between coloured men and white girls in exactly the same ruthless fashion that they do in their own country... and any English girl who walks out, however harmlessly, with a coloured American soldier should be made to understand that she will very probably cause his death![104]

This long comment reveals some of the nuances of the attitudes to race, and to sexual relations between people of different cultures, of a prominent member of the Royal Family, and their closeness to those of many of the wider population during the war.

Fathers who wished to adopt the child and take it to their families abroad were refused because the Adoption Acts did not allow British children to be adopted abroad, though a few exceptions were allowed. A new problem emerged at the end

---

[103] Rose, *People's War*, 74–6; Reynolds, *Rich Relations*, 276.

[104] Cynthia Colville, Lady in Waiting to Queen Mary to Violet Markham, 24 Aug. 1942, from Helen Jones (ed.), *Duty and Citizenship: The Correspondence and Papers of Violet Markham, 1896–1953* (London: The Historians' Press, 1994), 170–1.

of the war due to the ban on British women marrying foreign prisoners of war (many of whom were in work-camps in Britain), even if they were pregnant.[105] And pursuing fathers who were British servicemen could be difficult if they were serving abroad. In such cases a mother applying for an affiliation order had to deposit with the court the cost of his return fare, which was impossible for many women. The NC made grants for this purpose.[106]

The war experience reinforced the NC's growing belief that, much as it believed in forcing fathers to face up to their duties, affiliation orders were an unreliable means of securing the financial position of mothers and children. In 1936 there were 24,895 'illegitimate' births, but only 4,349 successful affiliation orders. By 1945 the numbers were 63,420 and 4,464. The NC was ready to consider other forms of support including from the state.[107]

William Beveridge's official report on social insurance of 1942, which so influenced the construction of the post-war welfare state, recognized the extent of poverty among 'unmarried persons living as a wife' and divorced and deserted wives, and their lack of access to public support except under demeaning conditions. Though he has been criticized for overlooking such women,[108] Beveridge in fact recommended 'further examination' by the Government of ways to provide state support for them. He could not easily fit them into the system of social insurance that was strictly the purpose of his report, especially where the male cohabitee and/or father was already married, or a divorced man had remarried.[109] Social insurance normally depends upon regular work and contributions by a woman or her partner calculated to cover the needs of no more than two partners. Like many of Beveridge's proposals, investigation of the issue was not taken forward by the post-war Labour Government. It met familiar opposition in Parliament and elsewhere for 'endangering marriage'.[110] However, his recommendation of a means-tested 'National Assistance' scheme to replace public assistance and help those who 'fell through the net' of the universal national insurance scheme could, and did, improve support for unmarried mothers when it was introduced in 1948.[111]

The NC set up a subcommittee to consider the Beveridge Report and in 1944 recommended to the Ministry of Reconstruction, that '13 weeks benefit should be paid to unmarried mothers without distinction',[112] after the birth, and any unmar-

---

[105] H. Macaskill, *From the Workhouse to the Workplace: 75 years of One-Parent Family Life, 1918–1993* (London: NCOPF, 1993), 23.

[106] Sue Graham-Dixon, *Never Darken My Doorstep: Working for Single Parents and Their Children, 1918–1978* (London: NCOPF, 1981), 21.

[107] Ibid.

[108] Elizabeth Wilson, *Women and the Welfare State* (London: Tavistock, 1977), ch. 7. See discussion of views of contemporary women's groups in Jose Harris, *William Beveridge: A Biography*, 2nd edn (Oxford: Oxford University Press, 1997), 391–7.

[109] William Beveridge, *Social Insurance and Allied Services*, Cmd 6404 (London: HMSO, 1942), paras. 347–8.

[110] Harris, *Beveridge*, 397.

[111] See pp. 107–8.

[112] Graham-Dixon, *Never Darken*, 21 NC Annual Report 1943–4, 5/OPF/10/1a, 10; CMM, 14 Oct., 2 Dec. 1943, 5/OPF/2/1/1/1f.

ried mother should be able to apply for an allowance for her child under the proposed National Assistance scheme; and that the children's allowance proposed by Beveridge should be paid to the first child of an unmarried mother. Beveridge proposed that the allowance should not normally be paid to first children, except where the responsible parent was on state benefit or a pension.[113] For the first time, the NC advocated state benefits for unmarried mothers and their children. They had decided from their war experience that the state could and should provide support that was not stigmatizing or punitive. This was the only effective way to help the neediest families.

ADOPTION

For all the efforts of the NC and others to prevent mothers feeling forced to have their children adopted during the war, the number of adoptions increased to a peak of 21,000 in 1946. An estimated one-third of these were adopted by their mothers and most adoptions legalized existing relationships. But, as we have seen, many mothers were forced into adoption by adverse circumstances, including married women pregnant by men other than their husbands. The mother of novelist Ian McEwan had a baby by McEwan's father while her husband was serving overseas. She placed an advertisement in a local paper: 'Wanted home for baby boy aged one month: complete surrender', and gave the baby to a couple on Reading station. The law could not yet prevent such informal adoptions. Her husband was killed in the Normandy landings, she married the baby's father and had another son, Ian.[114] Similarly, Beatle John Lennon's mother became pregnant by a Welsh soldier while her husband was away at sea: she also gave the child up for adoption.[115]

Weaknesses in the 1926 adoption legislation, and fears that children were still suffering from unregulated adoption by unsuitable people, had persuaded Parliament to establish the Horsbrugh Committee,[116] which led to the Adoption of Children (Regulation) Act, 1939. This was designed to allow only local authorities or adoption societies to arrange adoptions. Individuals who assisted in placing children for adoption were obliged to inform the local welfare authorities. A child's parent or guardian could still make a direct arrangement with an adopter provided the appropriate authorities were informed. The Act was also intended to restrict advertisements for adoptive parents and sending children abroad for adoption. But it was not implemented due to the onset of war, which caused concern to the NC, among many others. With other voluntary organizations the NC monitored adoptions and put pressure on the Ministry of Health to implement.[117] Demand to adopt was particularly high during the war: adoption agencies were flooded with

---

[113] Beveridge, *Social Insurance and Allied Services*, para. 419.

[114] Keating, *Child for Keeps*, 181.

[115] Ibid. 181; Julia Baird, *Imagine This: Growing Up with My Brother John Lennon* (London: Hodder and Stoughton, 2007), 20.

[116] Departmental Committee on Adoption Societies and Agencies, 1936–7, Cmd.5499.

[117] Fisher, *Twenty-One Years*, 20.

requests, especially to adopt girls.[118] By 1943 rumours and press reports put the Ministry of Health under further pressure to implement. It was alleged that adoptions were casually arranged in pubs and fish queues and babies disposed of through newspaper advertisements. The NC sent the Home Office a pile of advertisements, including:

Wanted—some baby-lover to adopt baby girl: love only—Alderson, Flat 3, 182 Lavender Hill, Enfield, Middx (*Kentish Independent*, 22 August 1941).

Offered for adoption, 4 months old baby girl, all rights forfeited. Write P7428 'Guardian' Office (*Warrington Guardian*, 16 August 1941).[119]

Questions were asked in Parliament and there were deputations to the Home Office, the first from the Woman Power Committee (an official committee established by the Ministry of Labour to advise on the employment of women in wartime), led by its Chair, Irene Ward; another by the Charity Organization Society (COS) and representatives of the NC, the National Council of Adoption Agencies, and the Church of England Moral Welfare Council. The Home Office was reluctant to implement the law but was over-ruled by the Ministry of Health and it came into force from June 1943.[120] But the NC continued to express concern about abuses. In particular, individuals, including doctors, nurses, and midwives, could and did offer children for adoption provided that they notified the welfare authorities. The NC believed that some mothers came under undue pressure to adopt from doctors and nurses while they were in hospital.[121]

Again there were lurid press stories: 'Dodgers rushing to adopt babies—There is evidence to show that as June 1 draws near—when the law will take a hand—more and more unwanted babies are being sold to women anxious to avoid war service.'[122] Mothers of young children were exempt from service. There were some exaggerations but also serious concern about abuse of adoption, expressed for example in *The Times*[123] and at public meetings,[124] concerns only increased by a *Sunday Dispatch* campaign to make adoption still easier, because, it claimed, the system was enmeshed 'in a tangle of red tape'.[125]

The Ministry was aware of continuing problems from a battle it was secretly fighting with Mrs Elizabeth James, matron of a private home in Surrey. This started before the Act came into force and continued thereafter. Mrs James had an outwardly respectable image as a benefactress of women in distress, approved of by local doctors and Members of Parliament. But her unsavoury activities had been revealed to the Home Office by the NC and other organizations.[126] Unmarried mothers living in her home paid fees, but also staffed the home and it was understood that all their babies would be adopted. The Ministry had evidence that she sold the babies into adoption, but it could not prove conclusively that 'New-born

[118] Keating, *Child for Keeps*, 176.   [119] Ibid. 177.   [120] Ibid. 179.
[121] NC Annual Reports, 1943–5.   [122] *Sunday Chronicle*, 11 Apr. 1943.
[123] *The Times*, 7 Aug. 1942.   [124] Keating, *Child for Keeps*, 177.
[125] Ibid. 177.   [126] Ibid. 178–9.

babies were taken on long railway journeys sometimes in the depth of winter, and handed over to strangers without enquiries on either side', usually for cash.[127] Outwardly, Mrs James kept carefully within the law. The mothers would not testify in court though some made statements in private. Theoretically, Mrs James had to inform the welfare authorities when she placed a child, but the COS found evidence that she was still handing over children, pretending to the adoptive parents that she was the child's legal guardian.[128] Her activities appear to have continued until the home closed in 1948.

In 1945 Birmingham's health visitors reported on the 712 adopted children under their care. Seven per cent lived under unsatisfactory physical conditions, 8 per cent under unfavourable psychological conditions. Unsatisfactory placements were twice as frequent among those whose adoptions had been privately arranged.[129] Not all local authorities were so vigilant and effective. From 1944, Birmingham insisted upon a satisfactory statement of health from would-be adopters and some were excluded.

Such safeguards were not universal. In 1944, the writer George Orwell and his wife, Eileen, adopted a baby boy straight from hospital. Orwell's sister-in-law, a doctor, arranged it—in what circumstances is unknown. Orwell's wife had been suffering from a tumour for some time but delayed seeing a surgeon until the adoption was through, mainly, she said, because her husband was so eager to adopt. She then had her operation, but died nine months later. While Eileen was alive, Orwell was an enthusiastic parent, taking his turn getting up at night and changing nappies. Shocked by her death, he left the baby, Richard, with carers and went abroad for some weeks. When he returned, he found a nurse-housekeeper to help him and Richard while he looked for a new wife and mother for Richard. But Orwell was already suffering from symptoms of the tuberculosis which killed him in 1949. Richard was cared for from about a year after Eileen's death by George's sister Avril and her husband, who brought him up after his father's death.[130]

Adoption law, like so many aspects of law and administration vitally important to unmarried mothers and their children, needed further attention after the war.

CONCLUSION

The war experience brought to the surface much about the everyday experiences of unmarried mothers and their children and about deficiencies of the law and social services that had previously been hidden. It strongly influenced post-war policy changes and practice. Yet the belief that it was a time of unprecedented immorality and illegitimacy survived, impervious to solemn official statistics.

---

[127] Ibid. 136.   [128] Ibid. 188.   [129] Ibid. 137 n. 4.
[130] Bernard Crick, *George Orwell: A Life* (London: Secker and Warburg, 1980).

4

Unmarried Motherhood in 'Family Britain': Challenging Bowlby

Post-war Britain was a different place, initially constrained by austerity, as a Labour Government restricted consumption and kept taxes high in order to re-build the economy. But most people increasingly enjoyed higher living standards and better social conditions as the measures worked, there was sustained full employment in peacetime for the first time in modern history, and, as we will see in the next chapter, a 'welfare state' was established. For unmarried mothers and their children, this brought gains and losses. At the same time, social research, as the social sciences expanded and were increasingly institutionalized in universi-ties, increased knowledge and understanding of the diversity of their experiences. The expansion and increased influence also of professional social work and of psychology and psychiatry, especially in relation to children, affected understand-ing of and the discourse around 'illegitimacy'. Among psychologists, John Bowlby is often claimed to have dominated the thinking of professionals dealing with families. In reality many of them were sceptical about his work.

HOW MANY UNMARRIED MOTHERS?

After the war, 'illegitimate' births fell, but not dramatically and not back to pre-war levels, despite the apparent return to peacetime normality in relations between the sexes and increased opportunities for marriage. The numbers, and the responses of many people to unmarried mothers and their children, challenge popular percep-tions of the 1950s as rigidly sexually conformist. By the early 1960s the numbers were rising well above wartime levels. According to official statistics, pregnant brides were slightly fewer than in 1938: 20.4 per cent in 1950; the same, after minor fluctuations, in 1957; in 1965 the official numbers returned to the 1938 level of 22 per cent.[1] The gulf between private behaviour and public morality seemed to be gradually widening.

---

[1] K. Kiernan, H. Land, and J. Lewis, *Lone Motherhood in Twentieth-Century Britain* (Oxford: Oxford University Press, 1998), 35; V. Wimperis, *The Unmarried Mother and Her Child* (London: Allen and Unwin, 1960), table 11.

Table 4.1 Illegitimate births per 1000 unmarried women aged 15–44, England and Wales

1905–6	8.4
1911–15	7.9
1921–5	6.7
1931–5	5.5
1941–5	11.4
1951–5	10.7
1961–5	19.1

Source: A. H. Halsey (ed.), *Trends in British Society since 1900* (London: Macmillan, 1972), 51.

There were local variations that are hard to explain. In 1950 the urban district with fewest births to unmarried parents was working-class Barking in East London, with 2.5 per cent, followed by more socially diverse Wembley, north-west London, with 2.8 per cent. Highest was notoriously raffish Brighton, with 8.9 per cent, followed, less predictably, by respectable Bournemouth at 8 per cent. Other seaside towns, Margate, Morecambe, and Penzance, also returned 8 per cent. In 1957 the lowest numbers were in Hornchurch, Essex, not too far from Barking geographically though perhaps more prosperous, at 1.7 per cent, followed by industrial Wigan (Lancashire), 1.9 per cent. Highest was the north London suburb of Willesden, geographically close to Wembley, with 11.7 per cent. It was followed, again, by Margate with 10.1 per cent, while Brighton had fallen to 7.4 per cent. 'Illegitimacy' was generally lower in rural areas, though Merionethshire, in South Wales, hit 10.2 per cent in 1957.[2] These variations cannot be explained in class, cultural, or socioeconomic terms without more detailed background knowledge than we have.

As before, the ages of unmarried mothers were scattered across the child-bearing spectrum, though concentrated among women in their twenties and early thirties.

Some births, legitimate and illegitimate, probably resulted from failed abortions. How often is unknown since abortion was illegal and secret. An official report in 1939 had estimated 44,000–60,000 illegal abortions each year, 6–8 per cent of all pregnancies.[3]

Despite the low and falling numbers of pregnancies among young teenagers, there was a moral panic throughout the 1950s about a perceived rising tide of 'schoolgirl mothers' who were unavoidably unmarried because marriage was prohibited to under-16s. The National Council tried to cool the panic by pointing out that births to under-16s were falling, despite the fact that their numbers were rising due to the increase in births during and since the war.[4] They quoted a sixteen

---

[2] Ibid. tables 6, 7.

[3] *Report of the Inter-departmental Committee on Abortion* (London: HMSO, 1939); Wimperis, *Unmarried*, 346.

[4] NC Annual Report 1952–3, 16.

Table 4.2 Ages of unmarried mothers, 1950–7, England and Wales[5]

Year	Ages	%	Number
1950	Under 20	15	5,327
	13–15		218
	20–24	27.3	
	25–29	33.2	
	30–34	20	
	40–44	3.7	
1957	Under 20	19.6	6,887
	12–15		97
	20–24	30	
	25–29	20.4	
	30–34	15.3	
	40–44	3.5	

year old in the NC office: 'There are more of us doing things, in 70 years there may be more do-gooders like yourselves.'[6]

Still, some insisted that teenage births were symptomatic of the growing moral depravity of the nation, perhaps all the more because they occurred in all social classes.[7] This was part of a wider moral panic about 'youth culture' in the 1950s. Teenagers, as they were beginning to be called, were more numerous, more visible, had more disposable income and were developing distinctive pleasures, such as rock music, and lifestyles shocking to some, though by no means all, of their elders.[8] The serious causes of some teenage pregnancies—child abuse and rape— were not openly discussed in this, or any, context,[9] though they had long histories in Britain[10] and cases came to the notice of the NC.[11] They were among the many sexual secrets still hidden in families and from wider public discourse.

ATTITUDES AND EXPERIENCES

These moral panics erupted amidst what is sometimes presented as the 'golden age' of the long, apparently stable, marriage. This has sometimes been presented as an

[5] Wimperis, *Unmarried*, Tables 9a, 9b. There are no page nos for Wimperis' appendix of tables.
[6] NC Annual Report 1960–1, 14.
[7] Joan Bourne, *Pregnant and Alone: The Unmarried Mother and her Child* (Royston: Priory Care and Welfare Library, 1971), 59.
[8] Lesley Hall, *Sex, Gender and Social Change in Britain since 1880* (London: Macmillan, 2000), 158–9.
[9] Adrian Bingham, *Family Newpapers? Sex, Private Lives and the Popular Press, 1918–1979* (Oxford: Oxford University Press, 2009), 155.
[10] George Behlmer, *Child Abuse and Moral Reform in England, 1870–1908* (Stanford: Stanford University Press, 1982).
[11] NC Committee of Management Minutes (hereafter CMM), 11 June 1937; 10 Dec. 1947.

historical norm, but, in all previous times, all too many marriages were broken by the early death of one partner, more often the male, leading to single parenthood and/or new partnerships and complex step-families. By the mid-twentieth century, life expectancy was rising and fewer mothers of young children were left as impoverished widows. There were more divorces than before the war but fewer than later in the century, because divorce was still expensive, difficult to obtain, and stigmatizing, especially for women. As we have seen, the difficulty of obtaining a divorce did not prevent some marriages breaking up, followed sometimes by unmarried cohabitation with a new partner. Also, a high proportion of people had never married (in the 1930s, 15 per cent of women and 9 per cent of men).

The post-war period, by contrast, was an historically unusual time of near universal marriage, perhaps due to greater prosperity as well as an evening of the sex ratio in the population. Average marriage ages were exceptionally low (21 for women by 1971 compared with an historical norm of around 25[12]), due again, probably, to higher living standards enabling earlier marriage and, perhaps, to earlier sexual maturity in a healthier population. This 'golden age' was to last only until the 1970s when divorce and cohabitation rose dramatically.[13]

In the post-war years, the work of psychologists, most influentially John Bowlby, reinforced the view that the two-parent family was the bedrock of a stable society and any deviation should be condemned. Such views perhaps raised expectations of marriage, which seems to have been more widely idealized as a site of companionship, communication, and perfect parenthood.[14]

How widely such views were held has been questioned repeatedly.[15] It is possible to exaggerate their dominance in this much stereotyped but little understood period. How many marriages were indeed stable and contented is unknown, as is to what extent striving to meet the ideals put them under new strains. There was another moral panic about a supposed increase in adultery. In 1954, Lord Denning, Lord Justice of Appeal, 'feared that we had unfortunately reached a position where adultery, or infidelity or misconduct as soft-spoken folk called it, was considered to be a matter of little moment'.[16] In 1959, the Archbishop of Canterbury spoke of a 'tide of adultery' and asked whether it had 'become such a public menace that the time has come when it ought to be made a criminal offence' because 'the immense damage that adultery does to the public welfare in broken homes,

---

[12] Jane Lewis, *The End of Marriage?* (Cheltenham: Edward Elgar, 2001), 30.

[13] Pat Thane, *Happy Families? History and Family Policy* (London: British Academy, 2010); Hall, *Sex*, 150–2.

[14] Hall, *Sex*, 151–6.

[15] Janet Fink, 'For Better or For Worse? The Dilemmas of Unmarried Motherhood in Mid-Twentieth Century Popular British Film and Fiction', *Women's History Review*, 20:1 (Feb. 2011), 145–60; Elizabeth Roberts, *Women and Families: An Oral History 1940–1970* (Oxford: Blackwell, 1995); Hera Cook, *The Long Sexual Revolution: English Women, Sex and Contraception, 1800–1975* (Oxford: Oxford University Press, 2004); Liz Heron (ed.), *Truth, Dare or Promise? Girls Growing up in the 1950s* (London: Virago, 1985); Hall, *Sex*, 150–66.

[16] Quoted in Claire Langhamer, 'Adultery in Post-war England', *History Workshop Journal*, 62 (Autumn 2006), 86–115.

and to the children of broken marriages, does constitute a very grave social danger'.[17] In 1959 Eustace Chesser, psychiatrist and champion of sexually progressive
causes, including legal abortion, published an article 'Is Chastity Outmoded? Out-
dated? Out?' in the BMA annual booklet *Getting Married* and caused a furore:
'Doctors in Free Love Storm' screamed the popular press. The BMA withdrew the
booklet.[18] There was no convincing evidence whether there was indeed more adultery than before. However, during the late 1950s and 1960s, the popular press
expanded its coverage of sexual matters and was increasingly explicit, e.g., in discussing the transgressions and divorces of prominent people. The *Daily Mirror* and
the *Sunday Pictorial* campaigned for greater openness and the democratization of
sexual knowledge.[19] This sharing of what had traditionally been upper-class secrets
with the masses, and a sense that established public conventions were increasingly
being publicly challenged, perhaps helped trigger the many moral panics of the
period about sexual transgression.

Contemporary social surveys[20] and oral histories[21] indeed suggest relaxed attitudes to infidelity in some sections of the population, cutting across classes and
challenging notions of a dominant sexual and marital conventionality, though it
is uncertain whether these were new or long established. Geoffrey Gorer commented following his survey *Exploring British Character* (1955): 'Most people's
views on sexual morality are more rigid than their personal practice,' suggesting
how widely public secrecy about transgressive private behaviour still prevailed.[22]
There were now clearer signs of a division between those who expressed moral
panic in public and a quieter, quite widespread, acceptance of unconventional
behaviour, provided it did no obvious harm.[23] Janet Fink's study of popular novels
and films in the late 1940s and 1950s suggests a degree of popular tolerance of
unmarried mothers, especially those who behaved respectably and could support
their children.[24]

Sexual matters were discussed more openly than before, though this was still
limited and often controversial. In 1957, the report of the official Wolfenden
Committee on prostitution and sexual offences made unprecedented recommendations for decriminalization of homosexual acts between consenting adults in
private. This followed several years in which the press had overcome their previous
silence about homosexuality, as about other sexual matters, mainly to publicize
sensational cases.[25] There were scandalized responses to Wolfenden. The recommendations for stricter regulation of street prostitution by women became law,
whereas those on homosexuality had to wait until 1967. But the topic had come
out into the public arena from a long silence.

---

[17] Quoted in Langhamer, 'Adultery', 99.   [18] Hall, *Sex*, 156.
[19] Bingham, *Family Newspapers?*, 12–13 and *passim.*
[20] G. Gorer, *Exploring English Character* (New York: Criterion Books, 1955).
[21] Roberts, *Women and Families.*   [22] Gorer, *Exploring*, 94.
[23] Hall, *Sex*, 150–67.   [24] Fink, 'Dilemmas'.
[25] Bingham, *Family Newspapers*, 185–8.

The 'problem pages' of mass circulation women's magazines, such as *Woman's Own* and *Woman*, provide abundant further evidence of private deviation from public norms. 'Evelyn Home' (real name Peggy Makins), 'agony aunt' of *Woman* (circulation 3.5m in the mid-1950s), worked closely with the National Council, guiding correspondents to them, promoting their services and keeping them informed of the types of problem she encountered.[26]

The NC itself kept close watch on changing public attitudes. Its Annual Report for 1956–7 commented:

Since our Council was founded in 1918, the whole social scene has changed and with it the position of the unmarried mother. She is no longer 'ruined' as a matter of course, but can usually go back fairly easily, after her confinement, to whatever employment she had before.[27]

But even this statement produced 'unfavourable comment from people who thought "we were making light of sin" '[28] and the following year, the Report acknowledged how divided attitudes still were, commenting that even if some were more liberal, there still were parents who rejected their erring daughters.[29]

The experiences of unmarried mothers themselves were equally diverse. It perhaps became easier for some middle-class women to keep their children, due to the gradual improvement in their employment opportunities, but it was harder for many working-class women. It was more difficult to find daily childminders or foster mothers. Older women took better paid work at a time of unprecedented labour shortage and demand for their labour, and, due to the housing shortage, fewer people had room for foster children. Day and residential nurseries were all too few, after their brief wartime expansion.

Middle-class women were also often better prepared to avoid pregnancy before marriage. When northern, working-class Margaret Forster went to largely middle-class, southern, Somerville College, Oxford, in 1957, 'the best thing was being in touch with girls who knew about birth control and abortion. Oh dear, how funny it was, how sweet, to have their little north-country friend so ignorant.'[30] Following their advice, she was fitted with a cap at Helena Wright's clinic in London, though in her innocence did not know that she was expected to pay. But she was delighted that, unlike her great-grandmother and grandmother she would not have an illegitimate child, or, like her mother, an unwanted child after she thought her family was complete.

A growing volume of social research produced a clearer understanding of the everyday lives of unmarried mothers who kept their children.

---

[26] NC CMM, 24 Apr. 1957. And see problem pages of these and other magazines.
[27] NC Annual Report 1956–7, 11.
[28] Ibid. 13.
[29] NC Annual Report 1957–8, 13.
[30] Margaret Forster, *Hidden Lives: A Family Memoir* (London: Penguin, 1996), 247. Central to the memoir were the pregnancies outside marriage of her great-grandmother and grandmother and the family secrecy surrounding these and other matters, including mental illness in the family and domestic violence in the neighbourhood.

THE FAMILY LIVES OF UNMARRIED MOTHERS

The research showed that the living arrangements of mothers and children were as diverse after the war as before, but it provided far more detail. A fairly consistent picture emerged from several studies that of every 100 'illegitimate' children, 3 died in their first year; around 20 were adopted by people other than their parents; 3 entered voluntary or public care. The largest group, about one-third, grew up in 'unofficial families' with cohabiting, unmarried parents. A smaller number lived with grandparents, with or without their mothers, while a still smaller group lived with their mothers alone. A possibly quite high, but uncertain, number of mothers later married the father or another man and kept their children.

This general picture emerged from a series of local studies. Sixty-seven children born in Newcastle upon Tyne in May and June 1947 were surveyed to the end of their first year where possible: 27 'lived with both parents as members of unofficial families'; the parents of 6 children had subsequently married; one mother had married another man; 17 lived with their maternal grandparents. Only 3 mothers were living alone at the time of delivery. Twelve children were adopted.[31]

A larger survey by the Ministry of Health in Leicester in 1954–5 followed up 284 'illegitimate' children born in the city in 1949, when the extramarital birth rate was 5.6 per cent. The Leicester MOH reported that, of the mothers whose circumstances at the time of conception were known, 141 were single, 64 married, 35 widowed or divorced; 42 were aged under 20. Half of the single mothers, and three-quarters of those who were widowed, married, or divorced were living with the father at the time of conception. Half of these were cohabiting because one or both partners was already married; the other half had chosen not to marry. Forty per cent of fathers were married at the time of the child's birth, 29 per cent living apart from their wives. Only 20 children were the result of casual relationships. Five years later, 30 per cent of the mothers were married, 40 per cent were cohabiting. Fifteen per cent had parted with the child, 11 per cent for adoption, c.3 per cent to institutions, the remainder to live with relatives, usually grandparents. Fifteen per cent of mothers were bringing up the child alone. Ninety-five mothers gave their occupation as 'housewife', 91 as factory work, 8.6 per cent were domestic workers, 6 per cent shop assistants, 4.3 per cent clerks or typists.

Mothers and children living in stable two-parent partnerships, whether or not this was based on formal marriage, appeared to have few problems. The study also found that, although 90 per cent of the mothers had left school at 14 (like most British people before the school-leaving age was raised to 15 in 1947, when very few went on to further or higher education), few were of low intelligence, as some psychiatrists asserted was typical of unmarried mothers (see below). Home conditions were good and the children's development satisfactory. The study was unusual

---

[31] Wimperis, *Unmarried*, 244–6; Sir James Spence et al., *A Thousand Families in Newcastle-upon-Tyne* (Oxford: Oxford University Press, 1954).

in shedding some light on the (resident) fathers. They too mostly were not the unstable 'neurotics' who figured in the psychological literature. Most were aged 30–34; many were engaged to the mother when she became pregnant or were family friends; most were employed, skilled, workers.[32]

Studies in Scotland reached similar conclusions. A survey of 582 mothers of 'illegitimate' children in Aberdeen in the 1950s found that one-third were older women who were cohabiting.[33] Cyril Greenland, a psychiatric social worker based at a hospital in Dumfries, also found that one-third of a sample of unmarried mothers were older and cohabiting and more than one-third of fathers were married, often living with a woman other than their wives. He pointed out that about 21 per cent of women giving birth in Scotland in 1953 did so within nine months of marriage, and there appeared to be little difference between young unmarried mothers and those involved in 'shotgun' weddings.[34]

Greenland carried out two further studies of 3,444 women helped by the National Council in 1953. They were not a representative sample of unmarried mothers but were drawn from those who had sought help from the NC and were likely to be those with fewest other sources of support.[35] Twenty-two per cent came from London. Again, he found that one-third of the mothers were living with the father, 41 per cent lived with their parents or other relatives, 23 per cent were in lodgings, 5 per cent were in a hostel, 5 per cent were resident hospital staff, and 1 per cent were of no fixed abode. Greenland concluded that the most important factors associated with unmarried motherhood among this group were not psychological but social, including age, social class, membership of large families, lack of family support, and living away from home. He concluded that women were in particular danger if they worked closely with men.[36] Forty-seven per cent of the known fathers were married, but he could find information on only 5 per cent of fathers. Twenty-five per cent just disappeared from their lover's life, 9 per cent denied paternity, and 27.5 per cent refused to marry the mother. Those who could be traced were of similar age to the mothers.[37]

Most of the mothers had worked as domestics, followed by clerical workers, hospital domestics, and nurses. These were among the most common occupations for women at this time. Others worked in factories, as shop assistants, in the armed services, as teachers or waitresses, or were students. Three-fifths were under 25.

---

[32] Wimperis, *Unmarried*, 51–75; E. K. Macdonald, 'Follow-up of Illegitimate Children', *Medical Officer*, 196 (1956), 361–5; Jane Lewis and John Welshman, 'The Issue of Never-Married Motherhood in Britain, 1920–70', *Social History of Medicine*, 10:3 (Dec. 1997), 411.

[33] Lewis and Welshman, 'Never-Married Motherhood', 411–12; B. Thompson, 'Social Study of Illegitimate Maternities', *British Journal of Preventive and Social Medicine*, 10 (1956), 75–87.

[34] C. Greenland, 'Unmarried Parenthood: Ecological Aspects', *Lancet* (19 Jan. 1957), 148–51.

[35] NC Annual Report 1957–8, 17. 'A Preliminary Report of an Analysis of Data Abstracted from 3444 Cases Dealt with by the National Council for the Unmarried Mother and her Child in 1953', TWL/5/OPF.

[36] C. Greenland, 'Unmarried Parenthood: I—Unmarried Mothers', *Medical Officer*, 99 (1958), 265–72.

[37] C. Greenland, 'Unmarried Parenthood: II—Putative Fathers', *Medical Officer*, 99 (1958), 281–6.

Most were single, but 4 per cent were married and 6 per cent separated or divorced. Greenland complained that the NC did not keep enough data on parents' attitudes to their daughters' pregnancy, but he discovered that 11 per cent of applicants to NC did not want to tell their parents. Research for the NC into records of 650 'illegitimate' births in Birmingham in 1955 found that 300 mothers were living with the father of the child.[38] Margaret Yelloly's study in 1964 of the backgrounds of 196 unmarried mothers found that most did not come from dysfunctional homes, as some psychiatrists believed, and about 80 per cent had a long relationship with the father. Ninety-seven parents accepted and supported their daughter, 13 rejected her, 3 were ambivalent, 13 were not told. About the remainder nothing was known.[39]

COHABITATION

As we have seen, a high proportion of 'illegitimate' children continued to be born to unmarried cohabiting parents. In 1964, 40 per cent were registered jointly by both parents.[40] This did not necessarily suggest that the parents lived together, but it did imply an ongoing relationship and that the father acknowledged the child. Most unofficial cohabitation was, still, due to the difficulty of gaining a divorce because of the limited grounds available, the slowness of the process, and/or the unwillingness of the other partner to agree.[41] 'Unofficial families' generally still lived covertly, pretending and often wishing to be married and, apparently often accepted as such. One researcher noted that:

one may meet a quiet and most respectable-seeming couple, a Mr and 'Mrs' Brown who have a thriving family and do not excite the curiosity of their neighbours at all, unless by their reticence about the past. Like thousands of other unofficial families they have faded quietly into the landscape and have taken on the protective coloration of marriage, without ever having been through a marriage ceremony.

These unofficial unions can be found at every social level and at very different moral levels.[42]

Historian Carolyn Steedman was born in 1947 to unmarried parents in South London. Her father had left his wife and two-year-old daughter in the North in 1934. He and Carolyn's mother had been together for at least ten years before her birth and they later had another daughter. The sisters discovered this, and their 'illegitimacy' only after his death in 1977. They never discovered why their parents had never married, though their mother clearly wanted this and the relationship became seriously unhappy, between two unhappy people, their father providing

---

[38] NC Annual Report 1956–7, 16.
[39] M. Yelloly, 'Social Casework with Unmarried Parents', MA thesis, University of Liverpool (1964).
[40] Kiernan et al., *Lone Motherhood*, 42.
[41] See pp. 8–9.   [42] Wimperis, *Unmarried*, 240.

for them, but living on his own in the attic from the mid-1950s. They only knew that they lived in a world of isolation and secrets. Carolyn didn't understand why she was withdrawn from Sunday School when Confirmation was in prospect and she was asked to show her baptism certificate—which would have revealed the family secret.[43]

Some couples hid their unofficial status through the female partner changing her name by deed poll to that of her 'husband'. These 'illegal wives' caused another moral panic. In 1947 the Lord Chancellor announced that this practice was becoming 'more and more frequent', indeed was 'undoubtedly becoming a common practice', though he gave no numbers and none seem to be available. In the same year, the Church of England Moral Welfare Council proposed legislation to curb the practice. Church representatives complained that the BBC had broadcast a radio programme, 'Changing your Name', suggesting that 'to the couple who are not married it means avoiding the embarrassment of ration books made out in the same address but in different names'. They argued that the wartime practice of awarding separation allowances to 'unmarried wives' had encouraged the belief that cohabitation was acceptable. They did not comment on why this practice in the First World War had not apparently had the same effect. Both the Lord Chancellor and the Home Secretary condemned name-changing by cohabitees as an 'abuse', but the Labour Government was reluctant to legislate.

In 1955 the London Housewives' Association complained that a 'Change of Name Deed' could be bought for a mere one and a half pence and that the practice

is a threat not only to the moral structure of society but also, in many cases, to the well-being of legitimate and illegitimate children, and a cruel embarrassment of injustice to a spouse whose rights and true position are overthrown by an imposter.

Again, the Government—now Conservative—refused to act on an issue seen as controversial. Popular views appeared to be divided and not widely supportive of such a measure.[44]

Many social researchers, social workers, and some social psychologists—the latter numerous, outspoken, and vigilant as never before concerning the family circumstances of young children—found the situation in cohabiting families 'surprisingly encouraging'.[45] Most were judged stable and content despite the reality that

[m]any of the families must live under a constant strain...generally the truth must be concealed from neighbours, who can be cruel if they find out, and often the children themselves are uncomfortably aware that some secret is being kept from them. Some families conceal their position, move to another district, which means that in times of crisis they may be far away from the friends and relatives to whom they would have turned for help.

---

[43] Carolyn Steedman, *Landscape for a Good Woman* (London: Virago, 1986).
[44] Langhamer, 'Adultery'.
[45] Wimperis, *Unmarried*, 251.

If the union should break down, the family is in a much less favourable position than a legal family: the mother cannot claim maintenance for herself at all, and for the children only if she has, or can obtain, an affiliation order.[46]

Experience suggested that breakdown was rare. In London at least, few children of such unions went into care, and the relationships seemed to be

[r]emarkably stable, perhaps because the men and women face the difficulties of such a relationship with deliberation and realism, or because they are generally older and more experienced, and do not face this path unless they are unquestionably devoted to each other. This might also explain why so many of the children seem, on the slight information we have, to be settling happily.[47]

A few fathers had custody, even when married to someone other than the mother. The father's right to custody was supported by the NC, the BMA, and the Magistrates' Association as being in the best interests of the child when the mother could not cope. The rights of fathers were increased by the Legitimacy Act, 1959 (see below), which for the first time allowed both the father and mother of an 'illegitimate' child custody or access, bringing the rights of the fathers into line with those of divorced and separated fathers.

Of course not every woman who bore a child after a failed marriage later formed a stable partnership. In 1960 the NC was approached by Valerie,

one of the older married women whose unhappiness through a broken marriage had made it easy for her to form an association with another man. She was nearly 40 and came to us when she was about five months pregnant; she had been a secretary and had considerable savings. She left her home in the North of England, determined to face the last few months of her pregnancy in a district where she was unknown. At her age and with her independent attitude she would have found it difficult to fit into the community life of a Mother and Baby Home. Valerie asked if we could find her private accommodation where she could stay until her confinement and return there afterwards with the baby until she had decided on the child's future. She could easily find temporary secretarial work and she was prepared to pay her own way. We were able to put her in touch with a woman who had written to say she was interested in our work and wanted to know how she could help. She had a spare room to offer and was glad to take an expectant mother. Within a few days Valerie had moved in and we know she spent several happy months as part of the household and yet with a certain independence.[48]

We do not know what happened to Valerie and her child thereafter.

LIVING WITH GRANDPARENTS—CHALLENGING BOWLBY

Children growing up with grandparents appeared to researchers and social workers also to be generally stable, despite the forebodings of some child psychiatrists.

---

[46] Wimperis, *Unmarried*, 251–2.   [47] Ibid. 252–3.
[48] NC Annual Report 1960–1, 32.

Some members of this increasingly influential profession were concerned about the traumatic effects on those growing up believing their grandparents to be their parents, then discovering the truth, rightly sometimes, as we have seen with Catherine Cookson and Eric Clapton.[49] Yet even John Bowlby, the most notorious child psychiatrist of this period, often cited as comprehensively critical of unmarried mothers,[50] conceded that there were occasions when 'the arrangement...worked well'. But he believed that 'this seemed to have occurred only when the mother was stable, had good relations with her parents, and was fond of the baby and his father—not a very frequent set of circumstances'—a conclusion challenged by the British research evidence discussed above.[51]

It is rarely noted that Bowlby also commented that

In Western communities two types of illegitimacy are distinguishable, the first of which is socially accepted and the second of which is socially not accepted. Among the illegitimacy which is relatively accepted in certain Western communities can be placed the convention that, before it is wise to marry her, the girl should demonstrate her fecundity. Another example is the convention for a couple to live together as though married despite not having gone through a legal ceremony. Finally there are the sub-cultures, usually among the poorer classes, where the possession of an illegitimate child is not held against the mother and both are given support within the greater family.[52]

This was an accurate enough description of the situations revealed by British social researchers. Bowlby regretted that official statistics did not distinguish between these 'socially accepted' illegitimacies and the 'socially unacceptable' mother, whom he described as 'often...from an unsatisfactory family background [who] has developed a neurotic character'.[53] These were the people who aroused his concern, though he was unclear about the numbers and this negative comment about some mothers has been cited as representing his view of all unmarried mothers.[54]

Bowlby, in 1952, noted the 'absence of satisfactory evidence for any country of Western Europe' of the long-term effects of growing up 'illegitimate', but concluded, confidently, that 'in some countries at least a large fraction of illegitimates, *perhaps* (our italics) more than half, under the present haphazard arrangements grow up suffering from some degree of maternal deprivation and into characters likely to produce more of their kind.'[55] His view was based on two small studies in North America, of 92 teenage 'illegitimates' in Toronto in 1943 and 30 in New York in the 1930s.[56] It was shortly to be challenged by the findings from the larger

---

[49] See pp. 7, 75.

[50] E.g., Kiernan et al., *Lone Motherhood*, 102; Lewis and Welshman, 'Never-Married Motherhood', 409.

[51] John Bowlby, *Maternal Care and Mental Health*, 2nd edn (Geneva: World Health Organization, 1952), 98, quoted in Wimperis, *Unmarried*, 257–8.

[52] Bowlby, *Maternal Care*, 93.

[53] Ibid.

[54] Kiernan et al., *Lone Motherhood*, 102; Lewis and Welshman, 'Never-Married Motherhood', 409.

[55] Bowlby, *Maternal Care*, 97.

[56] Ibid. 97–8.

British studies described above, though Bowlby appears not to have taken note of these in his later work. British social researchers and voluntary organizations working with unmarried mothers and their children, including the NC, undertook their research partly to put Bowlby's claims under empirical scrutiny in British environments. As a result they took a more optimistic view of the lives of most unmarried mothers and their children.[57] Bowlby's views did not persuade all professionals, as is often asserted.[58]

MOTHERS ALONE

However, based on their research and experience of working with mothers and children, social researchers and voluntary groups agreed that the situation of the minority of children living with their mothers alone was often precarious and insecure, and they needed more support than others. Lone women, abandoned by the father, are etched in popular memory as typical unmarried mothers. They indeed existed, though they were not typical. Elizabeth, mother of Rodney Bickerstaffe, later a leading trade unionist, born 1944, was a 24-year-old nurse in London who told her son that she had sex just once with one of the patients, a 23-year-old Irish carpenter. When he learned she was pregnant, he returned to Ireland and refused to marry her because she was not a Catholic. He rejected all pleas to return and married another woman. When Elizabeth told her parents, her father, a devout Christian and a very strict, sometimes violent, parent, according to her son, 'hit the roof and didn't want to know anything about her or the potential me or anything'.[59] She went to the NC for help and was guided to a nursing home for the confinement. Within two months of Rodney's birth she was a residential nurse using her skills caring for other people's children, so that she could keep Rodney with her. After a succession of such posts, her father relented and she and Rodney, now aged two, moved to live with her parents, sisters, and brother in Doncaster (Yorkshire). She adopted Rodney in 1950. Her mother was very supportive. They stayed until Rodney was 11. For him 'it was a phenomenally happy household as a youngster 'cos I was like the apple of everybody's eye.' He appears to have been unaware of the absence of a father until he was six and had 'a bit of a fight' with another boy who said that a father was needed to produce children. Rodney remembered replying: 'Don't be ridiculous. I haven't got a father. Look at me. I'm here aren't I?' When he told his mother, she gave him a photograph of a man, saying 'This is your dad, your daddy, and if anybody ever asks you, you know you can say, that's who it is.' His mother was then working in a day nursery of which she eventually became the matron. When Rodney was 11 she married a divorced man

---

[57] Wimperis, *Unmarried*, 258; Political and Economic Planning (PEP), 'The Unmarried Mother', *Planning*, no. 255 (1946).

[58] For a useful assessment of Bowlby's work and its reception see Denise Riley, *War in the Nursery: Theories of the Child and the Mother* (London: Virago, 1983).

[59] Tanya Evans, interview with Rodney Bickerstaffe, 27 June 2006.

with a son and they set up a new home, where there were initial tensions between the young stepbrothers. Thereafter the family appears from Rodney's accounts to have carried on contentedly.[60]

Other abandoned mothers came to the NC. In 1955:

A woman of 26 called at the office in a very distressed state. It was obvious her confinement was imminent and that her health was in danger. She had been living with the putative father who had promised marriage but he had left that morning saying he would not return... She had no money. Within two hours we arranged for her to be seen at a hospital where she was admitted at once and a Home vacancy to be found where she could go with her child for a few weeks and think out plans for the future.[61]

Like Elizabeth Bickerstaffe, mothers who were initially alone did not always remain so and those who did so were a minority of all unmarried mothers.[62] Social researchers and social workers who were in regular contact with families were often less pessimistic than the child psychiatrists and aware that few mothers remained alone for very long, since many married after the birth or returned to their parents.[63] But when they were unsupported by the father or their family, having perhaps grown up in institutions or in dysfunctional families, they could have difficulty finding a home, childcare, or adequately paid work. Some placed their children with foster parents, but good ones were particularly hard to find after the war. Bowlby was particularly critical of the effects of foster care on children.[64] Poor fostering could indeed be harmful, especially if the child experienced frequent changes, though there is no sign that this was widespread in Britain.[65] Some local authorities paid grandparents to foster, while the mother lived with them, which eased family finances.

The status of children whose parents subsequently married was eased by the Legitimacy Act, 1959, which allowed legitimation even if one or both parents were married to another at the time of the birth. This was the subject of a succession of Private Members' Bills and was considered by a Royal Commission on Marriage and Divorce, which reported in 1956. A majority (12) of the Commissioners rejected it, arguing that:

Legitimacy is the status held by a lawful child of the family. Any departure from that conception can only be made by ignoring the essential moral principle that a man cannot, during the subsistence of his marriage, beget lawful children by another woman. It is unthinkable that the State should lend its sanction to such a step for it could not fail to result in a blurring of moral values in the public mind. A powerful deterrent to illicit relationships would be removed, with disastrous results for the status of marriage as at present understood. The issue is fundamental but perfectly plain. If children born in adultery may

---

[60] Ibid.

[61] Sue Graham-Dixon, *Never Darken My Doorstep: Working for Single Parents and Their Children, 1918–1978* (London: National Council for One Parent Families, 1981), 27.

[62] Wimperis, *Unmarried*, 258–60.

[63] Ibid.   [64] Bowlby, *Maternal Care*, 113–14, 117–18.   [65] Ibid. 96.

subsequently acquire the status of legitimate children, an essential distinction between lawful marriages and illicit unions disappears.[66]

But a minority of commissioners (7) considered that

there was no evidence that the law did deter couples from forming illicit unions. Even if the law did have this effect, the hypothetical risk of promoting immorality had to be weighted against the real benefits which legitimation conferred on a child. It was difficult to see why parents should be allowed to confer the consequences of legitimacy by the 'circuitous and somewhat absurd process' of adopting their own children rather than achieving the same result by marrying. Moreover it would be wrong to allow an adulterous couple to regularize their position by marriage as and when they became free whilst denying any possibility of such regularization to the innocent offspring of the cohabitation.[67]

Opinion was deeply divided. In 1959, Labour MP John Parker introduced a Private Member's Bill in Parliament, strongly backed by the NC who worked with him to draft the Bill.[68] Parker argued that MPs' postbags showed that the existing law 'caused grievous hardship and mental suffering to people at all social levels'.[69] The Conservative Government did not oppose the Bill. It passed easily in the Commons but was rejected in the Lords, on the grounds put forward by the majority commissioners three years earlier. The Lords were over-ridden and the Bill became law. The number of birth re-registrations for purposes of legitimation increased from 6,506 in 1960, the first full year that the new law operated, to 13,043 in 1967.[70] As we have seen, natural fathers could now apply for custody of an 'illegitimate' child, but the law still did not give the children equal legal rights, in particular to inheritance, with those born 'legitimate', since their legitimacy was officially from the date of legitimation rather than from birth.

In 1964 Parker also successfully introduced a British Nationality Act, which granted British nationality to children of British mothers born overseas if they would otherwise be stateless, for which the NC had also campaigned and worked with Parker to bring about.[71]

ADOPTION

Adoption was the last resort for many mothers, chosen by some, forced on others by parents, by the father, or by the difficulty of bringing up a child independently. Wartime separation caused some hard cases. A married woman first approached the National Council in 1948:

---

[66] Stephen Cretney, *Family Law in the Twentieth Century* (Oxford: Oxford University Press, 2003), 552; Royal Commission on Marriage and Divorce, *Report*, Cmd 9678, para 1180.
[67] Ibid. paras 1182, 1174–8.
[68] NC CMM, 24 Apr. 1959.
[69] Cretney, *Family Law*, 553; House of Commons, Official Reports, 30 Jan. 1959, col. 1403 ff.
[70] Cretney, *Family Law*, 554.
[71] NC Annual Report 1964–5, 17.

She was expecting a child by a man she had grown fond of during the husband's absence. She was the mother of three little boys and the complications are obvious. A great many discussions took place and help of a specially valuable kind was received from the Almoner of the local hospital. Mrs A came to the conclusion after discussion that it would be best to tell her husband of her plight. This Council through another agency made arrangements for the boys to spend their summer holidays in a children's home and the baby was born in the local hospital so that Mrs A could remain with her husband until the last moment. Then she spent a few weeks in a mother and baby home with her baby, Elizabeth, while she was considering whether she would leave her family or have her baby adopted. Finally she decided upon adoption and returned to her children. We were very happy when she came to the office not long ago with a new baby daughter, Frances, now about six months old. There is no doubt about it, she is still seeking in her mind to justify having allowed Elizabeth to be adopted. Thanks to the co-operation of the adoption society, we have been able to give her a very good impression of her little girl's new home and parents. This is now easing her mind and making the inevitable strained relationships within her own family less difficult as time goes on.[72]

About one-fifth of 'illegitimate' children were adopted by people other than their mother or other relatives.[73] The NC continued to encourage and support lone mothers to keep their children rather than have them adopted by others, and to adopt them themselves where this seemed realistic. They campaigned against the reluctance of some magistrates to make adoption orders in favour of unmarried mothers and of some local authority social workers to support them.[74] The advantage for a mother was that she did not have to pretend to be married and could escape embarrassing situations, such as an application for a passport in the child's name prompting a request for the husband's consent, or an application for a university grant or tax allowance causing enquiries about the 'husband's' means. The NC pointed out that

Where an adoption order is in force the mother can if she wishes, retain her status of spinster quite openly and exposure, painful both to child and mother, cannot arise. The mother should, of course be advised when the order is made that she should explain the true position to the child when he or she is old enough to understand it.[75]

Social workers in the public and voluntary sectors generally saw their duty as keeping mother and child together, if possible, at least for the first weeks after birth, so that she was not rushed into a decision and had time to reflect on her options, take advice, and bond with her baby. Bowlby disagreed, arguing that it should be obvious before or very shortly after the birth whether the mother had the 'stability of personality' necessary for good mothering, that it was wrong to allow a possibly

[72] NC Annual Report 1954–5, 17–18.
[73] Kiernan et al., *Lone Motherhood*, 39.
[74] NC Minutes, 28 Oct. 1953; 27 July 1955; 25 Jan., 23 May 1956; 26 Mar. 1958; 21 Jan., 25 Mar. 1959.
[75] NC Annual Report 1955–6, 13.

unsuitable mother to spend long enough with her baby to become attached and adoption was the best outcome for a 'socially not accepted' illegitimacy.[76] Again, his influence on the professionals in the public and private sectors was less than is sometimes thought; their day-to-day experience of working with mothers and children outweighed his assertions.

The NC and others were disturbed by the pressure on some mothers from doctors and nurses in maternity wards to have their children adopted.[77] There were more complaints of this in the 1950s than previously, possibly because more unmarried mothers were giving birth in hospital following the foundation of the NHS in 1948. There were also complaints about churches trying to arrange private adoptions.[78] It was believed that demand for adoption from would-be parents was especially high after the war, encouraging adoption outside the law.[79] The Curtis Committee on the Care of Children reported in 1946 that fewer than a quarter of adoptions in 1944 (the latest year for which figures were available) were supervised and protected by the law.[80] The PEP think tank complained, also in 1946, that there was still 'far too much casual adoption arranged, sometimes in pubs or even in fish queues'.[81] Fish queues were a favourite shock-horror location for critics of informal adoption.

Such reports made the NC and others determined to have the adoption law strengthened to prevent informal adoptions. The NC used their supporters' influence in powerful places and had an article published in the *Lancet* informing doctors of the dangers of encouraging informal adoption. Their General Secretary appeared on BBC radio *Woman's Hour* and on the *Letter-Box* programme in 1948, and organized articles in *The Times*, and more popular papers, to inform the wider public. They worked with parliamentarians on a bill designed to tighten the adoption law, which was introduced in the House of Lords in 1949.[82]

The resulting Adoption Act, 1949, required all adoptions to be sanctioned by law and would-be adopters assessed. A mother could not consent until the child was six weeks old, and consent must be in writing, witnessed by a JP, though adoption orders could be made without consent if the mother could not be found, was judged incapable of giving consent, or if 'consent is unreasonably withheld'. Some Members of Parliament, especially women, expressed deep unease about removing a child from its family, especially from its mother. They called for greater support to enable unmarried mothers to keep their children, painting a picture of a distressed young woman, abandoned by the father and often by her family, who should not be rushed into giving up her child.[83] Others argued that it was adoptive

---

[76] Bowlby, *Maternal Care*, 101–8.   [77] NC Minutes, 14 Apr., 23 June 1948; 27 Apr. 1949.
[78] Ibid. 23 May 1956.   [79] Ibid. 27 Apr. 1949.
[80] Cretney, *Family Law*, 610.   [81] PEP, *Planning* 255, 7.
[82] NC Annual Reports, 1948–9, 11; 1949–50, 11; NC Minutes, 14, 27 Apr. 1948; 22, 27 June, 27 July, 23 Nov. 1949; 25 Jan., 28 June 1950.
[83] Fink, 'Dilemmas', 154; House of Commons, Offical Report Dec. 1949, 470, col. 1611; 466, col. 680.

parents who needed legal protection, for fear that the natural pa
mail them or seek to alienate the child's affection.[84] Under tl
mothers lost their right to know the identities of the adopters, anc
in England and Wales had no right to know the names of their na
was permitted in 1978). Non-British children adopted by Brit
matically gained citizenship for the first time.[85] Adopted childr
property inheritance rights to natural children. Adoption by single people became
difficult and rare.

The NC welcomed the legislation, with reservations, and kept close watch
on how it worked in practice. They continued to support mothers through
the decision whether to keep their child. Their *Annual Report*, 1953–4,
described how

We were approached...by a girl in her twenties who had read our address in one of the
women's magazines. She had lived at home with her parents in the Midlands, but on finding she was pregnant by a man she had hoped would marry her, came to London and
found a temporary clerical job. She was a capable person, who wanted to help herself as
much as possible without letting her parents know of her difficulties. We were able to
arrange for her to enter a Mother and Baby Home shortly before her confinement. By this
time she had taken her employer into her confidence and as she had done so well at her
job, she was placed on the permanent staff and asked to return after the baby had been
born. Mary had always talked of adoption, but when her daughter arrived, decided she
could not part from her. She then took her parents into her confidence, and was reunited
with them, but decided to remain in London. By great good fortune, we were able to suggest lodgings for her where her baby could be cared for during the day. Mary would not
approach the putative father for help and is now doing very well. She is in touch with an
old friend, who knows her story, and there is a possibility that they may shortly be
married.[86]

Sometimes adoption was the preferable outcome:

Another applicant called at the office one morning to ask advice about the child she was
expecting in two weeks time. Her home was in the north but when she found she was
pregnant, she had come to London, hoping that the putative father would honour his
promise to marry her. After a time she returned home only to find that he had already
married another woman. The applicant's elderly mother was recovering from an operation so she could not tell her family of her predicament. Arrangements were made for her
care in a Mother and Baby Home. When her daughter was born, discussions were held
with the mother and it became evident that adoption plans would have to be made so
that she should return home to care for her family. The child has now been adopted by
parents who will give her the security she needs. The applicant is at home but is still in
touch with us and is thinking, when her family responsibilities are less, of training for a
useful career.[87]

---

[84] Ibid. 470, col. 1608.   [85] Cretney, *Family Law*, 610–15.
[86] NC Annual Report 1953–4, 17.   [87] Ibid. 19.

the problem remained that unmarried mothers were sometimes discouraged by social workers from adopting their own children. The NC tried to negotiate with the London County Council (LCC) Children's Officer about this 'without any very satisfactory conclusion' and in 1953 again publicized the issue in a letter from their president, Lord Gorell, to *The Times*.[88] In 1955 he targeted further letters at social workers and magistrates in their respective professional magazines, *Case Conference* and *The Magistrate*, while committee members lobbied individual magistrates. Dissatisfaction with the adoption law persisted despite further modifications in the Children Act, 1958.[89]

Mothers who had their children adopted usually did so, often reluctantly, because they could not support themselves and the child, often because they were very young, especially if they had no stable home. A particularly sad young woman, Clare, came to the NC in 1959. She

came from a large family of younger brothers and sisters. It had been a hard struggle for her parents to manage throughout her training as a nurse as her father was often out of work through illness. When she obtained her first post and was able to send a little money home, they were immensely grateful for her help and proud of her achievements. It was only a few months after she started nursing that Clare knew she was pregnant. Her first thought was that her parents must never find out and she determined to work as long as possible and save every penny so that she could continue to help them while she was out of work. She told them she was moving to London (she had been working in a big Hospital near her home in one of the Southern Counties) and she determined that the baby must be adopted as early as possible.

Then the long deception came. Clare was utterly terrified that anyone near her home should know of her condition and she refused to consult the local moral welfare worker. Eventually we were able to find her a vacancy in a small Mother and Baby Home which would accept her on the national assistance payment and she went there before her condition was noticeable.... Throughout her pregnancy this girl had steeled herself to accept adoption as inevitable. But this was not to be the solution to Clare's problem: when the baby's medical form was filled in Clare explained that her father suffered from mental breakdowns intermittently all his life. Enquiries as to the nature of his mental illness were made and as a result the doctors felt that it was undoubtedly hereditary. The baby, a lovely little girl, could not be placed with adopters.

It was a terrible shock to Clare, but through the understanding help of the Matron a vacancy was found for her baby in one of the large Homes. Clare, will of course, have to shoulder some of the financial responsibility.[90]

Another agonized, but ultimately happier, experience was that of Pauline Tilston, who gave birth, aged 16, in 1955 in St Bridget's House of Mercy in Cheshire. The father was a 21-year-old US airman, her first love, who promised to marry her.

---

[88] NC Minutes, 28 Oct. 1953; 27 July 1955.
[89] Cretney, *Family Law*, 615–23.
[90] NC Annual Report 1959–60, 28–9.

When Pauline became pregnant, her mother discovered that he was married. He claimed he was divorcing his wife, but suddenly disappeared. Pauline's mother went to the airbase, but the commander denied all knowledge of him. He did not reply to Pauline's letters. She carried on hoping and working for a smart hairdressing salon in Chester. Her male, Sicilian employer was kind and supportive when he discovered her pregnancy, assuring her, 'We'll take care of you.' She later recounted that 'Bowls of nourishing soup were sent to me with the compliments of the chefs in the restaurant' attached to the salon. Her female colleagues 'made sure I didn't do too much or strain myself lifting anything. Most of the regular customers soon suspected and started to give extra tips to buy "something nice for the baby". Everyone was so kind and took such special care of me.'[91] She was one more of the teenage mothers who inflamed the moralists, but, even among those able to afford expensive hairdressing in a respectable, northern cathedral city, this working-class girl was evidently not an object of shame and contempt. Her colleagues knew she had expected to marry Jim. Little blame seemed to attach to an evidently innocent young woman betrayed by a man in a culture where sexual relationships were quite normal between couples intending to marry. Pauline cannot have been alone in knowing that 'it wasn't unheard of for women to become pregnant out of wedlock in Chester'. She described how a young girl living across the road from the Tilstons had a baby by a local boy and married him. Their next door neighbour became pregnant in her early twenties by an American airman long before Pauline met Jim. She didn't marry him but kept her daughter.[92]

Nevertheless, Pauline's mother worried about what the neighbours would think and arranged with the local social services for her to enter St Bridget's when she was seven months pregnant. Pauline later recalled that it never crossed her mind to have an abortion.[93] The 'House of Mercy' was austere, with one bath for twelve young women, compulsory chapel twice daily—'but we were never preached to and were mainly left to quiet prayer and contemplation'[94]—and all mothers had to work in the kitchen, laundry or scrubbing floors. But Pauline found that the Mother Superior and the other mothers were warm and friendly. The mothers were all teenagers, 'some the victims of sexual abuse, others (like me) too innocent to understand the consequences of what we'd done'.[95] Two had been raped by their fathers.[96] They were expected to take their babies home three months after the birth or have them adopted.

Pauline desperately wanted to keep her baby, Timothy Paul, at home. Her mother 'thought he was beautiful', had him registered in his father's name, but

[91] Pauline Prescott, with Wendy Holden, *Smile Though Your Heart Is Breaking* (London: Harper Collins, 2010), 1–28.
[92] Ibid. 26.
[93] Ibid.
[94] Ibid. 32.
[95] Ibid. pp. ix–x.   [96] Ibid. 32.

refused to take him. Her husband was dead and she had to work, in a shop, as did Pauline and her ailing brother, and they could not afford childcare. Still hoping, Pauline refused to have him adopted. The nuns arranged for him to go to a residential nursery in Derbyshire, which she could afford to visit only every few months, while he became 'more distant' from her. After two years, the nursery would no longer keep him and he was sent into foster care, without her permission, in even more distant Wolverhampton. His foster parents later adopted him, against Pauline's will but with the support and connivance of her mother.[97] Only more than forty years later did she discover that her mother had spent several miserable years in care as a child, when her father died and her mother took to drink, and she was desperate that this would not happen to her grandson when a good couple were willing to adopt him: 'just as I had been keeping secrets from those I loved for much of my life [about the existence of her first child] so had she.'[98]

Before Paul was adopted, Pauline met and fell for a handsome, charming steward on international liners, John Prescott. He knew about Paul, was not put off, and visited the nursery with her. But by the time they decided to marry, he was already adopted. They had two sons, from whom Paul was kept secret, and John progressed to become Labour Deputy Prime Minister in 1997. But Pauline never forgot Paul, despite her mother's urging to 'move on', kept his photographs, and hoped he would find her when this became legally possible in 1978. He didn't, but in 2001 the *News of the World* found him, having heard rumours of a Prescott secret. As a result, they met after 44 years and Paul became close to her whole family including her mother, who now revealed her childhood secret. He had had a loving upbringing, attended Sandhurst, and become a much decorated leading member of the Royal Military Police and a Conservative voter, who had served in Northern Ireland, Kosovo, and the Falklands. He had not sought his natural mother for fear of upsetting his ailing adoptive mother, Mary, but she and Pauline also were reconciled. The *News of the World* was persuaded (partly by leading Labour politician Peter Mandelson) not to splash the story until Mary's death two years later.[99]

When the story became public, Pauline found that 'everyone was kind and pleased' including Prince Charles, who had met Paul previously in his military role. She recalled that 'Strangers congratulated me in the streets; others wrote to me in droves...So many people in a similar situation sent me the most moving letters...one lady who was in her eighties...was [still] waiting to hear from her son, and wrote, "I was caring for my mother when I had him. I couldn't look after him as well." '[100] Five years later, Paul traced his father in America, who told him that he had been genuinely fond of Pauline but had been ordered to leave the country immediately he revealed the pregnancy to his superior officers. Father and son were 'happily reunited'.[101]

---

[97] Prescott, *Smile*, 41–66.   [98] Ibid. 204.   [99] Ibid. 193–205.
[100] Ibid. 212–13.   [101] Ibid. 222–7.

This is a rare life-history, from pregnancy, though adoption, to a long-delayed happy ending, as represented by Pauline through a ghostwriter, after many years; one more of the diverse surviving experiences of unmarried mothers and their children, suggesting greater day-to-day tolerance of unmarried motherhood, even in the 1950s, than is always assumed.

Adoptions of children born outside marriage increased from 10,441 in 1950 to 12,981 in 1961 and 19,348 in 1968, due, at least to some extent, to the tightening of the law in 1949, which brought more adoptions into the legal arena. The number then declined to 4,072 in 1993, as it became easier for unmarried mothers to live openly with their children.[102] Thirty per cent were adopted by their mothers in 1950, 29 per cent in 1957, most of them in partnership with their husbands, who usually were not the natural fathers. Just 0.6 per cent of adoptions in 1950 and 0.8 per cent in 1957 were by mothers alone. At both dates, about 5 per cent were adopted by relatives, often after the child had lived with them for some time, perhaps when the mother left to marry or the child started school.[103] In 1950, 25 fathers adopted their illegitimate children on their own, 40 with their wives.[104]

In the late 1950s, the NC was concerned about a growing number of requests by parents of 'legitimate' children to have their children adopted. These were often widows or separated wives who felt unable to cope, parents who were just too poor to support another child, young women forced into 'shotgun' marriages that they were desperate to escape, or 'the occasional psychopathic woman who was unable to face the responsibility of a child'—the kind of desperate people who would often in the past have had their children adopted informally, often by relatives, but this was now difficult due to the tightening of the law.[105]

A different story was that of Clare Short, later a Labour Cabinet Minister, who became pregnant in 1964, as an 18-year-old student. She married the father, but then contacted an adoption agency and the child was adopted at six weeks. She said later:

I just thought I would never go back to university, that it would be terrible all round, terrible for the baby, there would be no money, so what I was doing was best for everyone.[106]

Universities at this time were often unsupportive of students who were mothers, whether married or, especially, if they were not. Clare came from a Catholic family, who offered no other option. She later wrote: 'When they came to take him it was terrible. It's been terrible ever since.' She and her husband soon 'deeply regretted what they had done'. The adoption decision made it difficult for the marriage to work and they divorced in 1974. She remarried but had no more children. Her son

---

[102] Kiernan et al., *Lone Motherhood*, 39, table 2.7.
[103] Wimperis, *Unmarried*, 272, table 15.
[104] Ibid.
[105] NC Minutes, 25 Mar., 8 July, 25 Nov. 1959.
[106] Michael White, 'Short and Son Reunited', *The Guardian*, 17 Oct. 1996 [online]; available at http://www.guardian.co.uk/politics/1996/oct/17/labour.uk; accessed 18 Apr. 2011.

contacted her 30 years later, when he was a successful lawyer and they were happily reconciled.[107]

However, in the complex, secretive world of the 1960s and early 1960s, not every woman who became pregnant out of wedlock shared the same fate. Lorna Sage's autobiography calls in question the contented stability of some of the long-lasting marriages of the period, and the uniformity of public opinion about deviance from family norms. Born during the war in a village on the Welsh borders, she described the 'permanently unhappy marriage' of her grandparents.[108] It was an open secret that her grandfather, the local vicar, was a serial adulterer, including with his daughter's best friend, aged 16, and was rumoured to have fathered at least one illegitimate child. The marriage survived until his death in 1952, though they 'hated each other'. Lorna's own father had been damaged by his war experience and her parents also were not happy. Divorce was unacceptable in the village, except among the aristocracy. Women in the community were known to have children by more than one father, but it was not openly discussed.[109] One girl in Lorna's class at High School was of mixed race, born while her mother's husband was away at war, but he had accepted her, they were a respectable middle-class family and no one ever mentioned her colour or her origins.[110]

Then, at age 16 Lorna met Victor Sage at a dance and became pregnant after one sexual encounter, somehow—and to her own later bafflement—innocently not quite believing that they had full sex.[111] Her mother was angry with her for spoiling all her hopes, when she had been doing well at school, and her father was appalled. Vic's working-class mother was disappointed, believing he would have to leave school in disgrace when he was on course to being the first member of the family to go to university. 'Like my parents, she saw us as juvenile delinquents who'd forfeited our chance,'[112] reported Laura:

My parents' plan was that I should go to a Church Home for Unmarried Mothers, where you repented on your knees (scrubbed floors, said prayers) had your baby (which was promptly adopted by proper married people) and returned home humble and hollow-eyed and everyone would magnanimously pretend that nothing had happened so long as you never seemed to be having a good time or developing too high an opinion of yourself—from now on you could count yourself lucky if they let you learn shorthand and typing.[113]

Instead she and Vic decided to get married. Her parents were hostile, then relented and the young couple lived with them and stayed at school. Her headmistress said that no university would accept her, but that a 'truly Christian' teacher training college just might. Fortunately, some of the senior mistresses disagreed and supported her through examinations and university applications. The music teacher

[107] White, 'Short and Son Reunited'.
[108] Lorna Sage, *Bad Blood* (London: Fourth Estate, 2001), 24.
[109] Ibid. 141.   [110] Ibid. 201.   [111] Ibid. 238–9.   [112] Ibid. 242.   [113] Ibid. 237.

stopped my mother and me in the middle of the Bull Ring to tell us at the top of her voice that seventeen was the ideal age to have a healthy baby and get on with your life... These women, who were all around the same age as the century, all unmarried, were not only unshocked, but somehow pleased with me, it was their younger colleagues, of my parents' generation, who were censorious.[114]

Baby Sharon was born in May 1964 and her parents took their A levels. Lorna was rejected by all Oxbridge women's colleges 'since they only took mature married women', aged over 23. Other universities accepted her but the local education authority refused a grant, because she was married, while giving one to Vic. Instead she gained a scholarship to Durham University, where they both went. Once there,

Miss Scott at St Aidan's [College] turned out to belong to the same generation as Miss Roberts [at school] and shared her no-nonsense view of my offence. In future St Aidan's wouldn't be sending women students down for anything other than intellectual shortcomings... she took it in her stride, only warning me of the mind-rotting side-effects of the washing-up that she'd heard living with a man involved.[115]

Sharon lived with Lorna's parents and grew attached to them. Lorna and Vic both graduated with Firsts and became academics, but the marriage survived only until 1974. Lorna brought up Sharon and later remarried.

Clare Short's contemporary in politics, the Conservative Minister Virginia Bottomley, had an easier experience than either Clare or Lorna. She became pregnant, aged 19 and unmarried, in 1967, as a student at Essex University. But she came from a more prosperous and liberal background than either of the others, kept her son, stayed at university, and three months after the birth married the father, future fellow politician Peter Bottomley. This was not publicly known when she became Conservative Minister of Health in 1989, until it was revealed by the press in 1992.[116] Even in 1990 this past transgression had to be kept secret in some social circles.

CONCLUSION

Social norms were changing through the 1950s and 1960s, but slowly. Meanwhile, the lives of poorer unmarried mothers and their children were eased somewhat by developments in state and voluntary welfare, the subject of the next chapter.

[114] Ibid. 255–6.
[115] Ibid. 275.
[116] 'Virginia's Early Summer of Love, Books, and a Baby', *The Independent*, 12 July 1992 [online], available at http://www.independent.co.uk/news/uk/virginia's-early-summer-of-love-books-and-a-baby-1532773.html; accessed 22 Apr. 2011.

5

Unmarried Mothers in the 'Welfare State'

The lessons of the war contributed to real improvements for poorer unmarried mothers and their children as the Labour Government elected in 1945 reconstructed and expanded state welfare.[1] The greater role of the state did not, as some, then and since, assumed, or feared, crowd out the voluntary sector especially in specialized areas, such as that of the National Council in caring for unmarried mothers and their children. After a period of uncertainty, the state and voluntary sectors continued to cooperate and complement each other as they had since the beginning of the century, in a 'mixed economy of welfare', working together in new and changing ways that were gradually negotiated. The relationship between the National Council and the state exemplified this process.

STATE WELFARE

Public welfare support for mothers and children improved after the war. The Labour Government failed to implement Beveridge's recommendation for further investigation into the most effective means of supporting unmarried mothers and their children through the benefit system and it gave no serious consideration to providing a benefit specifically for them. Politicians thought this unpopular with voters. But mothers and children were better supported by the social services and the social security system partly due to lessons learned from the war. The official historians of wartime social services observed:

When the great enactments of the post-war period came into operation, the position of the unmarried mother in society changed beyond recognition. Over a wide area of needs, charity and poor law relief were replaced by defined social benefits.[2]

The National Council agreed:

All this means that [the unmarried mother] is no longer dependent upon charity for her maintenance, and that, with organization and money all available for her help, instead of having to search desperately for money, we can now explain to mothers the various public funds upon which they are entitled to draw.[3]

---

[1] For an accessible survey see Nicolas Timmins, *The Five Giants: A Biography of the Welfare State* (London: Fontana, 1996).
[2] S. M. Ferguson and H. Fitzgerald, *History of the Second World War*, Studies in the Social Services (London: HMSO and Longmans, 1954), 140.
[3] NC Annual Report 1949, 13.

This became an important aspect of the NC's role. It switched from r
ing information about charitable funds, and giving what it could it'
ing the system of state benefits to applicants often understandably confus___
changes,[4] publishing pamphlets informing mothers of their rights.[5]

With the foundation of the National Health Service in 1948, mothers and children benefited from free health care, including before, during, and after childbirth. Employed mothers could claim sickness benefit. Unmarried mothers became eligible for a maternity grant, raised for all mothers from £4 to £12.10s., plus 13 weeks maternity benefit of 36s. per week (as recommended by Beveridge). As a result, as Ferguson and Fitzgerald described, mothers were 'no longer tempted to stay at work almost up to childbirth' as all too many had before, contributing to the higher than average death rates of unmarried mothers in childbirth and their children in infancy.[6] They concluded, in 1954, that

The psychological and long-term result of this new situation is often as great as its immediate economic effect. The maternity allowance, more than any other single factor, has changed the position of the unmarried mother within her family. She need no longer be a financial burden while she is unable to go out to work, but can pay her way and preserve her self-respect. She has a greater chance of remaining at home, and the prospects for her own and her child's future are more hopeful than ever before.[7]

Local authorities now had a duty to care for the mothers and their children. The National Assistance Act, 1948, made statutory the advice embodied in Circular 2866 of 1943.[8] By the end of 1945, 108 local authorities had appointed social workers specifically to support unmarried mothers and their children, while 281 chose, as they were allowed, the cheaper option of subsidizing voluntary organizations to undertake the work on their behalf. Particularly at local level, cooperation between public and voluntary sectors became, if anything, more rather than less important then before.

The 1948 Act also placed a duty on local authorities to provide lodgings for the homeless. All too often this meant placing unmarried mothers and their children, along with other homeless people, in former workhouses, which had changed little from the pre-war era and provided no social work support. But it was Home Office and Ministry of Health policy that young children should not be placed in such institutions if alternatives could be found, and gradually provision improved. In 1945, 22 local authorities ran Mother and Baby Homes or Hostels and many others subsidized voluntary Homes. By 1956 there were 27 local authority Mother and Baby Homes, with 397 beds. Local authorities subsidized 107 voluntary Homes with 1,666 beds, for which mothers could be required to pay if they could

---

[4] Hilary Macaskill, *From the Workhouse to the Workplace: 75 Years of One-Parent Family Life, 1918–1993* (London: National Council for One Parent Families, 1993), 26.
[5] Sue Graham-Dixon, *Never Darken My Door: Working for Single Parents and Their Children, 1918–1978* (London: National Council for One Parent Families, 1981), 22.
[6] Ibid. 123.
[7] Ferguson and Fitzgerald, *History*, 140.
[8] See pp. 60–1.

afford it.[9] Local authority 'social' care, unlike that of the NHS, was not 'free at the point of delivery' and there was continuing confusion about the respective responsibilities of the two authorities.

Sickness and maternity benefits could be supplemented, in case of need, by the National Assistance Board (NAB), set up in 1948, the less punitive successor to the Poor Law providing means-tested benefits. Eligibility rules and levels of benefit were nationally uniform for the first time. In principle, unmarried mothers were no longer required to register for work before claiming National Assistance, if they had a school-age child at home, though women told the NC this was not always observed by local officials. It was official NAB policy to support mothers to bring up their children as securely as possible and to keep mother and child together, but benefit rates were so low that 'few self-respecting women who are capable of work wish to live on it independently'.[10] Additional payments could be made, e.g., for household equipment or clothing in cases of special need. The new system was helpful in times of crisis, imperfect but better than anything that had gone before.

The pre-war household means-test was abolished, enabling an unmarried mother living with her parents to claim benefit for herself and her child(ren) regardless of her parents' income and without affecting their benefit status. Ferguson and Fitzgerald assumed that it was normal for unmarried mothers and their children to live with the mother's family and that post-war changes made this arrangement easier for many, but that

No satisfactory way has yet been found in our industrial society for a mother without a breadwinner or a helpful family [i.e., Bowlby's 'socially unacceptable' mothers] to combine the two tasks of earning a living and making a home for her child. Local authorities and voluntary bodies are now experimenting with a new kind of social provision—hostels or residential clubs for working mothers, married or unmarried, where the children are in the care of skilled staff during the day. The greatest single need today, in the opinion of many informed people, is for more such hostels.[11] By 1950 six were known to exist in England and Wales and seemed to be working well. They may prove to be an answer to the question which faces every unmarried mother without a home.[12]

The number of hostels gradually increased.

From 1947, a shortened birth certificate that omitted details of parents' marital status, hiding 'illegitimacy' or adoption, was introduced. The National Council had long campaigned for this and it had been available in Scotland for some time. It provided the proof of age required by schools and employers, replacing the full birth certificate (which was still available) without revealing the secrets of birth. It

---

[9] V. Wimperis, *The Unmarried Mother and Her Child* (London: Allen and Unwin, 1960), 179–80.

[10] Ibid. 172.

[11] They cited *Report of the Ministry of Health for the Year Ended 31st March 1948*, Cmd 7734, p. 110.

[12] Ferguson and Fitzgerald, *History*, 141.

was cheaper than the full certificate, which appealed to many parents whatever their status. In 1968 it became free of charge, more widely used and even less a signifier of 'illegitimacy'.

Ferguson and Fitzgerald were optimistic that support for unmarried mothers had improved in the 'welfare state', though they rightly noted that

The voice of the unmarried mother herself has hardly been heard. She is rarely vocal and she shuns publicity. If she expressed her views, she does so in confidence and her testimony is hardly ever recorded.[13]

VOLUNTARY WELFARE

Though voluntary action continued to be an important source of support for unmarried mothers and their children and others, voluntary organizations, including the NC, went through a time of uncertainty about their roles as that of the state expanded and there was general optimism that the post-war 'welfare state' had abolished poverty. The NC anticipated that they might no longer be needed, though their case-load remained high.[14] Some donors thought so too and high taxation also took its toll of funds. The NC was kept afloat by the annual grant from the Ministry of Health, which clearly continued to value cooperation between the state and voluntary sectors. The grant rose to £750 in 1951–2.

Gaps in state provision soon became obvious and local authorities found it easier and cheaper to subsidize experienced voluntary support for unmarried mothers and their children than to develop it themselves when they were under pressure on many fronts. The voluntary sector revived and identified its role in the not so new order. By 1958 there were four times as many voluntary as statutory Homes, 45 run by the Church of England Moral Welfare Associations for mothers and babies, with 52 shelters for mothers needing emergency shelter, and 12 maternity homes providing for confinement and ante- and post-natal care. Homes were also run by other faith groups and a few by non-denominational organizations. They provided for about one in ten of all unmarried mothers, one in five of those under 25. The costs were normally covered by National Insurance maternity benefit or National Assistance, or, if these failed, by the local authority or a voluntary association, thus removing the worst financial problems of the later weeks of pregnancy and first weeks of the child's life for the neediest mothers.

Most Homes admitted mothers from six to eight weeks before confinement until three months after.[15] Conditions varied, perhaps even more than before. Some adapted under pressure of criticism:

---

[13] Ibid.
[14] N. Crowson, M. Hilton, and J. McKay (eds), *NGOs in Contemporary Britain: Non-state Actors in Society and Politics since 1945* (London: Palgrave, 2009).
[15] Wimperis, *Unmarried*, 192–3.

In one...the girls are encouraged to keep personal possessions and photographs in their bedrooms to help them feel at home; the baby's cot may be at the end of the bed. The mothers are encouraged to attend the classes arranged in cookery, sewing and childcare. A small chapel is the true centre of the Home's life but attendance is entirely voluntary. The children's fathers are encouraged to call and take an interest in their babies...

But...there are still some Homes pervaded by a strict, old-fashioned, almost penal atmosphere, where the mothers work in old-fashioned laundries, do exquisite embroidery that is not for their babies to wear, and live under rigid discipline, forbidden to go outside the gates without permission or to wear such luxuries as lipstick. In some of these Homes the babies' fathers might be assumed not to exist...

In visiting these Homes one is struck by the contrast between those where the girls creep around in passages avoiding every eye and those where they come up at once with a warm smile and loving pride in presenting their babies, sure of appreciation.[16]

In the 1950s fewer mothers would tolerate the stricter Homes. Also they wanted to spend less time in an institution after birth and felt more confident that they could cope in the community. The NC encouraged the voluntary agencies to be more flexible about length of stay.[17]

Then mothers had to face the world outside the Home. Now their financial problems began if they had to find their own home, a job, and childcare. NAB benefits and the new rules helped poorer unmarried mothers, but they were means-tested, which many found demeaning. The NC kept 'careful watch' on the new NAB system, concluding in 1953 that 'in spite of statutory benefits the unmarried mother still has a hard financial struggle. We have been asked for grants for all kinds of equipment from prams to sewing machines.'[18] They found that some women were still so frightened of revealing an unmarried pregnancy to family and friends that they failed to claim maternity benefit and fled from their home towns, often to the anonymity of London, where the NC tried to help them.[19] A woman was disqualified from benefit if she was suspected of living with a man, who was deemed responsible for supporting her. Mothers were visited regularly by NAB officials to check on whether they were illicitly cohabiting, surveillance that toughened in the 1960s, as we will see.

In 1949, the NAB estimated that 'the great majority' of unmarried mothers and separated wives 'succeed in keeping independent of assistance', because they 'receive a sufficiency from the person liable' (i.e. the father) or 'probably more often' because they 'maintain themselves by their own efforts'.[20] When the father did not help, either the mother or, now, the NAB (as recommended by Beveridge) could seek a maintenance and affiliation order against him. Maintenance payments were offset against benefit. But the maximum payment was still only £1 per week,

---

[16] Wimperis, *Unmarried*, 194–6.
[17] NC Annual Report 1956–7, 23.
[18] Graham-Dixon, *Never Darken*, 6.
[19] Ibid. 22.
[20] Ministry of National Insurance, *Report of the National Assistance Board for the Year Ended December 1949*, Cmd 8030 (London: HMSO, 1950), 21.

which just 20 per cent of successful claimants received. This was raised to £1.10s. (£1.50) in 1952, but only 10 per cent of claimants received it.[21] At this time the average weekly pay of women workers was about £4.30.[22]

In 1953 the NAB decided that pursuing fathers was not worth the effort and cost. They found, as the Poor Law authorities long had, that fathers were too hard to trace and, when found, often could not afford to pay. Thereafter, the NAB encouraged mothers to seek their own affiliation orders and paid their legal costs, but the old obstacles remained and few women did so. In 1945 there were 63,420 'illegitimate' births but only 4,464 affiliation orders; in 1959 38,161 and 4,160. Not all claims succeeded. Many fathers could not afford to pay: they were unemployed, were low paid, or had another family to support. Mothers shied away from the unfamiliarity and stress of the courts and from facing the father, especially if he had a history of violence, or they could not provide the necessary proof of paternity. Either party could demand a blood test, which was now routine in some countries, such as Norway, but either could refuse and it was still rarely used in Britain.[23] Still, however, an unknown number of fathers paid voluntarily.

There was little sign of public support for a state benefit for unmarried mothers and their children or any other special provision,[24] though pressure was growing. Margaret Wynn's *Fatherless Families* (1964) was a thorough study of the financial hardships of unsupported mothers, including widows and divorced and separated women and their children. She argued that the stress of poverty caused psychological problems for mothers and children rather than vice versa as some psychiatrists suggested. She proposed a minimum state 'fatherless child allowance' at the level already paid to foster parents; also that affiliation and maintenance orders should be underwritten by the state at an adequate minimum level and responsibility for collection transferred to the Inland Revenue. The NC campaigned in support of this proposal, which embodied principles they had long favoured,[25] but there was no sign of government action from any political party.

HOUSING

Finding a home was the biggest problem for many mothers. After the war, housing was run-down, overcrowded, and in short supply. It was still very hard for an unmarried mother to rent a home for herself and her child. The shortage was compounded by the hostility of some landlords and landladies. And it was harder for many families to find space for an unmarried daughter and child. Housing condi-

---

[21] Wimperis, *Unmarried*, 140.

[22] N. Crafts, I. Gazeley, and A. Newell, *Work and Pay in 20th Century Britain* (Oxford: Oxford University Press, 2007), 69.

[23] Wimperis, *Unmarried*, 137–8.

[24] Ibid. 176–7.

[25] Margaret Wynn, *Fatherless Families* (London: Michael Joseph, 1964); Joan Bourne, *Pregnant and Alone* (Royston: Priory Care and Welfare Library, 1971), 76–7.

tions improved in the 1950s, with the building of thousands of council houses. But these were often small, allocated according to family size, with strict rules about overcrowding, restricting the opportunities for mothers to return to their families with their children. Demand far outstripped supply, and unmarried mothers had difficulty qualifying for council housing in their own right because allocation systems gave preference to those needing most room, which favoured married couples with children over single parents, who were expected to share a bedroom with their child. Relatively few one-bedroom council homes were built. In some cases, the obvious housing need of some unmarried mothers may have outweighed other issues and increased their chances of being housed, though they tended to be allocated older, poorer quality housing, in locations with poor transport and few shops, increasingly so through the 1950s and 1960s as pressure of demand for housing grew. They and other single mothers might face discrimination by housing authority staff, though probably less than that suffered by the growing population of immigrants. Black single mothers fared worst of all.[26]

Sometimes mothers could not afford council rents or the upkeep of their homes.[27] The NC and other voluntary organizations helped them to negotiate applying for council housing. The NC reported in 1964 that 'even the professional woman earning a good salary found it was difficult for a single woman with a dependant to obtain a lease or a mortgage'.[28] There was an increased need for 'flat-lets', small homes where mothers and children could live independently at moderate rents. They helped women find them, but demand outstripped supply.[29]

Almost certainly it was still hard in the late 1940s and 1950s for an unmarried mother to support herself and her child, despite the easier benefit rules, unless she had substantial support from the father, her family, or a good job. Unmarried mothers were often young and poorly educated. Despite full employment it was often difficult for them to find work at adequate pay or childcare. Live-in domestic service had never been a popular option, though it had enabled some women to keep their children, but it dwindled after the war. Harder conditions forced more women to have their children adopted.

VOLUNTARY ACTION IN THE WELFARE STATE

As we have seen, the National Council continued to support and campaign for mothers and children very actively, despite limited funds and, despite the growth of state welfare, it remained indispensable for the support of all too many families. Staff and officers were, as ever, hard-working and enthusiastic, the latter using their influence in powerful circles whenever possible. Lettice Fisher remained 'Chairman' until 1955 (she died in 1956), succeeded by Zoe Puxley,[30] after she retired

---

[26] Daisy O'Brien, 'In No Man's Land', MA dissertation, Oxford University (2009).
[27] Ibid.
[28] NC Annual Report 1963–4, 21.
[29] Ibid. 23.
[30] See p. 60.

from the Ministry of Health, in 1953–8. She was Vice-President in 1949–53 and 1958–67. Presidents included, from 1930 to 1961, the third Baron Gorell, second son of the divorce campaigner of the early part of the century, who shared the family commitment to divorce law reform.[31] Vice-Presidents included the prominent physician and former Ministry of Health official Lord Amulree, 1958–66, and the Archbishop of York, 1933–55.

FUNDRAISING IN A COLD CLIMATE

However, the NC could not do as much as it wished due to the difficulties of raising funds and growing demands from mothers. The annual Ministry of Health grant rose to £750 in 1951–2, £1,000 in 1953, and £1,250 p.a. in 1957–8 and saved them in these hard times when private donors could be hard to find.[32] Zoe Puxley argued their case while she worked for the Ministry.[33] Women helped for the first time increased from 2,115 in 1952–3 to 4,570 in 1963–4.[34] This reflects the difficulties of many women and children at this time, also the success of the NC in publicizing its services and its growing capacity to help as the funding crisis eased from the later 1950s.

To gain publicity, they again used a range of media in imaginative ways. They had helpful advice and encouragement from Mary Adams, Vice-President from 1956 to her death in 1984.[35] She worked for BBC radio from 1930 to 1936, then became the first female BBC TV producer, controlling education, politics, talks, and culture. After her retirement in 1958, she had more time to devote to the NC and other causes, including helping to establish the Consumers' Association and supported feminist groups. In the mid-1950s, Adams with 'a group of experienced editors of women's papers', representatives of Citizens' Advice Bureaux and others concerned about getting key information to unmarried mothers, advised the NC on media strategy. She put them in touch with the popular writer Godfrey Winn, who wrote a series of articles in the *Sunday Dispatch* and other papers about the Council's work, which triggered a further flood of applications.[36] He became a Vice-President, 1956–63. In 1956 he broadcast a TV appeal. Regular appeals appeared in *Woman* and *Woman's Own*, promoted by their agony aunts, 'Evelyn Home' and 'Mary Grant' respectively, which produced initially offers of 'hundreds of prams',[37] then a 'steady flow of parcels... prams, cots, play pens and other baby equipment'.[38] Appeals in *Nursery World*, the *Manchester Guardian*, and *The Times*

[31] See p. 11. Stephen Cretney, *Family Law in the Twentieth Century* (Oxford: Oxford University Press, 2003), 789.

[32] NC Annual Report 1957–8, 23; Graham-Dixon, *Never Darken*, 31.

[33] The National Archives (TNA)/MH/1535, 1949–61.

[34] Compiled from NC Annual Reports.

[35] Sally Adams, 'Adams [*née* Campin] Mary Grace Agnes (1898–1984)', *Oxford Dictionary of National Biography* (Oxford: Oxford University Press, 2004).

[36] Graham-Dixon, *Never Darken*, 6.

[37] NC Annual Report 1953–4, 18.

[38] NC Annual Report 1954–5, 22; 1955–6, 24.

were also successful.[39] In 1955 a short publicity film—'a charming film of babies, their mothers and children'[40]—was shown in London suburban and provincial cinemas, initially with some difficulty, three years after it was made, using the contacts of the chair of the NC Finance Committee. Almost £2,000 was collected from cinemas where the film was shown. In the early 1950s, the NC gained £300 p.a. from the profits of Sunday cinema performances, which were still licensed only if they gave some of their takings to charity.

The NC cooperated in making a television programme, *Women Alone*, in 1955, after which

Many and diverse were the letters received. Many writers regretted bitterly that they had not previously known of the Council; some sent small sums of money; some told of abortions which had been grieved over ever since. But the great bulk of the letters and callers came from girls and women needing help.[41]

In 1953 the annual broadcast appeal was made on television for the first time, by well-known TV presenter Jeanne Heal, and raised £690. These appeals continued annually, that in 1963 by the film star Kenneth More raised £4,210, then the largest sum ever raised for a charity by an individual, though in 1966 an appeal by another film star, Dirk Bogarde, raised only £1,932. In the early 1960s, more funds flowed in from individuals, though the Council never felt it could satisfy the need for its services.[42]

FILLING HOLES IN THE 'WELFARE STATE'

By the mid-1950s it was clear that there were many holes in the welfare state 'safety net' that only voluntary action would fill, including support for unmarried mothers and their children. Giving and campaigning revived, spurred on in the early 1960s by the 'rediscovery of poverty',[43] especially among children and most of all among the children of lone mothers.[44]

The NC found that most mothers contacted them on their own initiative, 21 per cent were referred by another voluntary or social work agency, 14.5 per cent by an advice column in the national press, 3 per cent by their doctors. The Council felt under pressure, not least from its tireless work of supporting mothers of children of overseas servicemen who had returned home, and women overseas who had children by British servicemen. They urged the British Government to establish reciprocal overseas affiliation orders,[45] helped in parliament by Labour MP

---

[39] NC Annual Report 1956–7, 27.   [40] NC Annual Report 1952–3, 22; 1954–5, 14.
[41] NC Annual Report 1955–6, 10.
[42] Graham-Dixon, *Never Darken*, 31–2.
[43] By LSE academics Brian Abel-Smith and Peter Townsend in their research report *The Poor and the Poorest* (London: George Bell, 1964).
[44] Tanya Evans, 'Stopping the Poor Getting Poorer: The Establishment and Professionalization of Poverty NGOs, 1945–1995', in Crowson et al., *NGOs in Contemporary Britain*, 147–63.
[45] TNA/Foreign Office (FO)/1060/1098, 1948. Denmark TNA/FO/371/56143, 1946; Canada TNA/AIR/7290, 1943–5; US TNA/FO 371/51617-51623, 1946; Germany TNA/FO/937/136, 1946–7, TNA/FO/371/64929, 1947, WO/32/14950, 1952–4.

Reginald Sorensen, who asked frequent parliamentary questions on the issue and wrote to the Foreign Office about individual cases.[46] The Council heard of mothers in need from the British Control Commission and relief organizations in occupied Germany, German social workers and German mothers directly requesting help in tracing the fathers of their children. NC representatives wrote to and met Lord Pakenham, Chancellor of the Duchy of Lancaster, who had special responsibility for post-war Germany and was a supporter of the cause of unmarried mothers, pressing him to help mothers in Germany.[47] But the Foreign Office was unhelpful, stressing the 'insuperable' complexity of formulating reciprocal agreements with other countries,[48] and arguing that the illegitimate children of foreign nationals, even when fathered by British men, were the responsibility of foreign governments, since, under the law of many countries, if their mothers were unmarried the child acquired the mother's nationality.[49]

The armed forces of other countries could connive in protecting fathers from acknowledging their obligations. When 16-year-old Pauline Tilston (later Prescott) became pregnant by a US serviceman in 1955, he disappeared without warning and without further contact, after promising to marry her and divorce his wife.[50] Pauline discovered fifty years later, when her son tracked his father down, that when her mother visited his base and told his commanding officer of the pregnancy, 'Jim' was ordered to leave the country immediately and, with no time to pack, was put in a fast car to the airport.[51]

Through all the difficulties, the NC negotiated with the US, British, and other armed services, embassies, and representative organizations to get financial support for British mothers, and channelled over £2,000 each year in the 1950s to mothers overseas.[52] By the end of the 1950s they were concerned about the numbers of young women coming to Britain from abroad to work, especially from Germany, often encouraged by the Government to help fill the labour shortage, who became pregnant by British fathers. They tried to persuade the fathers to support the mothers and children before they left the country.[53] Sometimes there were happy endings, such as the 'foreign girl who married the father of her child; the General Secretary [of NC, Isabelle Granger] acted as interpreter and pushed the pram to the Registry Office'.[54]

The circumstances of British women pregnant by British men who asked for help were as diverse as ever. There were many requests from

---

[46] TNA/FO/371/64730, 1947; FO/371/70845, 1948.
[47] TNA/FO/371/70845, 1948.
[48] TNA/FO/371/54453, 1945; TNA/FO/950/210, 1947.
[49] TNA/FO/371/70845, 1948.
[50] See Pauline Prescott, with Wendy Holden, *Smile Though Your Heart is Breaking* (London: Harper Collins, 2010), 27. See pp. 100–2.
[51] Ibid. 216.
[52] NC Annual Reports, 1957–8, 20; 1958–9, 17.
[53] NC Annual Report 1958–9, 23–4.
[54] NC Annual Report 1955–6, 16.

mothers of older children who have struggled on for years bravely facing immense difficulties, and not knowing whom to approach for advice and help. The initial approach is often for material help from mothers who are unable to clothe their children adequately, particularly where Grammar School places have been obtained, and uniform has to be bought. We have been able to obtain grants from various trust funds, and the providing of this material help has often led to other less tangible difficulties coming to light. There can be no doubt that the unmarried woman who tries to be both mother and father to her child has much to contend with. Unlike the widow—who may be economically in much the same situation—the unmarried mother often has a burden of guilt that she has brought a child into the world who will be subject to emotional and social handicaps. This is increasingly brought home to her as the child gets older, and has to be told the truth about his origin. These women often need support given by a friendly social worker who is prepared to listen to their problems. As one of them said to the Case Secretary recently: 'I felt a lot better after talking to you, and don't take it out on Bobby so much now.'[55]

The NC was increasingly concerned about what it described as the 'West Indian problem', the numbers of women coming from then British colonies in the West Indies, often to work as nurses in the NHS with the encouragement of the British Government, who became pregnant or were pregnant on arrival. The NC tried to fund the return of the babies to their maternal family homes in the Caribbean. The Colonial Office helped provide escorts, but not finance.[56]

Some babies stayed, with happy results. Wesley's mother arrived to work as a nurse in 1958, aged 18, then found she was pregnant. She had left another baby at home in Jamaica with her parents and felt she could not ask them to care for another. After the birth she had to work and was lucky, with the help of the local authority, to place Wesley with a white foster family in Middlesex, who later moved to the country. It was particularly hard to find foster parents for non-white children. Wesley's foster parents were devout Catholics who had previously fostered 30 children, including one mixed-race child, followed by another later. Wesley thought they were 'wonderful'. His mother visited frequently until in the 1970s she married and moved to Canada. In the early 1960s she gave birth to a third boy. The father abandoned her for a white girl, but this time she could keep the child; he went to boarding school while she nursed. Meanwhile, Wesley grew up happily, won a scholarship to a public school, then to Cambridge and had a successful career in the media and public life.[57]

But not all British people were so tolerant. In 1956 the NC reported that:

Barbara and her father came to the office in the late Spring; she was his only child, delicate all her life and now at eighteen she expected a baby. Her family had not shirked responsibility, an aunt in the Midlands had offered Barbara a home, well away from her father's dental practice on the South coast. It sounded easy to help, there was no real shortage of money

---

[55] NC Annual Report 1955–6, 16.
[56] NC CMM, 20 July, 27 July 1955.
[57] We are very grateful to Wesley for this private information.

and the only problem to be solved was an introduction to the l
would find a Mother and Baby Home for Barbara and keep an e
the family hoped, she would agree to adoption.

But when they were alone Barbara told the General Secretary
West African student she had met in a club. They wanted to r
forbade it; what was to be the future of the baby?

In the late summer Christopher was born prematurely—very ...,
puzzled eyes and wavy hair; his father visited Barbara regularly in the Moth.
Home, he loved them both and was prepared to wait until they could marry. Robert Mason
came from a region where mixed marriages were acceptable, his family were in a good position, and he was studying medicine and intended to go home when he had qualified. He
was proud of Barbara and Christopher and when they met all their hopes centred on marriage; the opposition of the family did not weaken, and once Barbara had left the Home to
enable her to finish her training, it became gradually apparent that she had not the strength
to oppose her parents, she needed their familiar support more than the prospect of a future
with her baby and his father in a new country.

Robert accepted Barbara's decision, since her parents could not bring themselves to
accept Christopher; his future was never in doubt—he must go to his father's family, but
how could a six months old boy go to Africa? Suddenly through a friend in the BBC came
an introduction to an African minister. Three of his parishioners were flying home, so there
were three pairs of arms to take Christopher to his uncle and aunt. Telegrams were sent 'will
you meet baby airport' and the reply 'yes please'.

Christopher had to be re-registered in his new name—a sad little ceremony at which
both parents were required to be present. Barbara and the General Secretary met Robert at
the Registrar's office and little Christopher became baby Mason. Next the passport. Finally
the nurse at the Babies' Home took Christopher to the Air Terminal where Robert and his
new friends were waiting. Christopher has gone to his aunt and uncle and cousins, and
Robert Mason will join his son later on.[58]

The experiences of mothers and children continued to be infinitely diverse, happy
and sad, defying all stereotypes.

HELPING MOTHERS INTO WORK

Increasingly, the NC devoted time and funds to helping mothers gain training, for
example in nursing and secretarial work, and further and higher education, to
improve their work opportunities. They had always believed that decently paid
work was the best form of welfare, as did the post-1945 Labour Government,
hence its strong commitment to full employment as an essential complement to
the welfare state.[59] They were assisted by £2,500 from the Lord Mayor of London's
children's fund, for which demand soon outstripped supply.[60] When Lettice Fisher

---

[58] NC Annual Report 1956–7, 20–1.
[59] Pat Thane, 'Labour and Welfare', in D. Tanner, P. Thane, and N. Tiratsoo (eds), *Labour's First Century* (Cambridge: Cambridge University Press, 2000), 80–118.
[60] NC Annual Report 1950, 13.

n 1956 a Memorial Fund was established to pay for training. It paid out
3 in 1956–7.[61] In 1950,

An unmarried mother of a two-year-old son . . . asked for help in gaining further education.
Since the birth of her son she had been happily employed as a resident domestic. She came
of a good family, was well-educated and felt keenly the lack of training and her loss of
standard. She had made enquiries about a part-time secretarial course for which she
appeared eminently suitable. The obstacles were many: financial difficulties, care of her son
during training and loss of working hours. After much discussion and correspondence with
the local Moral Welfare Officer and Local Authority, satisfactory plans were made. The
employer agreed to part-time employment and only a slight reduction in wages; a day nursery was obtained and the mother accepted the course at a reduced fee. We gave a little
financial aid to cover initial expense of books and stationery, and have now been rewarded
by news of the applicant's good progress. This mother has gained confidence and feels she
will now be able to realise her ambition of providing a really good education and training
for her son.[62]

Many of the women the NC encountered now were better educated and set their
professional and personal sights higher than before the war. In the 1920s and
1930s it dealt mainly with domestic servants. By the 1950s,

Applications continue to come from almost every walk of life and range from university
student to the girl brought up in the old-fashioned children's home who left school at 14
with no particular training.[63]

As the decade went on they felt that mothers increased in confidence:

The present day unmarried mother is no longer the girl brought up in the care of Institutions, or earning her living in domestic work. She may be professionally trained, an office,
shop or factory worker. She will be earning good money, be attractively dressed, and osten-
sibly self-confident. She will either live at home with her family whose material standards
of living are high, or more likely in the big urban areas, independently on her own, or with
a girl friend. She will quite often consider pre-marital intercourse to be part of the normal
relationship between the sexes, or at any rate between a couple who intend to marry. She
will hope for marriage herself, but not until she and her partner have been able to achieve
a certain standard of living, which will involve her keeping on her job for a few years.[64]

CONCLUSIONS

At no time can unmarried mothers' lives be reduced to simple stereotypes and this
was as true in post-war Britain as before and after. The NC's Annual Reports regularly illustrated their diversity of backgrounds and the difficulties of mothers seeking its help, and how essential voluntary action such as theirs remained in the

[61] NC Annual Report 1956–7, 19.
[62] NC Annual Report 1950–1, 13.
[63] NC Annual Report 1952–3, 17.
[64] NC Annual Report 1959–60, 29.

'welfare state'. They provided highly personalized support that state agencies, often with huge responsibilities, could not. For example, in 1953,

Mary, an attractive girl of 17, arrived at the office one day, having read our address in the advice column of a woman's magazine. She was three months pregnant and had run away from her home in the country the previous week-end, fearing that her parents would learn of her condition. She had never been to London before, and had very little money. While she was having a meal in a café near the station, she was approached by a man and woman who said they could see she was 'in trouble'. They soon won her confidence, offered to look after her, and took her to their flat. When she arrived there, she was introduced to a man of dubious character who made advances to her. Luckily she left at once and made her way to us. During a talk with the Case Secretary, Mary revealed that she was on very good terms with her parents and was, in fact, engaged to the child's father, a young man of 21 with a steady job and good prospects. There was no reason at all why they should not marry, and Mary's flight to London was undertaken in a mood of panic when she first realised she was pregnant.

The Case Secretary made arrangements for Mary to stay at a hostel for a few nights and got in touch with the parents. They at once left for London and took Mary home with them. The last that was heard of her was that she was happily preparing for her wedding which was to take place within a few weeks.[65]

More sadly, the NC reported that

Lily has had two illegitimate children (both, according to Lily, 'whisked off' for adoption) before she found herself in further difficulties—married, pregnant, deserted and in trouble with the law. This baby died a few months after she was released from prison. Everything seemed lost. Lily's husband divorced her and she drifted from job to job until she met and married a steady man considerably older than herself. Although no longer an unmarried mother, Lily brought her baby, Sheila, to see us and gave us her outgrown clothes to pass on to other babies. A second child was happily waited for this spring. In May Lily brought the twelve day old son to the office—a mongol idiot [*sic*]. The grief of both parents was harming little Sheila, but we are trying with expert help them to face the future; last time they left the office Lily said 'We've come through worse things together than this, you and me and Jack.'

Perhaps, commented the Annual Report, 'this explains why the Council exists. No case begins or ends with us.'[66] They did what they could, and helped clients connect with other services, state and voluntary.

Just as the post-war 'welfare state' did not displace the voluntary sector, so also the 1950s was not quite the sexually conventional decade, centred wholly on the married two-parent family, that is often portrayed. A society in which living standards and standards of education had never been higher was changing and slowly bringing to the surface attitudes long buried in secrecy. Change moved still faster in the 1960s.

---

[65] NC Annual Report 1956–7, 19–20.   [66] NC Annual Report 1955–6, 16.

6

The Permissive Society? Unmarried Motherhood in the 1960s

In the 1960s, legend has it, unprecedented sexual 'permissiveness' swept the UK. Undoubtedly there were important shifts in behaviour and attitudes during the decade, which speeded up in the 1970s and 1980s, but historians and other commentators have questioned just how revolutionary, and how pervasive, the changes of the sixties were, especially in the context of often underestimated shifts in preceding decades.[1] The evidence of the experiences of unmarried mothers supports that scepticism.

There were demonstrable changes. The proportion of extramarital births rose, especially in the early 1960s, then fell somewhat through the 1970s before rising sharply in the 1980s and 1990s.

The numbers of divorces rose through the 1960s from an average of 37,657 petitions per year in England and Wales in 1961–5, to 57,089 in 1966–9, even before the change in the law in 1969. Then it soared to 121,772 petitions in 1971–5, 162,481 in 1976–80, and 176,969 in 1981–5. A growing proportion of divorces were initiated by wives. Through the 1920s and 1930s an average of 59 per cent of divorces were initiated by women. The proportion fell to 44–45 per cent during the war, then resumed pre-war levels. It then rose from 63 per cent in 1966–70 to 73 per cent in 1981–5.[2]

From the early 1960s a much more secure form of contraception, and one controlled by women, the pill, became available. But it was not free of charge or at all easily accessible to unmarried women until the Family Planning Act, 1967, allowed local authorities to provide free family planning services. Only about one-quarter did so until in 1974 contraception became freely available to all on the National Health Service. In 1968 the independent Family Planning Association allowed its branches, for the first time, to provide contraception to unmarried women, then in 1970 required them to do so.[3]

By the end of the 1960s there were more public statements of tolerance for unmarried motherhood and cohabitation and less private secrecy on this and other

---

[1] Lesley Hall, *Sex, Gender and Change in Britain since 1880* (London: Macmillan, 2000), 167–84; Adrian Bingham, *Family Newspapers? Sex, Private Lives and the British Popular Press, 1918–1978* (Oxford: Oxford University Press, 2009); Hera Cook, *The Long Sexual Revolution: English Women, Sex and Contraception, 1800–1975* (Oxford: Oxford University Press, 2004); Frank Mort, *Capital Affairs: London and the Making of the Permissive Society* (New Haven, CT: Yale University Press, 2010).
[2] A. H. Halsey and J. Webb (eds), *Twentieth Century Social Trends* (London: Macmillan, 2000), 62; Pat Thane, *Happy Families? History and Family Policy* (London: British Academy, 2010).
[3] Cook, *Long Sexual Revolution*, 290.

Table 6.1 Extramarital births per 1000 single, divorced, and widowed women, aged 15–44, England and Wales, 1955–2000

1955	10.3
1960	14.7
1965	21.2
1970	21.5
1975	17.4
1980	19.6
1985	26.7
1990	38.9
1995	39.4
1998	40.3
2000	38.4

Source: Jane Lewis, *The End of Marriage* (Cheltenham: Elgar, 2001), 32. 2000 ONS *Birth Statistics*, 2002 series, FM1 no. 31.

personal issues. But expressions of intolerance continued and there were continuing practical difficulties, even tragedies, affecting unmarried mothers and their children. Lifestyles changed through the 1960s, but slowly and unevenly.

FATHERLESS FAMILIES

From the late 1950s, there was a shift in the social policy discourse from representing unmarried, widowed, divorced and separated lone mothers as distinct groups with distinct problems, to emphasizing what these *Fatherless Families*, or *Mothers Alone*,[4] had in common, in particular their material difficulties, poverty, and poor housing. This represented a shift from the dominant professional concern of the late 1940s and early 1950s with the psychological causes and consequences especially of unmarried motherhood, to a focus on the material causes and, particularly, consequences for mothers and children of lone motherhood whatever the cause. Some social workers continued to stress the 'emotional instability' of unmarried mothers in particular,[5] but, as before, this was contested throughout the 1960s. In 1971 a report from the National Children's Bureau, *Born Illegitimate*, summed up views that were by then widely accepted, concluding: 'It is not possible to discuss the extent of the emotional problems of a child of a one-parent family until the financial and social problems have been solved.'[6]

[4] Margaret Wynn, *Fatherless Families* (London: Michael Joseph, 1964); Dennis Marsden, *Mothers Alone: Poverty and the Fatherless Family* (London: Allen Lane, 1969).
[5] K. Kiernan, H. Land, and J. Lewis, *Lone Motherhood in Twentieth-Century Britain* (Oxford: Oxford University Press, 1998), 105.
[6] Sue Graham-Dixon, *Never Darken My Door: Working for Single Parents and Their Children, 1918–1978* (London: National Council for One Parent Families, 1981), 25; E. Crellin, M. Kellmer Pringle, and P. West, for National Children's Bureau, *Born Illegitimate* (London: National Foundation for Educational Research, 1971).

The new approach brought separated and divorced mothers into public view more prominently than before, often in a sympathetic way. And Peter Marris's *Widows and Their Children* (1958) explored the material and emotional difficulties of a group of lone mothers who aroused greater sympathy than others, though the numbers of younger widows with children were falling as death rates of younger men declined.

The idea that unsupported lone mothers, whatever had caused separation from the father, had more in common than divided them was promoted by the Report of the Ministry of Health Working Party on Social Workers in Local Authority Health and Welfare Services (1959) chaired by Eileen Younghusband. Younghusband had long experience of voluntary social work and social work training[7] and was particularly concerned that social workers should be trained to help unsupported mothers. She alerted the National Council to her views at a meeting in 1959, but aroused there 'some doubt whether the problems of unmarried mothers and other "unsupported mothers" were really so similar.'[8] The doubts persisted in the NC, though they did not prevent Younghusband becoming a Vice-President, 1963–81.

From the late 1950s there were fewer social studies of the circumstances in which unmarried mothers, alone or not, kept their children and more surveys of mothers living alone with their children, for whatever reason, without, or with minimal support from, the fathers or their families, i.e. the minority of poorest lone-parent families. Particularly influential was Margaret Wynn's *Fatherless Families* (1964) based on analysis of statistics, official publications, social surveys, social policies, and the experiences of voluntary organizations. She stressed the similarity of the experiences of families headed by lone mothers and the poverty of many of them, focusing on income, housing, and the availability, or not, of day-care. She pointed out how little was still known about the numbers of lone mothers due to the inadequacy of census and other data, not least because it was often not a long-term condition, since mothers married, re-married, cohabited, or moved in with relatives.

Wynn argued that more was known about unmarried mothers than others, due in particular to the work of Wimperis. Hence she focused on divorced, separated, and widowed mothers and gave less information about the incomes, rents, and housing conditions of unmarried mothers. Indeed she implied that the specific needs of unmarried mothers had received too much attention, commenting that even the Younghusband Report 'placed perhaps a little too much stress on the unmarried mothers who represent only about one-tenth of the total problem [of fatherlessness]', when it pointed out the difficulties experienced by unmarried mothers and their children were due to the particular stigma and shame of illegitimacy.[9] However, rather contradictorily, she showed that, in 1960, unmarried

---

[7] Lucy Faithful, 'Younghusband, Dame Eileen Louise (1902–1981)', *Oxford Dictionary of National Biography* (hereafter *ODNB*) (Oxford: Oxford University Press, 2004). Younghusband was author of *Social Work and Social Change* (London: Allen and Unwin, 1964).

[8] NC Annual Report 1959–60, 10–11.

[9] Wynn, *Fatherless*, 153–4.

mothers were 35 per cent of all mothers receiving National Assistance benefits, compared with only 9.1 per cent who were widows and 18 per cent divorced and separated.[10] She criticized the NC for proposing that mothers should be helped to stay at home when their children were young, on the grounds that

There is no good reason for treating unmarried mothers of young children any differently in this context from other mothers of young children where there is no father [which NC did not imply]. Indeed there are obvious objections to unmarried mothers having special privileges compared with separated or divorced wives or widows.[11]

She did not spell out the 'obvious objections'.

Wynn was concerned, above all, with the poverty of fatherless families, its effects and means to cure it. She criticized a popular tendency to blame lone motherhood for social problems whose real cause was poverty, for example the often repeated claim that fatherless boys were more at risk than others of 'juvenile delinquency' (as youth crime was then generally known), whereas, she argued, 'juvenile delinquency is more closely correlated with poverty than anything else.'[12] She regretted that Beveridge's proposals for the support of fatherless families had been rejected, and proposed a minimum state allowance for all fatherless children.[13] She recommended that maintenance under separation and affiliation orders and divorce settlements should be guaranteed by Government and collected by the Inland Revenue; also higher and more flexible income limits for National Assistance benefits, in order not to discourage mothers from working; employment training schemes for mothers; a proportion of local authority housing to be allocated to fatherless families; and more day nurseries.[14]

THE 'REDISCOVERY' OF POVERTY

Wynn's concern with the poverty of lone mothers was part of a growing recognition that the post-war 'welfare state' had not abolished poverty. This was particularly promoted by Richard Titmuss,[15] the most active academic champion of the welfare state and an advisor to the Labour Party, and his colleagues at LSE, Brian Abel-Smith[16] and Peter Townsend. A study by Abel-Smith and Townsend, *The Poor and the Poorest* (1965), estimated the extent of continuing poverty in the UK by reanalysing data from Ministry of Labour Family Expenditure Surveys (FES) of 1953–4 and 1960. They recognized that the absolute destitution described by Booth seventy years earlier had largely disappeared, but Townsend argued that as incomes and living standards had risen for the population in general, substantial

---

[10] Ibid. 24.
[11] Ibid. 87.
[12] Wynn, *Fatherless*, 147–9.
[13] See p. 152.
[14] Wynn, *Fatherless*, 162–3.
[15] A. H. Halsey, 'Titmuss, Richard Morris (1907–73)', *ODNB* (2004–11).
[16] Peter Townsend, 'Smith, Brian Abel- (1926–96)', *ODNB* (2004–11).

inequality remained, leaving those at the bottom of the income distribution substantially excluded from the life chances and living conditions most of the population took for granted. This he termed 'relative poverty', different from the 'absolute poverty' of Booth's day but in the modern world equally disabling.[17] For the purposes of the survey it was defined as living at or below the stringent National Assistance benefit rates.

Abel-Smith and Townsend shocked contemporaries by revealing that, by this measure, extensive poverty remained, and was even growing, while average living standards were rising as never before. The study was published just before Christmas (22 December) 1965, for maximum effect.[18] Most shockingly, it showed that poverty prevailed not only, as widely assumed, among older, retired, people, but among children, including many in families with resident fathers in full-time work. However, in 1953–5, poverty 'was worst where there was no male bread-winner',[19] afflicting 36 per cent of all households consisting of one woman and two children. Poorest of all—42 per cent—were women living alone, a high proportion of whom can be assumed to have been older women. Lone mothers and their children were a minority of those in poverty, though still a substantial number.

The numbers in poverty by the chosen measure totalled *c*.4 million people in 1953–4, about 10 per cent of households and 7.8 per cent of the UK population, an estimate the authors thought 'likely to be on the low side'.[20] About half of these impoverished people were in households headed by retired people, but over one-third had a male head, in full-time work, and most included four or more children.

Analysis of the smaller 1960 FES survey showed that about 7.5m persons, 18 per cent of households and 14 per cent of the population of UK, were then in poverty as defined by the authors. About 35 per cent were households primarily dependent on state old age pensions, 23 per cent on means-tested state benefits, and 41 per cent on earnings, many of the latter large families.[21] Five to 6 per cent of the population lived in households whose poverty was due to pay for full-time work being too low for a family to live on at a decent standard, even when supplemented by family allowances.[22] Abel-Smith and Townsend recommended increased family allowances especially for larger families and that national assistance should be extended to those in low-paid work.

One outcome was the formation in 1965 of the Child Poverty Action Group (CPAG) to campaign for implementation of these recommendations.[23] It was one

---

[17] P. Townsend, 'Measuring Poverty', *British Journal of Sociology* (June 1954), 130–7.

[18] R. Lowe and P. Nicolson (eds), 'The Formation of the Child Poverty Action Group' (Witness Seminar), *Contemporary Record*, 9:3 (Winter 1995), 612–37.

[19] B. Abel-Smith and P. Townsend, *The Poor and the Poorest*, Occasional papers in Social Administration no. 17 (London: G. Bell and Sons, 1965), 32.

[20] Ibid. 37–8.

[21] Ibid. 49.

[22] Ibid. 66.

[23] Rodney Lowe, 'The Rediscovery of Poverty and the Creation of the Child Poverty Action Group, 1962–68' (Witness Seminar), *Contemporary Record*, 9:3 (Winter 1995), 602–11; Lowe and Nicolson (eds), 'Formation of CPAG'.

of a new type of independent campaigning group that emerged in the 1960s, including Shelter (founded 1966, to help the homeless) and the Disablement Income Group (DIG, founded 1965 to campaign for disability pensions). These groups were more publicly assertive than older voluntary organizations, such as the NC, gaining publicity through mass media that also were more assertive and less deferential than before and more willing to publicize campaigns critical of authority.[24] They were staffed by a radical younger generation, often trained in the expanding social sciences, willing to challenge a new Labour Government (elected 1964, after 13 years of Conservative rule) that they hoped would be more responsive on social issues than its Conservative predecessors. They also challenged older campaigning groups, like the NC, which came to believe that they too had to become more assertive, media savvy, and professionalized if they were to continue to make an impact.[25]

MOTHERS ALONE

Another follow-up to *The Poor and the Poorest* was Dennis Marsden's *Mothers Alone* (1969). This was linked with a larger poverty survey led by Peter Townsend, which was eventually published in 1979.[26] Marsden was a colleague of Townsend in the Sociology Department at the University of Essex, where Townsend moved in 1963. Like Wynn, Marsden was interested in all lone mothers in poverty. Unlike Wynn, he interviewed mothers rather than relying on secondary data. He was more interested in the differences among the women according to the cause of their 'aloneness', and the differences within the groups of widowed, divorced, separated, and unmarried mothers. He wanted to explore their personal experiences as well as their material conditions. He aimed 'to illuminate the human situations of poverty and fatherlessness'[27] and stimulate public debate 'about the problem of fatherlessness and about how we treat the group among the poor who are dependent on the state'.[28]

Marsden admitted that his small sample of interviewees—just 116—was not representative of any group of mothers and was biased towards the poorest, without significant support from the fathers or from relatives, since the sample consisted entirely of recipients of National Assistance benefits, who were, by definition, very poor. Some of these refused to see him because they feared that he was a National Assistance Board (NAB) official trying to catch them out, or they felt too

---

[24] Bingham, *Family Newspapers?*

[25] Tanya Evans, 'Stopping the Poor Getting Poorer: The Establishment and Professionalization of Poverty NGOs, 1945–95', 147–63, and J. McKay and Matthew Hilton, 'Introduction', 1–20, in N. Crowson, M. Hilton, and J. McKay (eds), *NGOs in Contemporary Britain: Non-state Actors in Society and Politics since 1945* (London: Palgrave, 2009).

[26] P. Townsend, *Poverty in the United Kingdom* (Harmondsworth: Penguin, 1979).

[27] Dennis Marsden, *Mothers Alone*, 2nd edn (London: Penguin, 1971), 9.

[28] Ibid. 2.

depressed and ashamed of their lives to reveal them to a stranger. Marsden's methodology, including the sometimes censorious comments on his interviewees in his interview notes would today be regarded as suspect, but was normal at the time.[29]

The interviews were conducted in 1965 and 1966, half in Marsden's home town, northern, industrial Huddersfield ('Northborough' in the book) and the southern market town of Colchester ('Seaston'), home of the University of Essex and of substantial army barracks, the latter supplying the absent fathers of some of the families interviewed. He interviewed no fathers. The women were mostly, but not all, working class, aged 20 to 40. Unlike Wynn, he devoted separate chapters to exploring the experiences of families who had lived through either broken marriages or unmarried motherhood, though not widowhood, which his colleague Peter Marris had studied in detail and which Marsden rightly believed already had more public sympathy and support from public policy than other causes of fatherlessness.[30]

Contrary to Wynn, Marsden concluded that unmarried motherhood was a major cause of poverty among his interviewees. Almost half the mothers interviewed had 'illegitimate children', 26 when unmarried, 26 when separated or divorced, 2 as widows. Marsden emphasized that they were not representative of unmarried mothers, pointing out that 'nationally...40 per cent of illegitimate children are born into stable two-parent homes'.[31] They had 'the lowest incomes and the fewest possessions of any of the fatherless families'[32] and the worst housing. Those who had succeeded in getting council housing had done so only with 'exceptional backing from welfare authorities, doctors or health pressure groups...mothers were almost powerless without some kind of official support for their case'.[33] Larger families and older mothers were most likely to qualify, younger mothers and those with 'illegitimate' children had least chance, and all too often fatherless families were concentrated in the least favoured estates. Others were at the mercy of often unscrupulous landlords and landladies, though some were helped by voluntary organizations.

Marsden did not explore the routes into unmarried motherhood, believing the topic to be complex and little understood, and that, 'in particular, the psychoanalytical "explanations" of illegitimacy in terms of the mother's need to have a baby or to be revenged on her parents simply are not verifiable or predictive'.[34] Too many 'explanations', he thought, were based on atypical women in contact with agencies precisely because they had emotional problems. He was more concerned with the material consequences of lone motherhood and how to remedy them.

---

[29] Marsden, *Mothers*, 7–8. Tanya Evans and Pat Thane, 'Secondary Analysis of Dennis Marsden's *Mothers Alone*', *Methodological Innovations Online*, 1:2 (2006). Marsden's notes are available in the UK Data Archive, University of Essex, and were thoroughly analysed for this research.

[30] Marsden, *Mothers*, 322.

[31] Ibid. 104. In 1960 one-third of illegitimate births were jointly registered by both parents. Kiernan et al., *Lone Motherhood*, 163.

[32] Ibid. 104.

[33] Ibid. 174.

[34] Ibid. 105.

He was fascinated by the variety of the mothers' backgrounds. Thirteen of the unmarried mothers he interviewed came from broken or unhappy homes, which, he believed, explained their dependence on state benefits but not the 'illegitimacy'. Four more had their only children in their thirties, having lived with and often cared for ageing parents. These were some of the most desolate mothers. Three of them

had withdrawn from life outside the home and they lived very intensively through their children... the shock of the birth had been very great... [they] had no longer been able to face social relationships with workmates and neighbours... The births might have resulted from the despairing indiscretions of those who felt destined to be left on the shelf.[35]

Some women who had 'illegitimate' children after a failed marriage also reported that it happened because they were lonely or experiencing a 'sudden release after a bad or brutal marriage and needed some support'.[36] Three definitely middle-class mothers—a former nurse and two secretaries—had their children in their mid-20s, 'apparently due to a failure of contraception after safely having sex with a number of men'. The relationships had been short-lived and uncommitted:

Of all the unmarried mothers these women showed the greatest concern for secrecy. Two signed themselves 'Mrs', one had changed her name so that it was the same as the child's and all three had changed their address, two living in caravans for privacy.[37]

Most of the English-born mothers had only brief and casual relationships with the father, which made it difficult for them to claim support from him. Six mothers, all unmarried, all living in Huddersfield, had been born in the West Indies. They had larger families than the English-born mothers. They were more likely than other mothers to be in regular contact with the father and receive some support from him. Some expected or intended to marry when they could afford it. As one of them put it, 'To be quite honest with you we could be married but what's the use? He don't get enough wage. He only just get enough to keep himself and keep the children.'[38] West Indian mothers reported even greater difficulty in getting council housing than British-born mothers. There were suspicions of racism among officials and private landlords/ladies. They were more often overcrowded and moved more frequently from one private rental to another.

Many of Marsden's generation of social researchers designed their work not only to study social conditions but to influence policy. Marsden recognized that 'the poverty of fatherless families has continued throughout the last four centuries of policy development under the poor law'[39] and it would not change easily. He believed that a major obstacle to mothers and children receiving support in their own right was 'covert or overt fears that to provide adequate financial support for

---

[35] Ibid. 109.   [36] Ibid. 115.   [37] Ibid. 110.   [38] Ibid. 113.   [39] Ibid. 310.

women to live apart from their husbands, or to maintain illegitimate children, would effectively condone immorality or blameworthy behaviour in marriage, and so erode marriage as an institution'.[40] He noted, in the second edition of his book in 1971, that 'Even in the 1970s implementing Beveridge's proposals would represent an advance on the existing arrangements,' limited though these had been.[41] Even widows, who were more favourably treated than other lone mothers, received state pensions determined not by their own needs but by the occupation, contributions, and cause of death of their husbands, e.g., whether he died in war, at work, or in some other circumstance.

Marsden was well aware of the difficulties of delivering non-stigmatizing allowances to fatherless families as a right: the very fact of receiving such an allowance might create stigma. Rather, he recommended higher family allowances for all, plus an allowance to unsupported mothers to compensate for their inability to work while rearing children. Education, training, work opportunities, pay, and day-care should be improved for all women, to help remove disadvantages that hit unsupported mothers especially hard. Fathers should contribute through the tax or insurance systems and, in return, to encourage compliance, should have greater rights over their children.[42]

Marsden demonstrated clearly that the 1960s did not look 'permissive' to unmarried mothers in provincial towns who experienced as much stigma, shame, and exclusion as their predecessors in earlier decades.

LONE MOTHERS ON BENEFIT

By the time the first edition of Marsden's book was published in 1969, the Labour Government, elected in 1964 and re-elected with a more secure majority in 1966, had begun to consider the problems of fatherless families and of child poverty, under pressure from CPAG and from its own backbenchers. In 1964, the former Labour Minister Baroness (Edith) Summerskill promoted a bill to introduce a Fatherless Child's Allowance. This was supported by the NC, despite what they saw as its inadequacies, but not by the Government.[43] Officials at the Ministry of Health and Social Security were not convinced that fatherless families were worse off than others or deserved more favourable treatment.[44] Summerskill initiated a further debate on the topic in 1967, again unsuccessfully.[45] This was the year in which abortion and certain homosexual acts were legalized, but there were clearly limits to parliamentary liberalism.

---

[40] Kiernan et al., *Lone Motherhood*, 311.
[41] Ibid. 317. The second, Penguin, edition was published with recommendations updated to take account of policy changes since the first edition, 309–32.
[42] Ibid. 324–32.
[43] The National Archives (TNA) PIN 19/425 1964.
[44] TNA PIN 47/89, 'Statistics: Fatherless Families: Sample Reports 1965–70'.
[45] *The Times*, 22 Feb. 1967.

In December 1965 the Prime Minister was asked by a Labour backbencher to establish a Royal Commission to investigate 'the problem of deserted wives and fatherless families'. Harold Wilson refused on the grounds that a comprehensive review of social services (the Seebohm Committee on Local Authority and Allied Personal Services, which reported in 1968[46]) was under way. The request, and the response, was repeated in 1966 and 1967.[47] The Government, beset by an economic crisis, gave priority to helping pensioners, who were the majority of the poorest people, though the 'earnings rule', which reduced benefits once claimants earned above a certain, low, limit, was abolished for widows—only—in 1964.[48] Widows also gained new tax concessions in 1967.

In 1966 Labour followed the advice of Richard Titmuss and abolished the increasingly discredited NAB, replacing it with a Supplementary Benefits Commission (SBC), and a new scheme of means-tested, non-contributory benefits designed to provide a form of guaranteed income for long-term claimants. It was aimed mostly at pensioners and 'widows and others with dependent children' and was intended to be less stigmatizing than NA benefits, carrying an increased sense of entitlement.[49] From 1968 means-tested and National Insurance Benefits were both for the first time administered by the same Whitehall department, the new Department of Health and Social Security, with the aim of drawing them closer together.

In 1967 a government study, *The Circumstances of Families*,[50] supported the findings of Abel-Smith and Townsend, showing that large numbers of working families, especially larger families, were still in poverty due to low pay: at least 160,000 families, with 500,000 children. The Government responded to both studies, and to continuing pressure from CPAG, by raising family allowances for the fourth and subsequent children from 50 to 75p per week in October 1966, then, in April 1967, to 75p for the second child and 85p for each subsequent child. This did not help single mothers with just one child. Also Supplementary Benefit (SB) payments were reduced by the amount of this increase, and tax allowances were adjusted to recover the cost of family allowances from taxpayers, including some low earners.[51] Widows, only, were exempted from the tax.

In another respect, life was getting harder for lone mothers on benefit. From the days of the Poor Law, welfare administrators had suspected lone mothers of secret cohabitation, or 'collusion' with partners who pretended to be absent, to enable the women to claim benefits. Suspicion and surveillance of lone mothers for this reason became more intense in the 1950s and 1960s. The reasons are unclear, but may have been a response to the revelations in official and unofficial surveys of the extent of secret cohabitation.[52] The National Assistance Act, 1948, did not refer to

---

[46] *Report* of Committee on Local Authority and Allied Personal Services, Cmnd 3703 (The Seebohm Report) (London: HMSO, 1968).
[47] Kiernan et al., *Lone Motherhood*, 165.
[48] Ibid. 168–9.
[49] Ibid. 168–9.
[50] Ministry of Social Security, *Circumstances of Families* (London: HMSO, 1967).
[51] Kiernan et al., *Lone Motherhood*, 168–70.
[52] See pp. 88–92.

the issue, but in 1954 the NAB appointed its first special investigators to look into suspected abuses, including covert cohabitation. It was assumed that a man who shared a mother's bed, however occasionally, should be liable to support her and her children, even if he was not their father. Sixteen investigators were appointed in 1954. By 1963 there were 97, the number of prosecutions for the abuse of cohabitation rose (58 in 1963, 98 in 1964), and there was growing criticism of the surveillance to which lone mothers were subjected and the implications of the rule.[53] In 1965 there were 525 prosecutions for 'false desertion' or cohabitation, leading to 481 convictions, and the NAB reported that 'in more cases where it was not possible to obtain the evidence necessary for proceedings, the allowances were withdrawn or reduced.'[54] The small number of appeals was taken as evidence of guilt, though critics judged the appeals system inaccessible and inefficient.[55]

The Social Security Act, 1966, defined cohabitation as 'cohabiting as man and wife', with no further explanation. The clause was not debated in Parliament, though the SBC maintained there was popular support for it, and that 'it contains no element of moral judgement or of legal sanctions against informal unions which are not legalized.'[56] In 1968, 6,173 cases were investigated and 3,194 allowances withdrawn or reduced, in 1970 9,300 and 4,388 respectively, from a total of about 200,000 allowances. At the time the country—or at least the media and some politicians—was in the grip of one of its recurrent panics about fraudulent claimants, which the Minister David Ennals did his best to refute.[57] There were real concerns that vulnerable families could be victims of malicious neighbours or over-zealous officials and that, at the very least, the system required overhaul and greater transparency.

Labour came under growing pressure to do more for fatherless families. In January 1969 it published a White Paper proposing a radical, earnings-related, overhaul of the social security system, designed to bring it closer to systems in other West European countries, as first proposed in 1957[58] by Titmuss, Townsend, and Abel-Smith, the latter now a special adviser to Richard Crossman, Minister for Health and Social Security, and on rather distant terms with Townsend, who was closely associated with CPAG and an outspoken critic of the Government.[59] The White Paper also announced the establishment of

A committee to consider the general position of one-parent families in our society and whether there are further methods by which they could be helped.

This was appointed later in 1969, chaired by Morris Finer, QC. It reported in 1974.[60] In June 1970 Labour lost another General Election to the Conservatives.

---

[53] Kiernan et al., *Lone Motherhood*, 163–4.
[54] Marsden, *Mothers*, 224.
[55] Ibid. 229.
[56] Ibid. 222–3.
[57] Ibid. 224–6.
[58] Labour Party, *National Superannuation: Labour's Policy for Security in Old Age* (London: The Labour Party, 1957).
[59] Lowe and Nicolson (eds), 'Formation of CPAG'.
[60] See Chap. 7.

The Conservative Government also faced pressure from assertive interest groups, including CPAG, and from a new phenomenon: assertive benefit claimants. These were encouraged by a wave of feminist groups and Claimants Unions, both associated with international, post-1968 radicalism. They informed people, including lone mothers, of their rights to benefits and how to claim them. The Conservatives quickly responded with a new Family Income Supplement (FIS), a means-tested supplement to low incomes, payable to men or single mothers, even if the latter were living with relatives. Maintenance payments counted as income. The supplement increased with the number of children and included the first child. However, it fell as earnings rose and was criticized, by CPAG among others, for disincentivizing work. Take-up was low. By 1974 half of all recipients were lone parents, two-thirds with just one child. More than half the unmarried mothers claiming FIS lived with their parents.[61] At the same time, the costs of school meals and prescriptions rose, and free school milk was withdrawn from primary schoolchildren (Labour had already abolished it in secondary schools). The net benefits were limited.

WHAT CHANGED IN THE 1960s?

The shift to representing 'lone mothers' as a single category constituting a problem of poverty was part of a laudable campaign to improve support for them, in particular for a Fatherless Child Allowance and access to suitable housing. But it may unintentionally have reinforced stereotypes and prejudices. As Marsden put it: 'We must be sensitive to the problem that such categories [as fatherless families] may imprison groups as well as represent opportunities for them.'[62] Prejudice certainly continued against unmarried mothers in particular who were represented as isolated, poor, often from broken homes themselves and ill-equipped to cope. This was true of some but not all even of the poorest, as the surveys showed, and, as we have seen, was not typical of unmarried mothers.

The NC was well aware of the shifting focus to 'lone mothers', not least because it received increasing applications for help from married or formerly married single mothers and occasionally from fathers. In the early 1960s it considered returning to its intended focus at its foundation, on all lone mothers, but felt constrained, as it had in 1918, by its limited budget and the belief that unmarried mothers still had more difficulties and less support than others.[63] Nevertheless, it did just this in 1973, under pressure of appeals from parents and shifting public opinion, when it changed its name to the National Council for One-Parent Families. But it continued to insist on the differences among unmarried and divorced, separated and widowed mothers, commenting that 'It is a dangerous mistake to classify unmarried mothers as a homogeneous group referred to as "they".'[64] Above all, they were

---

[61] Kiernan et al., *Lone Motherhood*, 171–4.   [62] Marsden, *Mothers*, 322.
[63] NC Annual Report 1964–5, 14.   [64] Ibid. 12.

not all 'alone'. Many had support from their families, though so had many other lone mothers. Many, as before, were stably cohabiting with the father or with another man, often due to the difficulty of getting a divorce before 1969. The Registrar General recognized this when he concluded from an investigation of the 1961 census data that 'nearly one illegitimate child in three may be born to a married woman or, at least, to a woman who would describe herself as married in the census'.[65] Thereby, perhaps, he encouraged NAB surveillance.[66] But the NC insisted that unmarried mothers and their children, even if they were not alone or poor, faced specific problems, in particular prejudice and legal barriers, which continued through the supposedly liberated sixties, against which they had little support and about which the Council went on campaigning.

The NC's records and publications again provide exceptional insights into the shifting and conflicting attitudes to and the experiences of unmarried mothers through the 1960s. In 1960, before the 'sixties' of 'permissive' legend had begun, the NC commented, as we have seen,[67] that many unmarried mothers were far more independent than in the past. More surprisingly, in the same year, the Annual Report asked, in the context of rising numbers of births out of wedlock:

why are an increasing number of our young people caught in a web of irresponsibility and misunderstanding of so much of the true values of life?[68]

Adding:

some mothers are unable to learn from experience and re-plan their lives in wider terms. They are often those most affected by... the less responsible papers, films and advertisements.[69]

In 1961–2 it hoped for 'the lowering of the illegitimacy rate and a higher standard of moral responsibility throughout the country'.[70] The Council's own views were conflicted, apparently more critical of unmarried mothers than in the past and of changes in the wider society that they perceived were influencing them.

Meanwhile, the moral panic about teenage mothers persisted and was discussed at an Extraordinary Meeting of the NC in January 1961. The Council continued to argue that the increasing numbers of teenage mothers was not disproportionate to the size of the age group due to the increased birth rate since the war. This too was supported by the Registrar General's sober statistics. He pointed out that it was not surprising that teenagers contributed substantially to the number of 'illegitimate' births since they constituted most of the unmarried women of reproductive age and marriage was prohibited before age 16. However, he reported in 1964:

It remains clear that extra-marital conception is not specifically a teenage problem; the probability that an unmarried woman will conceive in the course of a year is one in

---

[65] *Registrar General's Statistical Review of England and Wales for the year 1964, Part III, Commentary,* 64.
[66] See pp. 129–30.
[67] See p. 118.
[68] NC Annual Report 1960–1, 22.
[69] Ibid.
[70] NC Annual Report 1961–2, 10.

thirty-four if she is under 20, rises to a peak of one in fifteen if she is 20–24, falls to one in twenty if she is 25–29 and to one in forty-five if she is 30–39.[71]

The NC agreed, and asked:

What type of girl has an illegitimate baby? They come from every background and all standards of education: frightened fifteen-year-olds, sophisticated women of forty; in all stages of pregnancy (often between the fourth and fifth month, perhaps just as the child has quickened). They write or arrive at the office without an appointment. Although the national figures show an increase in teenage pregnancies, most of the applications that come to us are from girls between the ages of eighteen and twenty-two.[72]

It noted that applications for help were increasing faster than the rate of illegitimacy, notably from women who were or had been married rather than from teenagers. This may have owed much, as they recognized, to their continuing successful media campaigns.[73]

In 1966 the Council returned to the theme that society was becoming more tolerant—up to a point:

Our society is more compassionate to the unmarried mother than it was a generation ago, but she and her illegitimate child are still seen as a threat to normal family life.[74]

A year later the Annual Report referred to an apparent 'more permissive' shift in public attitudes to sexual behaviour, but noted that these were not generally more benign towards unmarried mothers. It noted the 'continued unpopularity of unmarried parents as a group' and that much of its work was

directed towards trying to break down the generalized hostility of the public to illegitimacy into an appreciation of the fact that it concerns innumerable human and often tragic individual histories, many of which could have had a more satisfactory outcome had there been more public understanding, more social provision and more easily available professional counselling. The unmarried mother remains a symbol of our fears and guilt about ourselves and our children. She illustrates the hypocrisy of a society which condemns her, as her predicament may be the inevitable result of the more permissive code of sexual behaviour which the public in fact now accepts while still preserving a different standard of morality for men and women.[75]

As the Council suggested, the woman still generally bore the responsibility and shame of the pregnancy if the father abandoned her, while there was a continuing popular disposition to believe that 'men were men' and to exonerate them from responsibility for unmarried parenthood.

The NC felt concern that schoolgirl and student mothers were still poorly treated and should be helped to complete their education. Too many were expelled

---

[71] *Registrar General's Statistical Review of England and Wales for the Year 1964, Part III, Commentary,* 67.
[72] NC Annual Report 1961–2, 12.
[73] NC Annual Report 1963–4.
[74] Ibid.
[75] Ibid.

from school and university, and services were poor for younger mothers, who were least equipped to help themselves.[76] A year later, the Annual Report commented again that children born out of wedlock 'are born to a hard and hostile world'.[77] It repeated in the following year, 1968, its fiftieth anniversary:

Although society is less punitive towards the mother than when NCUMC was founded fifty years ago, there is still considerable residual hostility to single mothers.... She and her child should be accepted as integrated members of the community. Society should provide financial and practical services that will give the child the maximum chance of a stable and settled upbringing.

However, the Report noted 'welcome signs of a trend towards tolerance. Some credit must go to the press, television, and radio for their sympathetic presentation of the problem.' Nevertheless, 'simultaneously...there appears to be a new hardening in attitudes towards unmarried mothers'.[78]

In 1970, as the 'permissive' decade drew to a close, the NC noted a strengthening of the 'welcome trend', though it was still not unmitigated:

Hostility to unmarried mothers still exists...but public feeling has moderated during the past five years and the decreasing number of children offered for adoption bears out the contention that more mothers are able to keep their children.[79]

The NC's assessment was confirmed in the perhaps surprising setting of the civil service. In early 1970 it was proposed to abolish a rule introduced in 1963 that an unmarried woman who had a second 'illegitimate' child should 'normally' be dismissed. It was decided that there should be no decision before the coming General Election because, still, 'there was some danger of public criticism if the change we were proposing became known.'[80] The proposal was put to the new, Conservative, Government in July 1970. It was informed that paid leave was allowed to unmarried mothers for one confinement but, in the case of a second, the decision to retain her should normally be taken at a high level. However, departments were clearly not operating the rule strictly. A recent triennial review of disciplinary cases found only two cases in the entire service in which a woman was dismissed after a second 'illegitimate' child, 'in one case the woman's work had long been unsatisfactory and the other had been convicted of theft.'[81] There was no comment on how many were kept on.

The change was proposed because

The climate of public opinion towards unmarried mothers has perhaps changed since 1963 [The same social stigma does not seem to apply to them]. Many would question whether it is reasonable for an employer to take disciplinary action on moral grounds against unmar-

[76] NC Annual Report 1966–7, 28–9.
[77] NC Annual Report 1967–8, 4.
[78] NC Annual Report 1968–9, 2.
[79] Graham-Dixon, *Never Darken*, 13; NC Annual Report 1969–70.
[80] TNA BA 19/5/5, A. Duke to Mr Watson and Mr Morrison, 27 July 1970. We are very grateful to Kath Sherit for this reference.
[81] Ibid.

ried women who have children; many would argue that to take such action against an unmarried mother but not against the father of an illegitimate child is a form of illogical discrimination against women. And the State does not discriminate against unmarried mothers and their children in terms of social security benefits.

Moreover there have been changes in the law relating to abortion. Departments will not always know when a woman civil servant has had a pregnancy terminated and it seems unreasonable to treat a woman who has had a second illegitimate child more harshly than another who has had the pregnancy brought to an end.[82]

It was recommended that, in future, departments should deal with such cases at their discretion, taking account of 'whether a woman's conduct has brought the Department into disrepute' and any security implications.[83] The rule was modified as recommended, as part of a wider review of the position of women in the civil service in 1971, perhaps anticipating possible future sex discrimination legislation (introduced in 1975).

The NC faced increased requests for information about terminations following the legalization of abortion in 1967. Women found the law confusing. The NC feared that 'especially very young girls may be subject to pressure by their parents or their boyfriends'[84] to have abortions. Yet, for all the change, much remained the same. They reported in 1970:

We are glad that many mothers are able to live with their parents. Often the shared resources of the family takes the edge off the mother's poverty, relieves her loneliness and gives her an adequate amount of freedom to meet her own needs as an adult while providing the child with a family circle.

But still they were concerned that

Sometimes these children are adopted by the maternal grandparents, who do not tell them the truth about the situation. This may cause great confusion to a child who may grow up believing that his mother is his sister, or his aunt. It can be disastrous when the child reaches adolescence, not only because he is confused about his own identity, but because he finds that those he most trusted have concealed the truth from him.[85]

Material problems also continued. Grandparents received no financial support to house their daughters and grandchildren unless they were already on benefits. There were still many families too poor and with too many other children to help:

The problem our clients most often bring to us is their failure to find somewhere to live with their children...

...An increasing number of unmarried mothers get in touch with us because they have acute financial difficulties. It is clear that in a time of rising prices very many unmarried mothers, especially as their children grow, are finding it harder to manage on earnings which frequently do not bring them up to supplementary benefit level....

---

[82] Ibid.
[83] Ibid.
[84] NC Annual Report 1969–70, 9.
[85] NC Annual Report 1970–1, 11.

...We know of one mother who has a little boy of six. She comes from a professional middle class background, but she is living in sordid slum conditions unable to provide her child with the sort of home that she herself was used to, fearful of inviting his school friends home, and too proud to let her family visit her because she feels that the sort of life she is living for her child indicates gross failure on her part.

Another mother of 48, a cleaner with a daughter of 13 to support, earns a gross wage of £10 a week. With deductions and fares to work, her net income is approximately £8; yet she decided that the advantages of the social contacts made at work, her independence and the pride that her daughter showed in her ability to manage far outweighed the disadvantages of living on £3 a week less than she would have received in supplementary benefit![86]

Whatever change there might have been in the 1960s, sad experiences of impoverished mothers and their children, of shame and exclusion, persisted.

WORKING WITH THE MEDIA

Insofar as attitudes *did* change, the Council played a role by continuing to work with the media both to change representations of unmarried mothers and their children and to inform mothers of their rights and sources of help. From the early 1960s representatives of the NC were increasingly invited onto radio and TV programmes—part of the increased media awareness of many voluntary organizations and greater receptivity to them by an expanding range of media. The NC built up its media contacts including 'with a group of reliable journalists' who in 1964–5 contributed articles on unmarried mothers to an eclectic array of journals including *Readers Digest, Honey, The Guardian, News of the World, Daily Mail*, and *The Irish Times*. The BBC was particularly supportive. Its willingness to broadcast 'progressive' views on sexual matters prompted Mary Whitehouse's widely publicized 'Clean-up TV' campaign, initiated in 1964 to challenge the 'disbelief, doubt and dirt that the BBC projects into millions of homes through the television screen', dedicated to promoting 'Christian values', good taste, and moral purity.[87]

In the mid-1960s, the NC noted 'the growing tendency in both television and radio for members of the group whose problems are being discussed to speak for themselves rather than to have *experts* speaking on their behalf.'[88] This was part of a wider tendency, as marginalized people—women, ethnic minorities, disabled, gay people—started new self-help organizations that became more prominent over the following decade.[89] A notable example was Gingerbread, founded in 1971 by Tess Fothergill, a London mother whose marriage broke down and who found being a lone parent such a struggle that she set up a support group.[90] She was the

---

[86] NC Annual Report 1969–70, 9–10.

[87] Lawrence Black, 'There Was Something about Mary: The National Viewers' and Listeners' Association and Social Movement History', in Crowson et al., *NGOs in Contemporary Britain*, 182–200. Cook, *Long Sexual Revolution*, 285.

[88] NC Annual Report 1966–7, 46.

[89] Pat Thane (ed.), *Unequal Britain. Equalities in Britain since 1945* (London: Continuum, 2010).

[90] 'Our History', *Gingerbread: Single Parents, Equal Families*, available at http://www.gingerbread.org.uk/content/442/Our-history

subject of a *Sunday Times* article that encouraged hundreds of single parents to get in touch, and Gingerbread was formed as a charity to provide mutual support and lobby for better provision. It originally included only divorced and separated women, but the NC noted in 1972, with approval, that 'One result of the acceptance of illegitimacy has been that unmarried mothers are being accepted as members.'[91]

The staff of NC now spent more time advising on radio and TV programmes and assisting participants who were themselves lone parents rather than participating themselves. They had reservations about this, since women willing to appear often were not representative, especially of those with greatest problems. They commented that, however hard the media strove for authenticity, 'it is often difficult to present a true picture of the variety of girls and women who become unmarried mothers when many do not wish to be identified because of the distress this will cause to their children and their families.'[92]

Another sign of changing times was that, in 1971, 24-year-old Bernadette Devlin became the first serving female MP to give birth to a child out of wedlock, causing particular shock in her, sexually conservative, native Northern Ireland, where her constituency was located. She married the father, Michael McAliskey, in 1973, had two further children and remains married to him in 2011. Still, in 1974, pregnant unmarried teachers were dismissed,[93] but not MPs: there was no precedent in a still overwhelmingly male institution. But Bernadette McAliskey lost her seat in the next election in 1974.

Perhaps a more significant indicator of cultural change was that in 1972 the NC made the landmark decision always in future to refer to 'natural' rather than 'illegitimate' children, their parents as 'natural 'parents, and all single parents, whatever the reason, as 'lone' parents. It determined to

cease using language that is offensive and wounding to a group of people who have enough disadvantages without suffering the indignity of being referred to in pejorative terms.[94]

It went further: announcing its change of title to the National Council for One Parent Families from 1973, explaining:

all lone parents share one crucial characteristic: the responsibility of bringing up children single-handed in a society that is geared economically, socially and emotionally to two-parent families.[95]

It hoped that focusing on 'lone parents', including fathers, would lessen prejudice against unmarried mothers by merging awareness of their needs with groups who aroused more sympathy. But it remained alert to their specific difficulties, commenting:

[91] NC Annual Report 1972–3.
[92] NC Annual Report 1966–7, 46.
[93] *The Times*, 19 Apr. 1974.
[94] NC Annual Report 1972–3.
[95] Graham-Dixon, *Never Darken*, 26.

If unmarried mothers are treated as part of the wider group of one-parent families this will encourage social workers, as well as society, to see them as people first and unmarried mothers second[96]

but

The opinion is sometimes expressed unjustifiably that there is now little need for agencies concerned with single mothers because it has become acceptable, even fashionable, to have a child out of wedlock.[97]

It believed there still was such a need, and described some of the serious problems that persisted:

This year Cathy Charlton and her baby both died when her delivery took place without medical attention in a London bedsitting room. During the next two weeks, two babies were still-born because their school-age mothers gave birth without daring to tell anyone they were pregnant.[98]

Material problems had not gone away, concerning housing and employment as well as access to benefits. Finding suitable housing was still a major problem even for many well-paid professional mothers. Mothers were ever more resistant to the rigours of traditional residential homes, which were closing for lack of demand. Some Homes were converted to group flatlets with support services for mothers.[99] Council housing, especially good council housing, was still hard for unmarried mothers to access. The NC still campaigned for more flatlets, or bedsitting rooms, where mothers and children could live independently, and for increased day-care. The NC was pleased that some former clients 'offered rooms and friendly support' to women in circumstances they had themselves come through.[100]

As well as accommodation, mothers needed adequately paid work or benefits. Women who appealed to the NC had higher ambitions in the workplace than in the past. They would no longer work in residential service jobs.[101] Instead the NC joined the wider, growing campaign for more training, education, better pay, and work opportunities for all women. In a 1972 memorandum to the House of Commons Select Committee on Women's Employment, it recommended equal training grants for men and women; flexible working hours; more day nurseries, after school and school holiday care; and higher 'disregards' to increase the incentive for mothers on benefits to find work.[102]

Despite the change of name, the NCOPF, or One Parent Families (OPF) as it became known—modern, media-friendly charities had snappier titles now— remained dedicated to the needs of unmarried mothers and their children because no other agency was concerned specifically with their welfare.

[96] NC Annual Report 1971–2, 4.
[97] Graham-Dixon, *Never Darken*, 26.
[98] NC Annual Report 1972–3, 3.
[99] NC Annual Reports, 1967–8, 19; 1969–70, 13.
[100] NC Annual Report 1965–6, 28.
[101] NC Annual Report 1970–1, 18.
[102] NC Annual Report 1973–4, 3.

CONCLUSION

The alleged, but much disputed, shift to more relaxed sexual attitudes in the 1960s is not so evident from the perspective of unmarried mothers, particularly those who lacked support from family or partner and were alone and poor, those who had always lived at the margins. The myth of the 'permissive sixties' rests on over-estimation of both the sexual conformity of society in previous decades and the extent of change in the 1960s. Change there was, in particular towards greater openness in acknowledging and discussing such issues as unmarried motherhood and cohabitation, and towards at least the potential for greater sexual freedom for women with the coming of the pill,[103] but it was slow, uneven, and contested. Change moved faster in the 1980s and 1990s, as we will see. It was resisted by campaigners speaking an older language of social purity, and there were still casualties: women and children living, and even dying, alone and in poverty. Some new forms of hypocrisy replaced the old, not least in some popular newspapers, particularly the *Sun* (after its re-launch as a Murdoch-owned tabloid in 1969) and the *Star*. These papers gossiped about celebrity transgressions—particularly the Profumo affair in the early 1960s—and, following changes throughout the popular press since 1945, encouraged greater sexual explicitness, but still 'maintained a vocal defence of "family values", and vigorously denounced anyone who did not adhere to them...while [they] embraced certain aspects of modern "permissiveness" they were keen to ensure that it did not go "too far".'[104] As Mort has put it in his discussion of gay culture in London in the 1950s and 1960s:

The permissive society was neither a revolution in English social life nor a radical break with the sexual cultures that preceded it; rather it was an extremely uneven acceleration of shifts that had a much longer period of incubation.[105]

The experience of unmarried mothers entirely supports this judgement.

---

[103] Cook, *Long Sexual Revolution.*   [104] Bingham, *Family Newspapers?*, 2.
[105] Mort, *Capital Affairs*, 4.

7

A Finer Future?

The Finer Committee on One-Parent Families was set up in 1969 to advise the Government about this growing social issue and how best to respond to it.[1] It sat for four-and-a-half years, causing some impatience among those who had long campaigned, and hoped, for such a review and subsequent change in government policy. It worked against the background of the demographic, cultural, and political changes discussed in other chapters, discussing and responding to them in their report, as we will see. The outcome was an outstandingly clear, well-written, and thorough review of the past and present of the material and legal circumstances of single parents. Completion was slow mainly because the chair and leading members of the Committee wanted a thorough, meticulous report, as it was.

The Committee was appointed in November 1969 by the Labour Minister of Health and Social Security, R. H. S. (Richard) Crossman, and consisted mainly of Labour sympathizers. Labour lost the election of June 1970 and was replaced by a Conservative Government led by Edward Heath. Sir Keith Joseph took over at the Department of Health and Social Security (DHSS). There were rumours and fears that the new government would wind up the Committee, but Joseph was seriously concerned about family deprivation and sympathetic to the Committee and it survived. He was already on cordial terms with the chair, Morris Finer. A researcher for the Committee, himself a Conservative, commented: 'He did not wear the Tory philosophy that the only good thing is a two-parent family that goes to church on Sundays. He was prepared to accept that a one-parent family was not a personal sign of failure.'[2]

At the outset, hopes of the Committee were high. The official historian of the National Council wrote that 'a dream was realized' when it was established, after decades of urging successive governments to investigate the whole question of unmarried motherhood.[3] It welcomed the Committee's remit to investigate all one-parent families, organized a conference on the subject,[4] and prepared a memorandum that was submitted to the Committee and published as *Forward for the Fatherless* (1971). This detailed document made recommendations for relieving the

---

[1] For discussion of its establishment, see p. 130.

[2] Pat Thane, interview with Richard Balfe, April 2008; Tanya Evans, interview with Balfe, July 2006.

[3] Sue Graham-Dixon, *Never Darken My Door: Working for Single Parents and Their Children, 1918–1978* (London: NCOPF, 1981), 8.

[4] The National Archives (TNA)/BN/89/1.

poverty of one-parent families, including a cash allowance for the children and their carers; reform of affiliation and maintenance procedures and other aspects of family law, and of supplementary benefits, including the treatment of cohabitation by the Supplementary Benefit Commission (SBC); fairer housing allocation; improved health and welfare services and antenatal care; day-care, including of schoolchildren in the holidays and after school; and provision of home helps and subsidized holidays. It also put forward a comprehensive plan to support schoolgirl mothers, proposing financial support and the maximum educational opportunities. This document 'summed up the current thinking and future hopes of the Council for improving and safeguarding the lot of one-parent families and their children'.[5]

THE COMMITTEE

The Committee was chaired by Sir Morris Finer, a respected barrister from working-class Jewish origins in East London.[6] He was highly opinionated, with a strong personality and impatient with Committee members who did not share his views. As his biographer described him:

at a time when most practising barristers wore bowler hats and pinstripe trousers and perhaps tended to take themselves rather seriously, he presented a much more modern and undeferential image. No doubt as a result he was viewed with a measure of reserve by some of the more old-fashioned judges. His left-wing views were thought to have impeded his advancement...On the bench [of the High Court, Family Division, from 1972] Finer totally lacked pomposity and quickly demonstrated an ability to relate compassionately to the problems facing men and women whose personal relationships had broken down. He accepted that the policy of the 1969 divorce reforms was, save in exceptional circumstances, to crush the 'empty shells of dead marriages'.[7]

Finer believed that the greatest problem of one-parent families was poverty, not status.[8] He was hard-working and made a major contribution to shaping the work of the Committee and writing the report. He died of lung cancer in December 1974, just five months after its publication.

Leading members of the committee included O. R. McGregor, Professor of Social Institutions at Bedford College, University of London, who had researched and written on the history and present state of the divorce law and lone parenthood and made a major contribution to writing the report.[9] In 1967 the NC had helped fund research by McGregor and his colleagues at Bedford College into the maintenance system for single mothers. This had revealed that only 8 per cent of all single mothers received the maximum £2.10s. (£2.50) maintenance from the

    [5] Graham-Dixon, *Never Darken*, 25.
    [6] S. M. Cretney, 'Finer, Sir Morris (1917–1974)', *Oxford Dictionary of National Biography* (hereafter *ODNB*) (Oxford: Oxford University Press, 2004).
    [7] Ibid.
    [8] Thane–Balfe interview.
    [9] Robert Pinker, 'McGregor, Oliver Ross, Baron McGregor of Durris (1921–1997)', *ODNB* (2004).

father, half received less than 35s. (£1.75) and one-third 25s. (£1.25p). The researchers also found that 80 per cent of natural fathers of 'illegitimate' children had the low income of £14 per week, one-third had less than £10 per week at a time when male earnings averaged *c*.£23 per week.[10] They also revealed the difficulties women had in collecting payments, as McGregor described to the NC's Annual General Meeting in 1967:

If you wish to see misery and unhappiness queuing up before you in an abject parade, visit a Court Collecting Office. There are very often grave difficulties facing women who are collecting their payments. Some Courts for example will not allow them to telephone in advance to discover whether there is any money there for them; they have to come to the Court. This is troublesome and expensive—particularly if it means losing half a day's work. Only a very small number of Court offices are open for payment or collection outside working hours.[11]

The research supported the NC's belief that it was unrealistic in many cases to expect one man's income to support two families, or in some cases even one. It reinforced their demand for a state allowance for fatherless children and their carers and informed the work of the Finer Committee. On the Committee, McGregor was described as having an 'anti-Establishment attitude and distrust of official lines', a 'dominant personality and intolerance towards other members of the committee and their views'.[12] McGregor concentrated on the liability of fathers to maintain and the impact of divorce and separation on women's lives, and on injecting what some believed was an excessive amount of history into the Committee's report and analysis.

Also prominent on the Committee, until his death in 1973, was Richard Titmuss, Professor at the London School of Economics (LSE), the leading social policy scholar of his day, adviser on social security to Crossman.[13] Titmuss was deputy-chair of the SBC when it was established to replace the NAB, which he was very powerful in shaping. He believed that it was substantially reforming NAB practices and removing the legacy of the Poor Law. For example it referred no longer to 'applicants' but 'claimants'—though not yet to 'clients'—and all those with no other means of support now had a right to claim benefit. He was somewhat defensive of the SBC in the face of criticism from witnesses and his fellow-committee members, particularly McGregor.[14] However, Titmuss, McGregor, and Finer were long acquainted and on most matters could cooperate. Titmuss focused his attention for the Committee on benefits and cash allowances. He died of cancer in 1973, before the Committee reported.

D. C. H. Abbot, a civil servant, just retired as Undersecretary in the Ministry of Social Security, who had been 'given the work as a retirement job', was a member of the Committee's steering group with Finer, McGregor, and Titmuss. He was very active though not thought highly influential.[15] Less active were Jessie

---

[10] N. Crafts, I. Gazeley, and A. Newell (eds), *Work and Pay in Twentieth Century Britain* (Oxford: Oxford University Press, 2007), 69.

[11] NC Annual Report 1967–8; Graham-Dixon, *Never Darken*, 24.

[12] Thane–Balfe interview.

[13] A. H. Halsey, 'Titmuss, Richard Morris (1907–1973)', *ODNB* (2004–11).

[14] Thane–Balfe interview.   [15] Ibid.

Scott-Batey, an expert on education from Newcastle, representing the North-east; W. B. (Wally) Harbert, Director of Social Services in Hackney; Sidney Isaacs, a solicitor, the Welsh representative; N. Murchison, a former headteacher representing Scotland; and Marjorie Proops, 'agony aunt' of the *Daily Mirror*. Baroness Macleod, wife of the Conservative politician Iain Macleod, was appointed by Joseph after her husband's death in 1970, apparently because he felt that something should be done for her.[16] She was a JP and the only known Conservative on the Labour-dominated Committee. She was not very active and resigned in September 1972.

More involved was H. G. (Harry) Simpson, innovative Chief Housing Officer of Lambeth, where he had worked hard to ensure that single-parent families were not discriminated against, supported by the then Chair of Housing in Lambeth, Councillor John Major, the future Conservative Prime Minister.[17] Simpson largely wrote the housing section of the report. Also active were Barbara Kahan, one of the first Children's Officers to be appointed following the Children Act, 1948, and at this time Assistant Director of the Social Work Service in the DHSS, and Marie Patterson, the most prominent woman in the Trade Union Congress (TUC). Kahan and Patterson disagreed strongly about whether mothers should take paid work: Patterson favoured it, Kahan, who was influenced by Bowlby and Winnicott, thought they should not work more than, at most, part-time.

EVIDENCE

Committee members, especially McGregor, were aware of the vast gaps in knowledge about one-parent families. A Research Sub-Committee was established, consisting of Finer, Titmuss, McGregor, and Abbott.[18] It was provided with full-time research officers who initiated and analysed research, much of which was commissioned by the DHSS.[19] Following an invitation published in the press in November 1969, the Committee received evidence, mainly written, over two years, from 171 organizations, including a large number of local authorities; professional associations, including the Associations of Chief Police Officers of England and Wales, Children's Officers, Headmistresses, Educational Psychologists, Magistrates, the British Medical Association, and the Institute of Housing Managers; voluntary organizations, including the NC, which was invited to give oral and well as written evidence, the Scottish Council for the Unmarried Mother and Her Child, Barnardo's, Gingerbread, Mothers in Action, the Mothers' Union, the National Citizens' Advice Bureaux, the National Council of Women; also the Labour Party, the Scottish National Party, and the Women's National Advisory Committee of the

[16] Ibid.   [17] Ibid.
[18] London School of Economics (LSE) archive, Minutes of the Finer Committee (hereafter MFM), 1/1/a, 11 Dec. 1969.
[19] TNA/BN 898/249.

Conservative Party. Fifty individuals submitted evidence, including Margaret Wynn, who was the only individual to be interviewed.

She and the representatives of the NC were interviewed in January 1972. The NC's representatives were Lady Stross, its current Chair; Professor Leonard Schapiro, an academic lawyer, previously a member of the legal committee and Chair of the Committee of Management, later a Vice-President; Della Nevitt, housing expert and colleague of Titmuss at LSE; Stephen Lloyd, a solicitor experienced in family law and advocacy for one-parent families, later Chair of NC, 1975–85; and Margaret Bramall, the General Secretary. They provided a history of the organization and elaborated on the problems of one-parent families, stressing the discrimination they experienced in a society founded on the two-parent family unit. They described at length the poverty of lone-parent compared with two-parent families, and the humiliating experiences of many mothers when applying for Supplementary Benefit (SB) or local authority housing. They asked for equal treatment for unmarried mothers with other social groups in the allocation of housing and reiterated that the system of providing maintenance was unsuited to the needs of unsupported mothers and their children, since most mothers avoided the intimidating formality of the court system. Also, most knew nothing about legal aid and could not afford costly proceedings. The NC believed that the system should be completely overhauled.[20] They proposed Children's Aid (CHAID), a special financial allowance to be paid as of right to one-parent families.[21] The Committee acknowledged that the help they had received from Wynn and the NC concerning proposals for a special social security benefit for one-parent families 'was particularly valuable', though, as we will see, they did not adopt either proposal.[22]

Gingerbread, which worked closely with the NC, described the discrimination mothers suffered from officers of the SBC, and in the housing market, the shortcomings of the maintenance system, and the lack of information about their rights to benefits and legal advice. It proposed closer collaboration between the DHSS, the courts, and social services departments.[23] It strongly influenced the Committee's proposals.[24]

The Committee also considered published research, including that of Dennis Marsden. Titmuss in particular was highly critical of Marsden's *Mothers Alone* and that of Peter Marris on widows[25] because of their statistically unrepresentative evidence and findings. The SBC agreed and apparently had no respect for Marsden's research, thinking it irrelevant to current circumstances. They argued that their organization and the treatment of lone parents by the benefits system had changed enormously since Marsden had conducted his research in the mid-1960s, in the

[20] LSE/7/4, 10 Jan. 1972, and LSE/7/14, Apr. 1972.

[21] LSE MFM/1/1/a, 24 June 1971.

[22] DHSS, *Report of the Committee on One-Parent Families*, Cmnd 5629 (hereafter *Finer Report*) (1974), vol. 1, 2–3.

[23] LSE/5/6.

[24] *Finer Report*, vol. 1, 443.

[25] Peter Marris, *Widows and Their Families* (London: Routledge and Kegan Paul, 1958).

days of the NAB of which he was highly critical, as we have seen,[26] and he was guilty of 'tendentious generalization based on inadequate evidence'. They claimed that the SBC now informed claimants fully about their rights and about the different types of benefit available to them and emphasized that benefits had become more generous since Marsden's book was published, though the evidence of the NC and Gingerbread called this into question. They also criticized what they believed was Marsden's failure to cooperate with the NAB as he had promised and to recognize the difficulties of officers carrying out their jobs. They argued that '[he] seems determined to believe the worst of the Board's officers whilst presenting the mothers in the best possible light', though they acknowledged that Marsden's sympathy and compassion for the women he interviewed threw light on their circumstances and their difficulties in rearing children on their own.[27] These comments were a warning to the Committee to tone down their criticisms of the SBC, in order to avoid fierce opposition from a key government department. Finer and McGregor took note when writing the final report.[28]

A major problem was that, still, no one knew how many one-parent families there were. An essential starting point for the Committee was to find out. As they realized, the census was unhelpful since the only lone parents to be enumerated as such were heads of households. Those living with their children in the households of their own parents or of other relatives and friends generally did not show up.

At the Committee's request, the Statistics and Research Division of the DHSS provided the first reliable numbers of one-parent families.[29] The 1971 census was the first to try to define and count one-parent families, which was by no means easy.[30] It listed 49,000 unmarried lone mothers with dependent children, which, as the Finer report put it, 'can be seen to be unrealistic when compared with the 61,000 such mothers receiving supplementary benefit at the end of 1971'.[31] The General Household Survey (GHS) identified 73,000 unmarried mothers in 1971, 30,000 of them working full-time. The GHS, instituted in 1971, was an annual sample survey of the entire population of Great Britain, more frequent and reliable than the census, but still vulnerable to sampling error and failing to account for those who wished to hide their status through shame or for any other reason, and also likely to undercount younger and more mobile people, which included many one-parent families. But it was the best count available. Adding together the 30,000 the GHS found to be working full-time and the 60,000 receiving SB brought the total of unmarried mothers to what the Committee described as a 'more realistic figure' of around 90,000.[32]

Another study by the Office of Population, Censuses and Surveys of a sample of households in the 1971 census containing grandchildren of the head of household

[26] See pp. 162–4.
[27] TNA/BN 89/47, 10 Mar. 1970, and BN/89/16, 24 June–31 Dec. 1970.
[28] LSE MFM/1/1/, 22 and 23 Sept. 1972.
[29] *Finer Report*, vol. 2. App. 4, 78–83.   [30] Thane–Balfe interview.
[31] *Finer Report*, vol. 2, App. 4, 79.   [32] Ibid. vol. 1, 70; TNA/BN/89/44, 1969–73.

estimated the number of unmarried mothers living with their parents at 40,000. Together with the 49,000 unmarried mothers who had been identified in the census, this confirmed the estimate of around 90,000. The statisticians could not estimate the number of covert cohabitees who were in fact unmarried mothers, but the Committee was concerned with one-parent, not illicit two-parent, families.[33]

The DHSS statisticians concluded that in April 1971 there were altogether 620,000 one-parent families in Britain, including over 1 million children, 520,000 of whom lived with their mothers. 90,000 of the mothers were unmarried, 190,000 separated, 120,000 divorced, and 120,000 widowed; 100,000 families were motherless. Unmarried mothers headed only about 15 per cent of all fatherless families.[34]

The Committee was critical of the DHSS and its predecessors 'for the inadequate and unsystematic statistical data provided in their annual reports' and other government publications. They recommended that estimates such as those provided in its Report should in future be published regularly.[35]

THE PROBLEMS OF ONE-PARENT FAMILIES

Another important starting point for the Committee was to establish the specific problems facing one-parent families and how they came about. This, they believed, required them to locate current experience in an understanding of cultural and demographic change and the historical development of family law and the welfare system as applied to lone-parent families. Or, as the Report put it, in McGregor's unmistakable resonant tone, 'by showing how much of the past still survives to darken the present'.[36] It surveyed the histories of the law and welfare in detail, too much detail thought some, including Titmuss.[37] The historical work was mostly by McGregor and his colleagues at Bedford College. They concluded that matrimonial law had greatly improved, especially following the 1969 divorce law, but separation and maintenance procedures, 'like other services fixed in their origins with the obligation to make discriminatory provision for poor people... had tended to provide a poor service'.[38] The Scottish Law Commission provided a survey of the different history of Scottish law.[39]

The Committee was interested in the recent as well as the more distant past. They rightly identified the recent growth of awareness of the problems of lone parents as an outcome of the 'rediscovery of poverty' of the previous decade, and its impact in reinvigorating voluntary action, including the formation of 'self-helpful agencies', as the Committee described them, such as Gingerbread and Mothers in Action.[40] They also stressed the role of demographic change, examining in detail 'the silent revolution in marriage habits in Britain in the last two generations':[41] the increasing rate and declining average age of marriage, falling family

---

[33] *Finer Report*, vol. 2, App 4, 80.　　[34] Ibid. vol. 1, 490–1.　　[35] Ibid. 221.
[36] Ibid. 5, 66–71.　　[37] Thane–Balfe interview.　　[38] *Finer Report*, vol. 1, 9–10.
[39] Ibid. vol 2, App. 6, 152–257.　　[40] Ibid. vol. 1, 5.　　[41] Ibid. 62.

size, and the concentration of childbirth into fewer, early years of marriage.[42] They pointed out that lengthening life expectancy had increased the average duration of marriage, so that divorce had replaced death of a partner, which had long been the major cause of lone parenthood. Hence, commented the Report, 'Marriage breakdown is as inescapable a fact of life today as it was in the later middle ages', though the reasons had changed.[43] They also pointed out that the difficulty of obtaining a divorce, until very recently, had not stopped marriages breaking down in the past, leading to separation and, sometimes, unmarried cohabitation. The Committee commented that 'the relationship between *de facto* and *de jure* marriage breakdown in the past or today cannot be measured and it is therefore impossible to know whether the stability of marriage has changed from one generation to another', though it found the current number of breakdowns 'formidable'.[44]

The Committee argued that 'One parent families are...not things apart: they are an integral product of the normal working of the institution of marriage,'[45] but, due to the historically unprecedented near universality of marriage since the Second World War, 'it is likely that a family in which a mother or a father has to bring up children single-handed will think of itself, and be treated by others, as a little cluster of deviants from the marital norm.'[46] Also, they believed that changing patterns of childbirth had altered and increased women's participation in the labour force from a pattern of full-time work until marriage or first childbirth, followed by full-time domesticity, to a two-phase working pattern, whereby many women resumed work, often part-time after a break for child-rearing. This was broadly true, though it underestimated the traditional need of poorer women to contribute to the household income throughout married life. They were concerned, however, that the lone mother was disadvantaged by the unequal earning power and more limited work opportunities of women compared with men.[47] The inequalities experienced by lone mothers were an aspect of inequalities experienced by all women, against which women, especially in the Women's Liberation Movement, were protesting vociferously as the Committee sat, which the Finer Report firmly argued should be eradicated. As we will see,[48] the Equal Pay Act, 1970, was introduced while they were in session after long campaigns by women in trade unions, the Labour Party, and liberal feminist organizations such as the Fawcett Society, supported after 1968 by Women's Liberation.[49]

More positively, the Committee argued that, in the recent past, women had gained greater independence, social equality, and respect, though still not enough. The Report summed up recent cultural change, and the moral panics that accompanied it, highly positively:

The 1950s and 1960s witnessed the cumulative removal of customary and legal restraints upon certain forms of sexual behaviour...the sexual freedom of men and women has been enlarged. Some think of these developments as creating a 'permissive society'; for others, they represent no more than tardy social and legislative adaptation to new knowledge and

---

[42] Ibid. 22–36.   [43] Ibid. 62.   [44] Ibid. 21.
[45] Ibid. 62.   [46] Ibid. 6.   [47] Ibid. 6, 23–38.   [48] See p. 155.
[49] Elizabeth Meehan, 'British Feminism from the 1960s to the 1980s', in H. L. Smith (ed.), *British Feminism in the Twentieth Century* (Aldershot: Edward Elgar, 1990), 189–204.

to new notions of desirable relations between men and women within and without marriage...One result has been to confer new powers of self-direction upon women, so that
the double standard of sexual morality retains little vitality in law or in life...The collapse
of a marriage used to be denounced as causing shame, particularly to wives, no matter what
the cause might have been...In this climate of opinion, compassion for one-parent families
has grown quickly. The old tariff of blame which pitied widows but attached varying degrees
of moral delinquency to divorced or separated women or to unmarried mothers is becoming irrelevant in the face of the imperative recognition that what chiefly matters is to assist
and protect dependent children, all of whom ought to be treated alike irrespective of their
mothers' circumstances.[50]

Most people are brought up to think of marriage as central to their own personal security
and to the well-being of society. They are therefore quick to interpret changes in the institution as threatening evidence of moral decay.... The history of family law...shows that
such prophecies have always been falsified. We have no fear that the implementation of our
proposals to reduce 'the problems of one-parent families in our society' will weaken family
life or undermine the institution of marriage. Indeed we demonstrate...that the transition
from marriage in the past, buttressed by external compulsions, to marriage in the present,
based on the consent of the parties, has not been accompanied by diminished respect or
enthusiasm for the institution. On the contrary, it flourishes today as never before.[51]

The Committee examined in detail the reasons behind each route to lone parenthood, including 'illegitimacy', which it discussed relatively briefly, as the least trav-
elled route.[52]Th ey found that

the statistics of illegitimacy are extremely difficult to interpret...No convincing explanation has yet been offered for the change in England since the middle of the nineteen thirties
from 5.5 illegitimate births for each 1000 unmarried women aged 15–44 to 19.1 for each
1000 in the years 1961–1965, and none is likely to be forthcoming.[53]

They agreed with the Registrar General's rejection of 'teenage promiscuity' as the
main cause and recognized that 'Many of the babies born illegitimate do not become
members of one-parent families' because they were born to 'unmarried parents living in a stable union'.[54] They pointed to the Registrar General's investigation of the
1961 census, which showed that 'nearly one illegitimate child in three may be born
to a married woman, or, at least, to a woman who would describe herself as married
in the census'.[55] The numbers of children re-registered as legitimate had doubled,
1960–6, and had since fluctuated at around 12,000 per year. Some mothers of
illegitimate children married someone other than the father of the child. Other
children were adopted, but there were no good statistics of the number of illegitimate children placed for adoption. The Committee concluded that 'The number of
children who remain dependent upon their unmarried mothers is a small proportion of the total. Nevertheless the absolute numbers of children in this position at
any one time will be very large,' *c.*120,000, the DHSS figures suggested.[56]

---

[50] *Finer Report*, vol. 1, 7.   [51] Ibid. 7–8.   [52] Ibid. 60–2.
[53] Ibid. 60.   [54] Ibid. 61.   [55] *Finer Report*, vol. 1, 61. *Registrar General's Statistical
Review of England and Wales for the Year 1964, Part III, Commentary*, 64.
[56] *Finer Report*, vol. 1, 62; vol. 2, App. 4.

GUARANTEEING INCOME

The Committee's survey of the working of the SB system pointed out the inability of many divorced or separated men who set up new households to support two families on often low incomes. According to the law, they were obliged to maintain their former wives and families, whether or not they were divorced, and also their current families, whether or not they and their partners were married. The Ministry of Social Security Act, 1966, provided that, for the purpose of assessing benefit claims:

Where a husband and wife are members of the same household their requirements and resources shall be aggregated and shall be treated as the husband's, and similarly, unless there are exceptional circumstances, as regards two persons cohabiting as man and wife.[57]

The NAB had recognized the dilemma in 1953, concluding that:

Extracting money from husbands to maintain wives from whom they are separated is at best an uncertain business; it is easier to enforce the maintenance of those with whom the man is living than of those from whom he is parted.[58]

In practice, the SBC tried to establish whether, and how much, the father could pay for his first family. They generally found that people involved in such claims 'come from the poorest sections of the community', the father could rarely support two families and the SBC had to support one family.[59] But it was claimed by a number of witnesses, though SBC denied it, that even in such circumstances, women would often come under pressure from the SBC to institute legal proceedings for maintenance. This put them under great stress with little hope of success. The Committee concluded that this occurred, probably in a small proportion of cases,[60] but was 'a form of intervention in the matrimonial situation which, in our view, does much more harm than good'.[61] They believed that the current system was of 'enormous complexity' and delivered little.[62] They proposed instead that the SBC should pay an allowance to the female claimant, then investigate the circumstances of the father, taking legal action if necessary to recoup the cost of the allowance where he was judged able to afford it. A necessary corollary was reform of the legal system as it applied in such cases. The Committee recommended a new Family Court to take responsibility for all matrimonial and affiliation cases.[63]

There were tensions among Committee members over criticism, especially, by McGregor, of the SBC on these and other matters, including their treatment of suspected cohabitation. Titmuss, in particular, was concerned that members of the Government would perceive the Committee as too critical of the existing system of maintenance, and they might give too negative an impression of how social workers, institutions, and their staff carried out their duties in often difficult circumstances. Titmuss was also sensitive to any criticism of the SBC regarding the

---

[57] Ibid. vol. 1, 132.   [58] Ibid. 135.   [59] Ibid. 136.   [60] Ibid. 138–9.
[61] Ibid. 143.   [62] Ibid. 148–9.   [63] Ibid. 205.

cohabitation rule and keen to emphasize that any problems had been inherited from the NAB and were in process of reform.

Next, the Committee investigated the financial circumstances of one-parent families. A DHSS analysis of the Family Expenditure Survey (FES)[64] showed that for half of all fatherless families, other than widows' families, and one-third of all one-parent families SB was their main source of income.[65] The numbers in this situation had risen sharply since the mid-1950s, in all categories except widows, faster than among other family types, and faster than rates of divorce and illegitimacy and known numbers of lone parents. A possible explanation was improvement in the benefit system so that the additional income to be gained from full-time work was less for all but higher earning women.[66] About 300,000 fatherless families (100,000 of them widowed) were not drawing SB at the end of 1971, but they were not necessarily better off. About 15 per cent were estimated to have incomes below SB levels. None of the mothers were in full-time work, due mainly to child-care responsibilities, and they were mostly living on part-time earnings plus maintenance. Women with no preschool child had higher earnings.[67] The Committee concluded: 'with only a few individual exceptions, fatherless families are considerably worse off financially than two-parent families.' Widows tended to be better off because they had secure benefits that were not affected by earnings and were more likely than other single mothers to have inherited assets from the father, such as life assurance or a paid-up mortgage.[68]

The Committee was inclined to recommend a special one-parent family benefit to cut through the complexities and give greater security to one-parent families. First, they surveyed in detail the two main proposals put forward: the NC's CHAID and Margaret Wynn's Fatherless Family Allowance (FFA), which both described to the Committee. CHAID had two parts: a national insurance (NI) benefit and a discretionary scheme. The former would be payable in respect of all children living with just one parent, except children of widows, who already received national insurance pensions. The proposed benefits were designed to support the children, not the mother, because no blame could attach to the child for her or his situation. The NC pointed out that:

In the early twentieth century the death of one or other parent was a major cause of child deprivation and was recognized as an insurance risk; now it is the separation or divorce of his parents which puts the child at risk and a refusal to recognise this fact in the social security provisions is to deny the social changes which have occurred in marriage and the status of women.[69]

---

[64] This has been carried out for the Government each year since 1957. It surveys a random sample of private households in the UK, asking about household expenditure and income. Each member of the household aged over 16 is asked to keep records of expenditure for two weeks and is interviewed. Participation is voluntary and the survey is not necessarily representative of all types of household, nor do participants necessarily tell the truth about income and expenditure. A. H. Halsey and J. Webb (eds), *Twentieth Century British Social Trends* (London: Macmillan, 2000), 714.

[65] *Finer Report*, vol. 1, 244; vol. 2, App. 10, 326–56.

[66] Ibid. vol. 1, 244–50.   [67] Ibid. 254–5.

[68] Ibid. 261.   [69] *Forward for the Fatherless* (London: NCUMC, 1971), paras 633–4.

The benefit would be set at the same level as existing, short-term, NI benefits for dependents, e.g., sickness benefit, and would be taxable so that some of the cost would be returned to the Exchequer by higher income beneficiaries. The insurance principle was important because the NC believed that this ensured the benefit was perceived as a right, for which a parent had contributed, not as 'welfare hand-out'. It would be payable on the contribution record of father or mother or both. The period of qualifying contributions would be as short as possible, to take account of the fact that the employment careers of many women were broken by childcare. CHAID would cease on the mother's marriage or cohabitation. Like the, untaxed, widowed mothers' allowance, there would be no earnings rule to reduce the benefit as earnings rose. The NC was anxious that CHAID should supplement earnings to enable lone mothers who wished to work to do so. They believed that the lone mother

should be in the position of being able to decide whether it is in the best interests of her children and herself for her to go to work or to stay at home. She will have to weigh up her wish to be with her child and her child's need for her care against the depression and apathy and frustration from which many unsupported mothers suffer because of isolation and loneliness.[70]

NC recognized that some one-parent families would not qualify for insurance benefits, if, for example, the parents were very young with no employment record. For these, a means-tested CHAID allowance at the same level as the insurance benefit should be administered by the SBC. A cardinal principle of the scheme was that 'the position of the family within our society should not be undermined and fathers should continue to be responsible for maintaining their wives and children'.[71] A father should be required to make contributions, on a scale approved by Parliament, which would take account of income and family responsibilities, giving priority to the family with whom he lived. The contributions would be collected by the state, possibly through the tax system and could cover 30 per cent of the cost of the scheme. Mothers would retain their right to sue for maintenance in court, but courts would take account of the CHAID scheme in ordering payments. Only higher earning men were likely to be ordered to make additional payments. Mothers who were not in paid employment would also draw the means-tested benefit.

The Committee saw much to commend in the proposal but doubted whether the benefit would be

large enough to offer the lone parent a genuine choice whether or not to work, or that the proposal would be equitable as regards other groups and as between one-parent families themselves; and we have grave doubts whether the system suggested for recovering payments from fathers would be viable.[72]

They thought it 'most important that mothers, particularly when they have very young children, should not feel under any pressure to take paid employment'. Those who did not work were likely to end up with incomes below SB level. Also,

---

[70] Ibid. para. 137.   [71] Ibid. para. 631.   [72] *Finer Report*, vol. 1, 279.

like many of their witnesses, they saw serious disadvantages in SB as a source of support for fatherless families. They doubted that many mothers, or their former husbands, apart from the better-off whose need was least, would have paid sufficient NI contributions to cover adequate child benefits. They did not believe that the sums estimated by the NC could be recouped from fathers in the ways proposed. They concluded that the complex CHAID scheme would not meet the needs of one-parent families.[73]

DHSS officials were also critical, as was Titmuss.[74] The DHSS, while acknowledging the considerable effort that had gone into formulating CHAID, rejected it because they were unconvinced that the absent parent could be relied on to provide adequate contributions to prevent the scheme from becoming too costly. They also believed that it was too complicated and too expensive to police to prevent abuses, particularly in the case of unmarried mothers, whose circumstances changed more frequently than other social groups. They also emphasized that other groups in society would find it hard to accept that one-parent families had special needs requiring special treatment.[75] The Inland Revenue believed that the NC failed to understand the tax system and were unconvinced that the scheme was workable.[76]

Margaret Wynn's proposal, FFA, like CHAID, consisted of a child allowance and an adult allowance, payable as of right to all fatherless families, at a flat rate without an earnings rule, and taxable. Part of the cost would be recovered from fathers, partly through the tax system. However, unlike CHAID, it was non-contributory, not an insurance benefit, and not means-tested. It would be paid at a higher rate, equivalent to the widowed mothers' benefit. Courts would determine that a one-parent family existed and assess and recover maintenance from the father, which the court would pay to the administering authority.

Again, the Committee saw much to commend, but feared that it mainly benefited working mothers, who were already better off. They disapproved of the fact that the adult allowance would not be available to lone fathers. The proposal also ran counter to the Committee's determination to reduce lone mothers' dependence on court proceedings. They feared that the involvement of the courts would reduce the number of families likely to claim the allowance. They also doubted whether as much could be recouped from the father through the tax system as Wynn estimated.[77]

The Committee proposed, instead, a contributory Guaranteed Maintenance Allowance (GMA) for lone-parent families. It would be sufficient to bring a family off SB, even if the parent had no earnings, and tapered if they worked or had other income, 'so that it fell by considerably less than the amount by which income increased', so that there was no disincentive to work. It would vanish when it rose

[73] *Finer Report*, vol. 1, 279–81.
[74] TNA/BN 89/17, 27 May 1971. Letter from Sladden at DHSS to Elliott, Inland Revenue.
[75] TNA/BN 89/2, Nov. 1971 and BN 89/27, 15 Dec. 1971 and LSE/7/14, 21 Dec. 1971 and 2/5, Dec. 1971.
[76] TNA/BN 89/18, 17 Aug. 1971.   [77] *Finer Report*, vol. 1, 281–2.

above the level of male average earnings. It included a childcare allowance, subject to the taper and subject to review every 3 months, and a separate, fixed, allowance for dependent children up to age 19, payable to all lone parents whatever their income. Single parents under age 18 would be eligible on the same basis as others, in part to encourage them to stay in education. Maintenance payments would be assessed and collected by the administering authority and offset against the adult allowance so that lone mothers would rarely have to go to court to sue for maintenance.

The Committee believed that a 'cohabitation rule' was unavoidable, since the benefit was intended for parents living without partners. They had 'the strong disposition to recommend the abolition of the rule...We spent much time in this endeavour but failed' because of the 'overwhelming argument in its favour...that it cannot be right to treat unmarried women who have the support of the partner both as if they had no such support and better than if they were married.'[78] But they were anxious to avoid the problems arising from the existing rule and recommended that the 3-monthly assessment should be designed to establish the existence of serious cohabitation rather than casual relationships, though they recognized that some abuse was unavoidable. Claims and assessments would normally be made by post, avoiding the interviews that women often found intimidating. The system should not be administered by the SBC, which, witnesses had affirmed, 'is regarded with suspicion or hostility by some lone parents'.[79] GMA was devised by Finer himself and discussed carefully by the Committee. Its title was chosen because it was thought not to be as emotive or discriminatory as possible alternatives such as Lone Parent Allowance.

Under the GMA, all one-parent families would be treated alike, ending what the Report described as the 'squirearchical approach' inherited from the Old Poor Law, whereby the putative father of an illegitimate child was liable for benefit paid to the child, but not to the mother.[80] The Committee went into great detail about the operation of GMA, and was determined that it should be as uncomplicated as possible.[81] They noted problems with other benefits received by single-parent families, including inadequate pensions, but thought detailed consideration of these beyond their remit.[82]

Not all Committee members agreed. Titmuss, who was terminally ill by the time the proposal was finalized, expressed his views to Finer, who passed them to the rest of the Committee. He believed that any benefit for one-parent families had to be means-tested so they were treated equally with other low-income families, and that they should not, unlike other families, receive a benefit above the SB level. He was concerned about the likely opposition to any proposal that appeared to favour one-parent over two-parent, married, families. He thought that a combination of tax credits and a benefit along the lines of GMA was a step in the right direction, bringing together the tax and social security systems, but was not convinced that the benefit proposed was workable or likely to be effective. Rather, he

[78] Ibid. 340.   [79] Ibid. 308–9.   [80] Ibid. 317.
[81] Ibid. 284–335.   [82] Ibid. 334–55.

believed that the Committee should concentrate its attention on improving the SB system—his personal crusade.[83]

The DHSS was immediately concerned about the cost implications of the proposals. It was keen to avoid controversy and, like Titmuss and others, concerned that lone parents should not be treated more favourably than other low-income families.[84] Tension was exacerbated by disagreements between McGregor and the DHSS over his belief that SBC officers should be investigated for discrimination against unmarried mothers.[85] Officials were hostile to the idea of a universal benefit for lone-parent families, believing, wrongly, that the Committee failed to appreciate the diversity of their circumstances or the pressures on the Government to provide for other disadvantaged groups. In reply the Committee reiterated the special disadvantages suffered by lone parents.

HOUSING

Next, the Committee considered housing, having received much evidence of the difficulties of one-parent families. The introduction of rent rebates in 1972 and rate rebates in 1974 helped with housing costs, but the major problem was access to decent, affordable housing. The lone parents were more likely than two-parent families to share a home, usually with relatives. This was especially true of unmarried mothers, who shared homes in proportions varying from 85 per cent in Dundee to 2 per cent in Haringey, but in larger numbers everywhere than other single parents. In November 1972, 50 per cent of unmarried mothers, 20 per cent of separated wives, 11 per cent of divorced women, and 3 per cent of widows were not independent householders.[86] The remainder were more likely than two-parent families to be council tenants, but these were a small proportion of all one-parent families. They were more likely than two-parent families to live in privately rented, especially furnished, accommodation, which was relatively expensive and often of poor quality. They moved house more often than others. Conditions and amenities in their homes were inferior[87] and they were at particular risk of homelessness. The Committee agreed with a 1974 government circular, *Homelessness*, that local authorities should take responsibility for housing the homeless who currently were the responsibility of social services departments, though the two should work together to prevent homelessness.[88] Currently homeless families were all too likely to be placed in bed-and-breakfast accommodation, with limited facilities, which they had to vacate during the day and where it was impossible to create a home.

The Committee received much evidence from witnesses about discrimination in the allocation of local authority tenancies either against one-parent families in

---

[83] LSE Titmuss collection FCM, 18 Dec. 1972 and 1 Mar. 1972 and LSE/7/12, 26 Feb. 1973. Note of a discussion between the Chairman, Professor MacGregor, and Professor Titmuss.

[84] LSE MFM/1/1/a, 26 Nov. 1970. Evans–Balfe interview.

[85] LSE MFM/1/1/a, 28 Jan. 1971.   [86] *Finer Report*, vol. 1, 358.

[87] Ibid. 357–65.   [88] Ibid. 377–81.

general or unmarried mothers in particular, due partly to the operation of the points system (whereby a single parent could rarely build up as many qualifying points in respect of needs as two-parent families) and residence qualifications, though there were also suggestions of prejudice on the part of officials. The fact that many one-parent families had to move frequently made it particularly hard for them to satisfy local residence qualifications. The NC pointed out:

Some housing authorities impose on unmarried mothers special conditions that they would not impose on ordinary families. A member of our Committee of Management was present when an unmarried mother was offered accommodation in an outer London borough. The mother was warned that she must 'behave herself or be evicted'.[89]

They suggested that there had been a 'slight change' in the attitudes of housing authorities in the recent past, but there was still a tendency to allocate unmarried mothers the poorest housing. A representative of the Association of Directors of Social Work in Scotland told the Committee that in his area, when an unmarried mother asked for accommodation, the social work department might be asked for background information and perhaps a rent guarantee, as they would not for other applicants. The Institute of Housing Managers confirmed there was discrimination against one-parent families, especially unmarried mothers:

they can see no justification for this and recommend that all restrictions should be lifted that militate against families who are not only in housing need, but also have social and economic problems which make life difficult.[90]

The Committee was 'in no doubt that some discrimination exists and that it should cease'.[91]

EMPLOYMENT

Next, the Committee surveyed the difficulties of lone parents in the employment market, in the context of wider gender inequality, in particular the low earning capacity of most women, their limited employment opportunities and difficulty of getting training to improve their skills and earning-power, and of finding childcare during working hours. The Committee repeated that lone mothers of young children should be able to choose whether to take paid work and that flexible working hours and leave of absence to deal with caring responsibilities, of the kind recently introduced in the civil service,[92] should be available for all families, especially lone parents. They pointed out that the Equal Pay Act, 1970, passed while they were in session, would not help in the many occupations defined as gender-specific in a gender-divided labour market, since the law specified equal pay only for 'comparable' work, though they believed that the new law could help to 'promote progressive attitudes and policies'.[93] They also recommended the introduction of rights to

---

[89] Ibid. 382.   [90] Ibid.   [91] Ibid. 383.
[92] Ibid. 416.   [93] Ibid. 414–15.

e in the private sector to equal those already existing in the public
ued that pervasive gender inequality hit lone mothers hardest: 'As
y lip service to the ideal of equality for women while practising
...ation in the very area where it hurts most.'[94]

'THE SOCIAL AND PERSONAL LIFE OF ONE-PARENT FAMILIES'

The Committee also explored the 'social and personal life of one-parent families' based on the evidence they received and other research studies. They were aware that 'It is particularly important to avoid...any stereotyping of their condition.' They pointed to the isolation, loneliness, and stress parents could feel, the disapproval of others, as well as material deprivation, and the stress felt by children. They described the social work, childcare, and other services available to lone-parent families and the criticism by witnesses of their inadequacy, all too often, to meet the complex and variable needs of the families.

The Committee looked particularly into Mother and Baby Homes for unmarried mothers, which, they pointed out, 'have their origins in the penitentiaries and reformatories, residential charitable institutions established in the eighteenth and nineteenth centuries'.[95] Th ey concluded that

Modern mother and baby homes have moved far away from those grim beginnings. Some homes now exist—mainly those run by local authorities—which see their function solely in terms of the provision of accommodation and care; other homes may still have a reforming purpose, but pursue this end far less obtrusively than in the past. Although there are still restrictions, rules in the majority of homes are not as stringent as they were, and most homes are now prepared to allow a resident to stay for as short or as long a time as necessary.[96]

They found that in 1966 about one-sixth of unmarried mothers in England and Wales were accommodated in the 172 homes in England and Wales, 148 provided by voluntary (mainly religious) organizations, and 24 by local authorities. The number was falling. The NC told the committee that 'currently' (in 1972/3) there were just 65 homes in England and Wales, of which 10 were maternity homes and 55 provided care before and after confinement. The main reason seemed to be lack of demand, though there were difficulties in staffing the homes. The Committee commented that:

More mothers seem to prefer to remain in the community before and after confinement; the stigma attaching to illegitimacy appears to be less than it once was and parents may be more willing now to allow their daughters to stay at home with their babies. In addition, mothers who intend to have their babies adopted are more likely to have them placed with a foster mother or prospective adopters before they go to their adopted families than previously.[97]

---

[94] *Finer Report,* vol. 1, 425.   [95] Ibid. 480.   [96] Ibid.   [97] Ibid.

They added in a footnote: 'This would seem attributable to changes in attitude rather than to the reduction in the numbers of illegitimate births.' The latter had fallen since 1967 but numbers were still higher than in the 1950s and early 1960s.[98]

The Committee drew most of its information on Mother and Baby Homes from a research project undertaken by the NC, funded by the Ministry of Health and the Gulbenkian Foundation, examining policies and practices in the Homes. The report, by Jill Nicolson, was published in 1968.[99] She found that 'there was considerable confusion about the purpose and function of the homes among the persons running them…the mothers themselves and even among social workers.' Also, 'standards were generally below what would be tolerated in other forms of residential accommodation and that residents were faced with more rules, restrictions and invasions of privacy than would be found in, say, a hostel or a boarding house.' Nicolson found 'the two Homes where rules were most numerous and restrictive were also those in which an evangelical approach was most evident.'[100] Homes had, perhaps, improved, but not a lot. The NC tried, instead, to find 'friendly landladies' with whom mothers and children could stay, but they were all too few.

The Committee, Nicolson, and the NC believed that homes still had a role in providing accommodation, care and, sometimes, treatment. The Committee quoted the NC in *Forward for the Fatherless*:

Mothers who need them will be mainly those who have very special difficulties, in addition to the pregnancy. They will include mothers who are very young, or who have no families, or who have grave emotional problems, as well as mothers who are disabled or have histories of psychiatric or physical illness or delinquency.[101]

They recommended further investigation into likely demand for homes and the needs of unmarried mothers. Meanwhile,

Local authorities should squarely face the responsibilities that they already have, under Section 1 of the Children and Young Persons Act, 1963 and section 22 of the National Health Service Act, 1946…to ensure that there are adequate facilities for unmarried mothers who need them. What is required is a concerted plan with voluntary organizations; and we believe it to be particularly important that in tackling this local authorities should make efforts to see that non-sectarian accommodation is available for those mothers who prefer it.[102]

They recommended that the 'standard of provision must be raised', pointing out that in England and Wales (unlike Scotland) Mother and Baby Homes were one of the few forms of residential accommodation for which registration and inspection were not required and proposed its introduction. They recognized that this was no panacea. Jill Nicolson had pointed out that 'one of the worst voluntary homes had

---

[98] Ibid. 480 n. 3.
[99] Jill Nicolson, *Mother and Baby Homes* (London: Allen and Unwin, 1968); *Finer Report*, vol. 1, 481.
[100] *Finer Report*, vol. 1, 481.
[101] *Forward for the Fatherless*, para 281; *Finer Report*, vol. 1, 481.
[102] Ibid.

been inspected regularly for years'.[103] But they believed it would be 'a significant move in the right direction'.[104]

The Committee examined also the situation of certain 'special groups'. These included prisoners' families who, they believed, had specific difficulties that were beyond their remit, and 'immigrant families', whose problems had been described by a number of witnesses. The British Association of Social Workers described

the varying significance that illegitimacy has in different cultures. In Pakistani communities, a girl who has an illegitimate child may be cast out from her family, whereas for many West Indian girls it is the normal pattern to have one or more children before marriage, and a husband who may stay with her for only a short time. Whereas in the West Indies, however, the girl will have the support of her extended family, in Great Britain this is probably lacking, and instead she may have to turn to the Social Services for help.

The Committee included no representative of Britain's growing immigrant communities and did not feel competent to assess their difficulties. It recommended further study and joint discussions of the issues between social and education services at local and national levels.[105]

FINER'S CONCLUSIONS

The Committee's overall conclusions and recommendations were, firstly, that

The fragmentation of the law and the agencies through which it is administered is the result entirely of historical causes deriving from a society in which there was one family law for the rich, a second for the destitute, and a third for people in between. The triple system in modern form still bears the marks of its discriminatory origins. Its persistence is irrational and productive of much inefficiency and personal hardship. It needs thorough reform.[106]

These issues should be resolved by the institution of a new, independent 'family court' designed to 'apply a single and uniform system of family law'. This was not the first time such a court had been suggested. It had been proposed, unsuccessfully, by the 1965 White Paper *The Child, The Family and the Young Offender* and thereafter, according to the Finer Report, 'remained the subject of favourable if loosely structured comment and discussion'.[107]

Also, 'given that the community already bears much of the cost of sustaining the casualties of broken homes and of unmarried parenthood, and cannot avoid continuing to do so', there should be rationalization of the methods through which it made payments, 'primarily in the interests of the lone mother and her child, but also with the view of achieving a more satisfactory recovery from the liable relative where that is possible'. The Committee recommended that the SBC should take

---

[103] Nicolson, *Mother and Baby Homes*, 149; *Finer Report*, vol. 1, 482.
[104] *Finer Report*, vol. 1, 482.
[105] Ibid. 483–4.
[106] Ibid. 491.
[107] Stephen Cretney, *Family Law in the Twentieth Century* (Oxford: Oxford University Press, 2003), 746.

responsibility for assessing and collecting maintenance, relieving the mother of a difficult and stressful responsibility, whilst administering their other major recommendation, a new one-parent family benefit, the GMA.[108] In the end, the Committee had not thought feasible, or likely to be politically acceptable, a new body to administer the new benefit.

They set out procedures for reform in detail, proposing that:

The putative father of an illegitimate child should be a liable person subject to assessment and recovery by the GMA authority of an amount up to the level of State payment for mother and child.[109]

Where the absent parent was comparatively well off, the formula should enable the lone mother and the children to share in his affluence, while ensuring that he retained a reasonable share of his higher income for himself. It should also be such as would not cause the absent parent's financial position to be worse in relation to his commitments than that of the lone mother in relation to hers.

Before benefit is withdrawn on grounds of cohabitation from a claimant in receipt of weekly payments of supplementary benefit, she should be given a written statement of the alleged facts, and if she denies any of them, the case should go to the appeal tribunal, benefit being continued in the meantime. Where benefit is withdrawn because of cohabitation, but the cohabitee is not supporting dependent children of the claimant of whom he is not the father, the exceptional needs payment for the children which the Commission are now prepared to pay for four weeks should be continued for three months.[110]

The Committee urged that 'the utmost priority' be given to the introduction of the Government's proposed Child Benefit scheme. The Committee also recommended that the maternity grant be paid without any contribution conditions to all mothers, as the NC had proposed. They also advocated improved official statistics to provide accurate numbers of one-parent families.

The Committee stated that housing was 'the largest single problem of one-parent families...second only to financial difficulties and to a considerable extent exacerbated by them'. They acknowledged the recent improvements due to the national rent and rate rebate schemes, and the Committee supported the proposals in the 1973 Housing White Paper that housing authorities should have comprehensive responsibility for all housing needs in their areas, including responsibility for homeless people.[111] The Committee declared that 'Discrimination against lone parents in the allocation of council housing on grounds that they are "less deserving" than others should cease.'[112] Housing need should over-ride other qualifications such as residence. The SBC and housing authorities should help lone-parent families furnish their homes when needed.

The Report recommended that the GMA should be designed to give lone parents, 'whether mothers or fathers', the choice whether to take paid work, though, it stated, 'Wherever possible children under 3 should not be parted from their parents for long periods.'[113] Employers should be more flexible about

---

[108] *Finer Report*, vol. 1, 492. [109] Ibid. 504. [110] Ibid. 507.

[111] *Finer Report*, vol. 1, 508–9. [112] Ibid. 510. [113] Ibid. 516.

working hours and conditions: 'But the fundamental issue is the need to raise the pay and status of working women.' The Equal Pay Act, 1970, had made a start, but more comprehensive anti-discrimination legislation, as recently proposed (and introduced in the Sex Discrimination Act, 1975), was essential. Women should have wider employment opportunities, 'so that they are no longer concentrated in a relatively narrow range of low-paid jobs'. They recommended that employment rights be equalized between full- and part-time workers, including a minimum period of notice, remedies for unfair dismissal and redundancy payments. Maternity leave should be extended to 'at least' 3 months paid, 3 months unpaid leave in the public and private sectors. Also, 'Radical changes are required in the sphere of curricular and careers guidance for girls in secondary schools,' and employers should offer girls the same day-release opportunities as boys, extend them for both and make adequate arrangements for the training of women workers. Training arrangements should be flexible enough to allow for family responsibilities.[114] The Committee concluded, however: 'We emphasize...that all this must be accompanied by a change in attitude on the part of women themselves, who must be prepared to take a more active role in their own interests.'[115]

Social workers should be better trained to understand the needs of lone-parent families. The specialist local authority social services departments created in 1971 had taken over much of the responsibility for lone-parent families previously held by social workers employed by voluntary organizations. Important changes occurred while the Committee was sitting. It recommended 'considerable expansion' of day-care services, with priority for lone parents, and flexibility, taking account of parents' work commitments, with more play-groups in deprived areas, not necessarily provided by local authorities. Employers should be encouraged to provide day-care. Childminders and schoolteachers should be trained in awareness of the needs of children of lone parents and of pregnant schoolgirls, providing home tuition for the latter where appropriate. There should be investigation of demand for Mother and Baby Homes and tighter regulation.

Surprisingly, the Report made no recommendations about domestic violence though it identified this as a cause of partnership break-up, perhaps because, in theory, the courts provided redress. However, the publication, in the same year as the Report, of Erin Pizzey's *Scream Quietly or the Neighbours will Hear You*[116] and the high profile that the Women's Liberation Movement gave to the issue provided unavoidable evidence of how rarely the courts gave redress to 'battered wives' as they were popularly known.[117]

---

[114] *Finer Report*, vol. 1, 513–14.
[115] Ibid. 513.
[116] Erin Pizzey, *Scream Quietly or the Neighbours Will Hear You* (1974; repub. London: Enslow, 1978).
[117] Cretney, *Family Law*, 752–6.

THE RESPONSE

The Finer Report was published in July 1974, after the election of a Labour Government in February 1974. *The Observer* called it 'one of the major social documents of the century'.[118]The NC reported:

A sudden upsurge of hope when the Finer Report was finally published...many telephoned us, asking excitedly how soon the special one-parent family allowance was starting. When it became clear that it was recommendation and not a reality, the optimism gave way to despondency and fear.[119]

Poverty campaigners were generally supportive but not uncritical. Frank Field, then Director of CPAG, criticized the means-tested character of GMA, pointing out, rightly, the normally low take-up of means-tested benefits and consequent exclusion of many in need.[120] Peter Townsend feared, astutely, that 'to press too hard for a policy for the separateness of one-parent families, may be to damage their long-term interests and more attention should be given to measures that helped poorer two-parent families and all women'.[121]

Unfortunately publication of the Report coincided with the international economic crisis following the quadrupling of oil prices forced by the Organization of Petroleum Exporting Countries (OPEC) following the Yom Kippur war between Israel and Egypt—the 'Oil Shock'. Sharp cuts in public spending followed. It was a bad time to propose expensive welfare reforms.[122] Rising inflation and unemployment together with cuts in services worsened the situation of many one- (and two-) parent families. The NC reported in 1974–5:

The overwhelming dilemma for one-parent families this year has been their increasing privation. Many of them were already living in poverty. Nearly half were living at or very near subsistence level and throughout the year their situation deteriorated as a result of inflation...Now...the call for a reduction in public spending and for a halt in local authority expenditure threatens the housing and practical services essential to the welfare of these families.[123]

In the following year they recorded increasing hardship:

Punitively high food bills, increased taxation and transport costs, cuts in housing programmes and in the practical services, such as day nursery provision, have borne particularly harshly on one-parent families because their average income is half that of families with both parents.[124]

[118] Quoted Hilary Macaskill, *From the Workhouse to the Workplace: 75 Years of One-Parent Family Life, 1918–1993* (London: NCOPF, 1993), 35.

[119] NC Annual Report 1974–5, 1.

[120] F. Field, 'How Good a Model is FIS for a Means-Tested GMA?', *Poverty*, 31 (1975), 17–22.

[121] P. Townsend, 'Problem of Introducing a Guaranteed Maintenance Allowance for One Parent Families', *Poverty*, 31 (1975), 21–39.

[122] Jim Tomlinson, 'Labour and the Economy', in D. Tanner, P. Thane, and N. Tiratsoo (eds), *Labour's First Century* (Cambridge: Cambridge University Press, 2000), 65–6.

[123] NC Annual Report 1974–5, 1.　　　[124] NC Annual Report 1976–7, 8.

The NC faced growing pleas for help from lone parents, including increasingly from fathers.[125]They reported in 1974–5:

This year we have been horrified by the size of the fuel bills which parents had to face. The number of applications for help with gas and electricity debts has increased substantially...It is practically impossible for people with insufficient money to get by each week to save enough to pay large quarterly bills.[126]

But the NC itself was undergoing a financial crisis, hit by inflation while donations fell. Its annual grant from DHSS was now £40,000, having risen from £15,000 in 1970–1, and its total income was £86,594, but in 1975–6 it spent an additional £21,197. It decided to drop grant-giving until the position improved.[127] In fact, it stopped this permanently and thereafter focused on referring clients in need to social services departments and advising them how to negotiate the maze of welfare benefits, the legal system, and other hazards. For example:

In January 1978 Helen Takka received a [*sic*] electricity bill for £200 and was threatened with disconnection. Her flat was all electric, she was pregnant and her five-year-old daughter had bronchitis. She had been away from work because of her child's illness. Our intervention prevented disconnection and an arrangement was made to settle the account.[128]

The DHSS grant rose further to £50,000 in 1976–7. The NC tried hard to raise donations, continued its TV appeals, and appointed a full-time fundraiser in 1974, with no appreciable effect. The Friends of Fatherless Families, later Friends of One Parent Families, organized a succession of Ballet Galas from 1969, the fourth of which in 1977 raised over £19,000. The 'One-P Appeal' was launched in 1975, devised by an advertising executive on the Committee of Management, to raise funds for both the NC and Gingerbread, 'to arouse public awareness of the plight of one-parent families and to forge a closer working relationship between the two organizations'. This and the events associated with it gained wide press coverage but few donations. But the NC carried on.[129]

Shortly before publication of the Finer Report, there was a meeting between Brian O'Malley, the Parliamentary Secretary at DHSS, and Brian Abel-Smith, special adviser to the new Minister for Health and Social Security, Barbara Castle (Richard Crossman died of cancer shortly after the election). Castle described Abel-Smith and his colleague Tony Lynes as 'my conscience'.[130] She did much to move the DHSS and SBC further from its Poor Law and NAB heritage. After the deaths of Titmuss and Finer, Abel-Smith, Titmuss's colleague at LSE, took over the role of promotion of the Report in government. It was agreed at this meeting that a special benefit for one-parent families was needed, but its introduction depended on the timing of other government proposals for negative income tax and family endowment, both relevant to the needs of one-parent families. They also recognized

125 Macaskill, *From the Workhouse*, 42.   126 NC Annual Report 1974–5, 8.
127 Graham-Dixon, *Never Darken*, 27.   128 Macaskill, *From the Workhouse*, 37.
129 Graham-Dixon, *Never Darken*, 32.
130 Barbara Castle, *Fighting All the Way* (London: Macmillan, 1993), 461.

that the Treasury would oppose the benefit on grounds of cost. It was decided that it could not be introduced before 1977 at the earliest.[131]

Castle later described how, when she read the Finer report,

my heart sank…It proposed a new cash benefit, the guaranteed maintenance allowance, plus generous child allowances, and it admitted that the cost would be very high unless the new allowances were means-tested. I certainly did not want to create a new area of means-testing at the heart of social policy, but I also knew that my spending demands were making me unpopular in Cabinet. Dick Bourton, one of my deputy secretaries, who instinctively sided with the Treasury on everything, had already warned me sourly, 'The trouble, Secretary of State, is that your bids add up to the total amount of public expenditure available for all departments.' I therefore decided that my right course was to concentrate on introducing the party's 'child endowment' scheme designed to absorb both family allowance and child tax allowances in a new universal benefit payable to the mother for every child as of right.[132]

The Government did, however, quickly make the more popular, and necessary, move of increasing old age pensions, and took the innovative step of ensuring that in future they rose in line with average earnings. Widows' pensions were improved, although they were already better provided for than other single parents. Overall, the Government preferred to try to help all families in hard times rather than risking unpopularity by singling out one-parent families. But they came under strong pressure from the one-parent family campaigners (see Fig. 7.1).

In a letter to Denis Healey, Chancellor of the Exchequer, before the Finer Report was published, Barbara Castle acknowledged the difficulty of consigning a one-parent family benefit to the uncertain future. She believed the Report demonstrated that one-parent families needed extra help, though she was uncertain

Fig. 7.1 'Campaigning for the Finer Report', National Council of One Parent Families, The Women's Library, Box 120 Envelope 5/OFF/11/5/a.

---

[131] TNA/BN 89/268. Meeting, 21 May 1974.
[132] Castle, *Fighting*, 469–70.

what form it should take and at what level. She argued that 'To reject the Committee's main recommendations outright…would I believe bring us under intolerable pressure from the poverty lobby.' Healey replied that she should not make any promises about a future benefit because of the cost involved, which was estimated at about £190 million a year. The Treasury was unconvinced by the Finer proposals for recouping part of the cost from fathers. Castle was advised to insist that she could not accept the GMA. Any promise of such a benefit in future would, Healey argued, 'inspire immediately the maximum pressure on us to fulfil all the expectations thus aroused, and store up the maximum risk of embarrassment for us later on'.[133]

Castle was convinced, however, that she must say something positive about the Government's attitude to lone parents in her speech to Parliament announcing publication of the Report. Predictably, the Government came under pressure to hold a debate on the Report, especially following an early day motion by Helene Hayman, recently elected as a Labour MP and previously deputy Director of what was now NCOPF. But it avoided major debate for over a year. In a speech to the Commons on 2 July 1974 Castle stated that the Government accepted the need for additional support for one-parent families in principle, but it could not make any promises on the lines of the Finer proposals because it was already committed to diminishing poverty in all families by providing more generous Child Benefit for every child, in place of family allowances that excluded the first child, while abolishing child tax allowances which benefited the better off.

This was duly introduced in the Child Benefit Act, 1975, to be implemented in 1977. As a concession to the campaigners, the family allowance (£1.50 per week) was granted to the first child in one-parent families one year earlier. It was named Child Interim Benefit, was tax-free, and paid irrespective of the lone parent's income. When the full scheme was introduced in 1977 the payment for the first child was only £1, but one-parent families received an extra 50p. The Government discussed increasing the rate of Child Benefit from 1978 while removing the 50p premium for one-parent families. 'Following endless pressure' from the NC it was not only retained but increased to £1. The NC persuaded the Government to drop the parental age limit of 16 so that a younger parent—who would unavoidably be unmarried—could claim Child Benefit—the only cash social security benefit from which parents under 16 were not specifically excluded.[134]

From April 1975, a lone parent with taxable income received the same personal tax allowance as a married man, though less than a married couple in which the wife worked. By the end of the 1970s, it was estimated that this benefited 25,000 lone parents.[135] In 1976 the Government allowed lone parents on SB to earn £6 per week before losing SB, the amount allowed to the wife of a husband on unemployment benefit. This concession, which reduced the disincentive for those on

---

[133] TNA/BN/89/268, 26 June 1974. Note of a meeting in the Treasury.
[134] Graham-Dixon, *Never Darken*, 9.
[135] HM Treasury, *Taxation of Husband and Wife*, Cmnd 8093 (London: HMSO, 1980), 41.

benefits to work, was abolished by the Conservative Government led by Margaret Thatcher in November 1980.

In 1976 the SBC published a report, *Living Together as Husband and Wife*. This reiterated the need for a cohabitation rule, especially since one-parent families were now receiving more generous benefits than before, but stated that they had reviewed their guidelines and officers were now instructed to allow couples time to decide whether they wished to stay together, rather than withdraw benefit before establishing whether the relationship was stable. The 1976 Social Security (Miscellaneous Provisions) Act substituted the phrase 'living together as husband and wife' for 'cohabitation'. Nevertheless, appeals against the operation of the rule increased and a growing proportion were successful. Of the 340 appeals heard in 1974 16 per cent succeeded, compared with 747 and 22 per cent in 1978.[136]

In November 1975 Helene Hayman asked in Parliament when the Government would consult local authorities on implementation of the Report. Castle received a deputation from the Finer Joint Action Committee (FJAC) urging implementation. This was formed soon after publication of the Report by over 28 groups, including the NC, Shelter, Gingerbread, the Women's Institutes and MIND, who lobbied together regularly on poverty and welfare issues. The FJAC held marches and conferences and issued publications, including *Forward from Finer*, on the housing needs of lone parents, income, family courts, and other key recommendations of the report.[137] It wrote to all local authority Directors of Social Services and of Housing, pointing out the recommendations of the Report that they could implement without legislation.[138] It received some support in the press, particularly in *The Times*, whose respected social policy correspondent, Pat Healy, regularly reported its views and activities.[139]

The Committee's proposals for legal reform won much support among professionals involved in the family justice system, who formed pressure groups including the Family Courts Campaign.[140] But there was also strong, and on the whole successful, opposition from magistrates to the proposal that they should lose their responsibilities for family law.[141] The Inheritance (Provision for Family and Dependants) Act, 1975, incorporated important changes regarding inheritance and, at last, provided that blood tests should be used to establish paternity. Also, it committed Parliament to the principle of equal rights for children born in and out of wedlock, for which the NC had campaigned since its foundation. But it did not put these into law. In 1979 a Law Commission report 'tentatively' favoured 'the principle that the status of illegitimate should be abolished and that the law

---

[136] *Report of the Supplementary Benefit Commission for the Year Ended 1979* (London: HMSO, 1980). K. Kiernan, H. Land, and J. Lewis, *Lone Motherhood in Twentieth-Century Britain* (Oxford: Oxford University Press, 1998), 183.

[137] Macaskill, *From the Workhouse*, 35.

[138] NC Annual Report 1974–5, 12.

[139] TNA/BN/89/295/2, 11 Sept.–20 Oct. 1975. *Guardian*, 7 Apr. 1975; Peter Townsend, 'Money for a Million Children', *New Statesman*, 27 June 1975.

[140] Cretney, *Family Law*, 748–9.   [141] Ibid. 750–2.

applicable to the legitimate should apply to all children without distinction'. This came about at last in 1989, following the Family Law Reform Act, 1987.[142]

The Government was committed to improved housing and helping women combine work and motherhood through improvements in maternity leave and child care. Castle and the Government hoped, by focusing on these aspects of the Report, that the issue of the GMA could be avoided. The Employment Protection Act, 1975, introduced statutory maternity leave for the first time. Subject to being employed for at least 2 years for over 16 hours per week, or for 5 years if they worked shorter hours, women gained the right to 11 weeks' leave before the birth and 29 weeks after, receiving 90 per cent of their average pay for 6 weeks and statutory sick pay for 12 weeks. They were guaranteed reinstatement in similar work, though not to the same job, on their return. This was an important break-through though it was limited and benefited better-off women most. Many women found the continued lack of affordable childcare the main barrier to returning to work.

In August 1977 the Government issued a circular, *Housing for One-Parent Families*, based on the Finer recommendations. The most important proposals were for an end to discrimination against one-parent families in the allocation of council housing. Also, a lone parent in mortgage arrears could be granted payments to prevent their becoming homeless.[143] As a result, the 1977 Housing (Homeless Persons) Act, which the NC was closely involved in formulating, put responsibility for all but the 'intentionally homeless' onto housing departments. The NC welcomed this, as potentially increasing the chances of lone mothers, including unmarried mothers, gaining council housing. However, they were concerned that the 'intentionally homeless' clause 'could harm lone parents who are forced to leave atrocious accommodation where they are paying extortionate rents or who are unable to cope with living in the home of their parents when this becomes unbearably stress-ful'.[144] Or, they might have added, fled from violent partners. However, the 1976 Domestic Violence and Matrimonial Proceedings Act at last enabled women to gain injunctions against violent men.

The NC was severely disappointed at the Government's failure to implement the GMA in particular. It 'had dreamed of being freed from the struggle to achieve decent living standards for one-parent families and of being able to remove the legal disadvantages of illegitimacy. Instead it has had to carry on fighting.'[145] Supporters felt that

The virtual jettisoning of Finer has made it difficult for the Council to do more than bark constantly, in its role of 'watch-dog' for lone parents when legislation or decisions of the Supplementary Benefits Commission, or the petty-mindedness of local bureaucrats seemed to threaten the frail prosperity of its clients, and to wag its tail when any hoped for advance was made, such as the Housing (Homeless Persons) Act 1977.[146]

---

[142] Cretney, *Family Law*, 563–5.   [143] NC Annual Report 1976–7, 16–17.   [144] Ibid.
[145] Graham-Dixon, *Never Darken*, 8.   [146] Ibid. 27.

Parliament showed little interest. Neither Government nor opposition committed themselves to the GMA. After a further FJAC deputation to the Ministry in October 1975, Margaret Bramall and Jenny Levin (a lawyer, Committee member, and later Vice-Chair of the NC), who had represented NCOPF, expressed their disappointment at the lack of action on the Report, especially since the circumstances of many one-parent families were deteriorating due to rising inflation and unemployment. They were told that the Government was reluctant to implement the Report in a piecemeal fashion and that government departments were being extensively consulted.[147] Thereafter the NC worked with CPAG and other supporters, including Dennis Marsden, to try to adapt the lone-parent benefit proposal to make it more acceptable to the Government.[148]

A 'furious' Barbara Castle[149] was dismissed from DHSS in April 1976 in favour of David Ennals when James Callaghan replaced Harold Wilson as Prime Minister. Callaghan was said to oppose the new Child Benefit because he believed it would reduce male pay packets at a time of trade union protest about falling real wages, though, in reality, it gave benefits to women in families and was likely to have no net effect on household incomes at lower income levels.[150] Almost immediately, Ennals announced that the Benefit would be delayed indefinitely, while a family allowance of £1 per week would be introduced for the first child. Castle joined the outcry against this, supported by male trade unionists and women's organizations. Following the leaking of Cabinet papers on the subject by Frank Field, Director of the Child Poverty Action Group,[151] Callaghan was forced to accept a compromise whereby the Child Benefit was phased in over the following 3 years. Pressure from the NC ensured that one-parent families continued to receive the increased supplement of 50p per week. This acknowledged that one-parent families had special needs, though the NC thought it still too little and the rules too complex. It pointed out that over 100,000 qualified parents failed to claim—the normal weakness of discretionary benefits.[152] By 1979 the full Child Benefit was in place at a rate of £4 per week per child.[153] In the same year Labour lost another election and Margaret Thatcher replaced Callaghan at the head of a Conservative Government.

CONCLUSION

The Finer Report was the most thorough description and analysis of the situation of lone-parent families of the twentieth century. By no means were all its proposals implemented—such far-reaching proposals rarely are—but it led to significant

[147] TNA/BN/89/295/1, 10 Oct. 1975.
[148] NC General Papers, Benefits 1976–91, 5/OPF/12/1 1976–91.
[149] Castle, *Fighting*, 489.
[150] Howard Glennerster, *British Social Policy since 1945* (Oxford: Blackwell, 1995), 119–20.
[151] *Guardian*, 5 Oct. 2010.
[152] NC Annual Report 1975–6, 3, 7; 1977–8, 8.   [153] Castle, *Fighting*, 492–3.

changes in benefits, housing, and, probably, public attitudes. The Report also had a long-term impact on the legal system. Stephen Cretney has described the Report as Finer's most substantial memorial, a 'landmark in the history of the relationship between law and social policy', which 'engendered a great deal of enthusiastic support from many of those with knowledge and experience of the problems it had so clearly identified', and 'the long-term influence of the report has been greater than seemed likely in the late 1970s'.[154] The proposals for Family Courts were at last realized in the Children Act, 1989, and provision for conciliation rather than adversarial relations between divorcing and separating couples were given statutory recognition in the Family Law Act, 1996, 'and at the turn of the century had become part of the conventional wisdom'.[155]

The Committee achieved some changes in public policy which improved the lives of lone-parent families, but many problems continued.

---

[154] Cretney, 'Finer', *ODNB.*   [155] Ibid.

8

The Struggle Continues: 1980s–90s

INTRODUCTION

Much had changed and improved since the National Council for the Unmarried Mother and Her Child (NCUMC; since 1973, the National Council for One Parent Families, OPF[1]) was founded in 1918. Nevertheless, a report by a House of Commons Select Committee in 1980 reported that the infants of young, unsupported mothers were still more likely to die or suffer permanent handicap than other children. This had been the main trigger for the establishment of the NCUMC in 1918 and 62 years later it was still a scourge.[2] The report made 152 recommendations aimed to eliminate it. The new Conservative Government, elected in 1979, the first ever in Britain headed by a woman, Margaret Thatcher, challenged these conclusions and stated—rightly as it turned out—that the report raised 'unrealistic expectations' that this inequality would be reduced in the foreseeable future.[3]

In reality, the 1980s and early 1990s saw the most outspoken and persistent attack on lone mothers by representatives of any government of the century. It was coupled with exhortations to 'return' to supposed 'Victorian values', or, later, to go 'Back to Basics', meaning, ahistorically, universal chastity and long, stable marriages. It was also closely associated with the Conservative assault on the Welfare State. This was defined as encouraging the work-shy to idle in comfort on generous benefits. Poorer people were blamed for their situation rather than perceived as having needs that deserved support from the more fortunate. Increasingly lone mothers, and especially stereotypical teenage mothers living on council estates, were presented as archetypical welfare scroungers. The welfare system, in turn, was blamed for encouraging marriage break-up and lone parenthood. This rhetoric arose from another unprecedented trend of the period—which both triggered the attacks and challenged them—the growing number of unmarried mothers, openly cohabiting couples, and one-parent families. Yet everyday public tolerance of unconventional families was as evident, and as new, as the passionate official condemnation of them.

---

[1] See p. 131.
[2] See p. 14; House of Commons Social Services Committee, *Perinatal and Neonatal Mortality*, 1980; Hilary Macaskill, *From the Workhouse to the Workplace: 75 Years of One-Parent Family Life, 1918–1993* (London: NCOPF, 1993), 44.
[3] Macaskill, *From the Workhouse*, 44.

Births outside marriage in UK increased from 11.5 per cent of all births in 1980 to an unprecedented 27.9 per cent in 1990 and 33.6 in 1995.[4] In 1971, 45 per cent of these were jointly registered by both parents; in 1981, 58; in 1995, 78 per cent.[5] Many of these unmarried parents were living together with their child(ren) more openly than had been possible at any other time of the century. The percentage of non-married women in Great Britain, aged 18–49 who were officially estimated as cohabiting was 3 in 1979, 5 in 1985, 9 in 1991, and 13 in 1998.[6] It was a sign of cultural change in itself that official estimates of cohabitation in England and Wales were now provided for the first time.

Overall, the numbers of one-parent families rose from 940,000, 1 in 8 families with 1.5m children, in 1980, to 1.3m, 1 in 5 families with 2.1m children in 1992.[7] The numbers rose in all categories of single parents other than widows—single, separated, and divorced.[8] Lone parents, 90 per cent of them female, were regionally dispersed, but concentrated in the poorest districts. In 1985 Strathclyde, in Scotland, had the largest number in the UK, 48,672, mostly in Glasgow. The highest proportions in England lived in the poorest inner London Boroughs. In Lambeth in 1981 they constituted 32.3 per cent of all families, followed by Hackney (31.5), Hammersmith (29.6), Islington (28.5), Southwark (28.2), and Camden (28.2). The national average for England and Wales was 14.1 per cent.[9]

BLAMING THE VICTIM 1

In 1983, leaked government papers referred to support for one-parent families as 'subsidizing illegitimacy and immorality',[10] and such negative views were not only expressed by representatives of the Government. OPF became increasingly concerned that

It is not only 'the authorities' who must be watched—so must the 'caring' professionals, journalists and academics. The two-parent family is equated with normality and is widely regarded as a model of perfection for family life. …

The professional tendency is to label one-parent families as 'problem families' or not to regard them as 'proper' families. Academics and journalists who consider them as 'indicators' to a range of pathological ills such as child battering, inadequate parenting, shoplifting and juvenile delinquency (but not as 'indicators' of poverty) are being careless and unjust. Sadly this negative public image is too frequently internalized by the families themselves.[11]

Despite the supposed spread of 'permissive' attitudes since the 1960s the tendency to blame 'broken families' for social problems, including crime, indeed to blame

---

[4] K. Kiernan, H. Land, and J. Lewis, *Lone Motherhood in Twentieth-Century Britain* (Oxford: Oxford University Press, 1998), 56.

[5] Ibid. 42.

[6] Jane Lewis, *The End of Marriage?* (Cheltenham: Elgar, 2001), 34.

[7] Macaskill, *From the Workhouse*, 44.

[8] Lewis, *End of Marriage*, 36.

[9] NC Annual Report 1985, 16.

[10] Macaskill, *From the Workhouse*, 44.   [11] NC Annual Report 1978–9, 5.

the presumed effects of a presumed general spread of a 'culture of permissiveness' became much more overt. OPF spent much of the 1980s and early 1990s challenging the most sustained and influential public stigmatization of one-parent families of their existence. Whatever cultural changes there may have been, public attitudes remained deeply divided.

Noting this division, in 1986 the President of OPF, O. R. McGregor, now ennobled as Lord McGregor of Durris, wrote in his 'Foreword' to its Annual Report:

My pessimism about the future and fate of my vulnerable fellow citizens has grown deeper with every Annual Report that I have written in recent years…People at large seem to be becoming more impatient, less understanding and very ready to think and talk about problems in terms of moral blame.

But, he added:

Happily such views are not universal. In the course of dealing this year with temporary financial difficulties, we learned how much good will exists among politicians, civil servants and philanthropists.[12]

Though by 1988, OPF's seventieth year, he believed that 'the situation of one parent families has not improved since the publication of the Finer Report 14 years ago'.[13] The Annual Report commented: 'There can be few areas of public policy making so dominated by prejudice and ignorance and so little informed by fact.'[14]

HOUSING

One such area was housing policy. OPF was still concerned about housing for one-parent families, despite the improvements promised by the 1977 Housing (Homeless Persons) Act.[15] This concern 'inevitably deepened with the election of a government which was pledged to reduce investment in local authority housing'.[16] The more so when some local authorities seized the moment to press for reduction of their obligations under the 1977 Act, complaining of the 'burden' of homeless people, including unmarried mothers, who, they asserted, became pregnant only to qualify for council housing. When OPF challenged the London Borough of Brent for evidence of its claim that 'a significant minority' of women did so, the council was forced to admit that the claim was incorrect and 'not to be taken seriously'.[17]

Attacks by government supporters and Ministers became ever more explicit. In 1987 Conservative MP Rhodes Boyson was quoted as saying that 'one-parent families were bringing up hooligans and muggers'. In the following year, the Chancellor of the Exchequer, Nigel Lawson, was quoted in *The Times* as claiming that the

[12] NC Annual Report 1985–6, 1.   [13] NC Annual Report 1987–8, 1.   [14] Ibid. 5.
[15] See p. 166.   [16] NC Annual Report 1978–9, 14.
[17] NC Annual Report 1979–80, 13; Box 112 5/OPF/10/2/b, *One Parent Times*, 1979–80. Winter 1980.

benefit system was contributing to the rise in family break-up.[18] Also in 1988, Margaret Thatcher, in an address to the National Children's Home charity, referred to the 'growing problem of young single girls who deliberately become pregnant in order to jump the housing queue and gain welfare payments'.[19]

This became a Conservative refrain, despite a total lack of evidence. At the Party conference of 1988, Social Services Secretary John Moore declaimed:

Is the hope of a council flat and a guaranteed income a factor in unmarried teenage pregnancy? Is the knowledge that the state will provide a factor in fathers deserting their families? What is to be done about the nearly half million fathers who pay nothing at all towards the support of their wives and children?[20]

Observers had noticed that more single mothers had council homes than in the past, not that an important reason was how rarely they qualified for one before the change in the law in 1977.[21] There were rumours that the Government planned to open hostels to replace the housing entitlement of homeless unmarried mothers, as a disincentive.[22] In 1989, OPF commissioned a survey from the Trust for the Study of Adolescence, *Young Single Mothers Today*, which found no evidence that young women deliberately became pregnant to obtain a council home.

If any woman was desperate enough to become pregnant, persuaded by the public assertions that it would lead to a comfortable council home and generous benefits, she was likely to be disappointed. Housing problems prompted almost one-third of calls by mothers to OPF by the later 1980s. There had indeed been real changes following the 1977 Act. Most lone parents were now housed by local authorities—almost 60 per cent of all one-parent families lived in council housing, compared with 20 per cent of two-parent families. But the housing allocated to one-parent families was often 'unsatisfactory and sub-standard'.[23] This was due partly to allocation policies. OPF found that, in some London boroughs, one-parent families were automatically regarded as 'problem' families and housed in the least favourable accommodation. It was also due to the relative poverty of these families and the rapid growth of owner-occupation among those who could afford it. The sale of council houses in the 1980s predictably led to the best housing being sold off. The remaining homes were relatively less desirable, fewer in quantity, and increasingly confined to the poorest people with the greatest difficulties.

The experiences of mothers who appealed to OPF were very different from those broadcast by leading members of the Government. OPF's Annual Report described in 1980 the plight of Sally Medhurst, who

Lived in a small isolated seaside resort and in summer she had a living-in job at a hotel... every year she had to accept short-let tenancies [in winter] until she could return to the hotel in the summer.

---

[18] *The Times*, 10 Nov. 1988, quoted in Macaskill, *From the Workhouse*, 44.
[19] Ibid. 45.   [20] Ibid.   [21] See p. 166.   [22] NC Annual Report 1988–9, 15.
[23] Macaskill, *From the Workhouse*, 48.

She became pregnant whilst in a short-let tenancy and was given notice to quit. She approached the Housing Department who said there was nothing they could do. We telephoned them and were told they only had 130 council properties and that, as no more would become available, she would have to move to another area. We emphasized that even if they had no places available, they had a legal duty to place her as a homeless family in temporary accommodation until a place could be found. Even after her baby had been born, the Housing Manager argued that it would be impossible to place her in bed and breakfast accommodation because in such a tightly-knit community no landlady would accept an unmarried mother and child. However we persisted and in due course a tenancy was found for Sally and her baby.[24]

In 1983 OPF encountered Sarah Andrews, who

has spent eight months in bed and breakfast accommodation with her baby. She has been told she has to spend a year or more in halfway housing on a run-down estate reported to be infested with maggots and cockroaches. We are putting pressure on the local authority to rehouse her quickly and to improve its temporary accommodation.[25]

Two years later they reported:

Fatima Ali cares for her seven year-old child on her own. She lived in a ground floor council flat, and was subjected to severe racial harassment. The flat was burgled six times, windows were broken and excrement and rubbish were pushed through her letter box. Only after intervention by ourselves and the local Community Relations Council was Mrs Ali finally rehoused.[26]

Not conditions likely to encourage a woman to become pregnant. As the OPF commented in 1984:

Although Britain in 1984 is a very different society from 1918, many of the problems besetting single parents are remarkably the same: poverty, inadequate or inappropriate housing, difficulties in combining work and child care, and a hostile and unhelpful legal system particularly for children born outside marriage.[27]

In 1986 OPF described the experience of Lorna O'Malley, who, aged 18, came from Ireland to London 'to escape the stigma of her unmarried pregnancy'. She intended to have the child adopted, but, like so many mothers, changed her mind after the birth. The child was placed in unpaid foster care because Lorna's landlady would not let her bring the child home. The foster mother lived some distance away and would not allow Lorna free access to her baby. Lorna's landlady then served her a notice to quit, but the local housing department refused to accept her as homeless because the landlady had not obtained a court Possession Order. A vigilant and supportive health visitor, concerned that the baby would be taken into care when she considered Lorna a capable mother, worked with her social services department and OPF to put pressure on the Leader of the Council and the Chair of Housing. The housing department then accepted Lorna as homeless and she was given temporary accommodation with her baby and the promise of a permanent home.[28]

[24] NC Annual Report 1979–80, 66.   [25] Macaskill, *From the Workhouse*, 48.
[26] Ibid.   [27] NC Annual Report 1983–4, 1.   [28] NC Annual Report 1986–7, 7.

Despite all the evidence that unmarried mothers had great difficulty obtaining council homes, especially desirable homes, the peculiar myth of the feckless teenager getting pregnant just for the sake of a council flat persisted, and OPF continued to challenge it.

'BENEFITS'

The financial difficulties of one-parent families were at least as great as those due to housing. For all the public assertions about the comfortable lives of single mothers on benefits, a major role of OPF in the early 1980s was helping lone parents in poverty. They pointed out that the main reason why one-parent families were poor was that almost 90 per cent were headed by women and, despite equal pay and anti-discrimination legislation, women had more restricted employment opportunities than men and, in 1985, on average still earned only 66 per cent of average male pay.[29] Even in full-time work many of them were poor. In 1980, 42 per cent of one-parent families were mainly dependent on supplementary benefits, fewer than in the early 1970s;[30] in 1983, the percentage had risen to 51. By 1990, 80 per cent of lone parents, with 2 million children, received state benefits, despite repeated government assertions of their determination to reduce 'welfare dependency'. Most received no regular support from the absent parent. The numbers receiving maintenance through the courts fell from half of all one-parent families in 1979 to 30 per cent in 1989, mainly due to unemployment among fathers and inefficient collection by the Department of Social Security and the courts.[31] The average weekly income of the lone-parent family was 79 per cent of the average two-parent family at the beginning of the 1980s.[32] OPF's experience taught them: 'whether they are working or not, lone parents do manage money extremely well and it is the lack of money that causes them difficulties'.[33]

In 1980 2,000 parents, one-third of the total, contacted OPF about financial problems and much of its work involved chasing local social security offices because of slow or incorrect payments, and advising parents on their rights to benefits.[34] For example:

Janice Wrigley applied for SB and was asked for details of her child's father. When she refused to disclose his name, the social security office decided to assume that he was paying her maintenance of £5.20 a week for her child (equivalent to the SB rate) and reduced her benefit by that amount. OPF advised her that the decision…had been wrong and that she should have received her full benefit even though she did not wish to give details of the

---

[29] NC Annual Report 1985–6, 5; A. Weale, B. Bradshaw, A. Maynard, and D. Piachaud, *Lone Mothers, Paid Work and Social Security* (London: Bedford Square Press, 1984), 33.

[30] Kiernan et al., *Lone Motherhood*, 264.

[31] Helen Barnes, Patricia Day, and Natalie Cronin, *Trial and Error: A Review of UK Child Support Policy* (London: Family Policy Studies Centre, 1998), 9.

[32] Kiernan et al., *Lone Motherhood*, 264.

[33] NC Annual Report 1990–1, 3.   [34] NC Annual Report 1980, 5.

father. After representation, the social security office admitted the mistake and paid her the £5.20 a week, back-dated to the time of her claim.[35]

Also:

Tracey Bowen, aged 16, is a schoolgirl mother who read in Marjorie Proops' advice column in the *Daily Mirror* that from November 1980 she could claim SB. Her local social security office told her that she was not eligible and 'not to believe everything she read in the papers'. OPF contacted the local office and quoted the new SB regulations. It turned out that the office had not known about the change and had not even received a copy of the new regulations. After a further written complaint, Tracey received the full Benefit and an apology.[36]

The Conservative Government claimed to be dedicated to encouraging claimants to get off benefits on to paid work and in 1980 it introduced a tapered 'earning disregard' only for lone parents on benefit. Claimants working up to 30 hours a week could now keep up to £12 a week of their earnings, more than before and, importantly, after deduction of work expenses, including travel and childcare. This was a real, but small, incentive to find employment.

But the 1980 Social Security Act substantially reduced the discretion of local social security officials to decide on claims. Benefits were linked to the price index and no longer to average incomes, and gradually fell in real value.[37]

One mother wrote to OPF in 1985 about her situation following these changes:

The government allows us single parents no opportunity for improving our financial status...I'm just outside the earnings limit to qualify for any benefit whatsoever—suddenly I lost free school meals rent/rebate, FIS and health benefits. By the time I've paid these, I may as well be on Supplementary Benefits for all the hassles of work and being left with no spare money...it really isn't worth it.[38]

The decision to tax workplace nurseries in 1984—at which OPF protested[39]—did not encourage employers to provide them and further discouraged lone parents from working due to the major disincentive of the cost and scarcity of child care. Curiously, childcare was only subsidized for parents on benefits, not those in work, however low-paid. This decision was reversed in 1990 when it became clear that the numbers of lone mothers in employment was falling (see below). OPF campaigned to persuade the Government to support the European Economic Community (EEC) draft directive on parental leave, family leave, and flexible working, with little effect.[40] It worked with other voluntary organizations, CPAG and Project Fullemploy, on a study of the problems of mothers seeking work, training or education, which proposed more and cheaper childcare as the most effective way to help them. This won all-party support in the Commons, but no enthusiasm from the Government.[41]

There were rumours, rather, that the Government planned to abolish Child Benefit, which would have multiplied lone parents' financial difficulties. OPF

[35] Ibid. 6.   [36] Ibid.   [37] Box 112 5/OPF/10/2/b, *One Parent Times*, Feb. 1981, 17.
[38] Macaskill, *From the Workhouse*, 50.   [39] NC Annual Report 1984, 7.
[40] NC Annual Report 1985, 2.   [41] Ibid. 9.

worked with CPAG on a *Save Child Benefit* campaign.[42] It was not abolished, but nor was it increased in line with inflation, so it fell in value. OPF commented:

This year we have witnessed the re-emergence of an insidious view that one parent families are to blame for all the ills of society. Some popular and all too familiar myths seem to be gaining ground not just in fringe circles but amongst respected public figures. Single parents now not only have to cope with poverty and the problems that brings, but they also stand accused of bringing up delinquent children, of scrounging off the state, of encouraging immorality and of undermining the family. Indeed in a curious way they are not considered to be 'families' at all.[43]

With Gingerbread, they launched a campaign to dispel the myths and

urge decision makers and politicians to accept that the one parent family is a valid family form that is here to stay...we believe that OPF—working with other organizations that share our concerns—has a major role to play in ensuring that the facts rather than the fictions influence the debate about family life in Britain.[44]

With little effect, as we have seen. OPF pressed on, with other voluntary groups, including Barnardo's, Relate and the Family Policy Studies Centre, to challenge claims that only families headed by married parents could lead stable, successful lives and that punitive policies would reduce lone parenthood. They pointed out that the severity of the Victorian Poor Law had not prevented high levels of 'illegitimacy' and prostitution.

As the recession deepened, OPF received ever more requests from parents for financial advice due to the difficulty of finding work and the inadequacy of benefits.[45] In 1982, two additional staff were taken on to cope with the volume.[46] In OPF's view,

The current economic climate and the measures taken to restore the economy adversely affect poor families most of all. We do not share the government's view that social security benefits cannot increase until the economy revives, for this means that one-parent families and other poor families bear the brunt of the nation's economic ills.[47]

The difficulties were made worse by continued maladministration of SB:

Ms C became pregnant while age 16 and still at school. She wanted to continue her education and bring up her child at home with her mother and father. She applied for SB but was told she would not be eligible after her baby's birth unless she left school...Ms C was also refused a grant for essential items for the baby and told that she must give information about the baby's father...After reading *Single and Pregnant* she was able successfully to challenge all these points.[48]

The voluntary sector continued to play a crucial role in supporting claimants whose claims for benefit were unfairly refused.

The changes to benefits in 1980 were just a preliminary to a more radical overhaul of the social security system led by Norman Fowler, Minister for Health and

[42] NC Annual Report 1986, 4.   [43] Ibid.   [44] Ibid.
[45] NC Annual Report 1982, 10.   [46] NC Annual Report 1983, 1.
[47] Ibid. 10.   [48] NC Annual Report 1982, 11.

Social Security, in 1985. This was proclaimed as 'the most fundamental overhaul of our social security system since the second world war'.[49] One of its aims was to cut costs. It led to the Social Security Act, 1986, which came into force in 1988. This replaced Family Income Support (FIS), which was previously available for families with at least one member working for low pay for a minimum of 24 hours per week, with Family Credit (FC).[50]

The main stated aim of the reform was to reduce the complexity of the system and minimize the discretion which increased complexity. Exceptional needs payments and additional allowances for special circumstances were replaced by fixed rates depending on the age and household circumstances of the claimant. Loans— no longer grants—for special needs were available from a new Social Fund. The discretionary system had indeed become complex, mainly because, as it sought to respond to need, it became ever clearer that people had complex and diverse needs. The 'simplification' reduced the incomes of many claimants, especially long-term claimants, including many lone parents. OPF described one such parent:

Sandra Brown, aged 18, is a single parent living with her mother. In preparation for the birth of her baby, Sandra received £25 Maternity Grant [abolished under the new Act]. We also helped her to claim a single payment of £115.66 to cover the cost of nappies, baby clothes, cot and bedding, pram, feeding bottles and baby bath. She therefore received £140.66 to cover the cost of all basic items of clothing and equipment she needed for the baby... Under the new proposals Sandra would only be entitled to a flat-rate £75 [loan] from the social fund.[51]

They reported that 'Desperate parents contacting us for advice on how to buy clothing, shoes or other essentials for a growing family can only be advised to ask local charities and churches for help.'[52] More than before, the voluntary sector tried to fill holes in a shrinking welfare state.

The changes purported to 'encourage individuals to provide for themselves', but they created real disincentives to the main means of doing so, taking paid work, despite the Government's claim that this was precisely its aim. The 1986 Act raised the 'earnings disregard' to £15, but earnings were now assessed *after* payment of tax, national insurance, travel, or childcare costs so its real value fell. For families with dependent children, where the 'breadwinner' was in full-time work but with low earnings, FIS was replaced by the FC and the children lost their entitlement to free school meals or welfare foods and owner-occupiers were not eligible for housing benefit. This led to a net loss of income for many people and reduced the incentive to work for many women. OPF protested from the time the proposals were published in 1985 and found more to protest about after they were introduced. It sought to keep abreast of the new legislation in order to advise parents, but commented that 'The task is made more difficult by the fact that sometimes details of the new regulations are not announced until just before

---

[49] DHSS, *Reform of Social Security*, vol. 1, Cm 9517 (London: HMSO, 1985), 'Preface'.
[50] Kiernan et al., *Lone Motherhood*, 189.
[51] NC Annual Report 1985, 14–15.   [52] NC Annual Report 1989, 8.

they are implemented and by staff shortages in DHSS local offices [due to cuts in public expenditure] which delayed claims, often leaving claimants with no money.'[53] Younger parents suffered from the withdrawal of benefits for 16 and 17 year olds not on a Youth Training Scheme (YTS).[54] Those on such schemes received no help with childcare costs, though these were allowable to older people on Employment Training Schemes (ETS). However, ETS were not open to lone parents with children under school age who had not been registered unemployed for six months and those who did enter the schemes were hampered by a shortage of registered childminders.[55] Better day-care provision appeared not to be a priority for the Government: 'Day care will continue to be primarily a matter of private arrangements between parents and voluntary resources except where there are special needs,' stated a Government Minister in 1985.[56] A reform claimed to reduce complexity in the social security system had in fact increased it while failing to improve benefits or to increase incentives to work.

Rising unemployment made it still harder for lone parents to find work. The numbers in work fell. In 1981–3, 41 per cent of lone parents were employed or seeking employment, full- or part-time, compared with 39 per cent by 1991–3. At both dates 30 per cent of never-married mothers were working.[57] Over the same period the proportion of all women in employment rose from 56 to 62 per cent. Until the early 1980s, lone mothers' employment rates were higher than those of mothers living with partners and most worked full-time. Those who could combine work with childcare had long been under pressure from the social security system to do so, evidently with some success.[58] By 1992 three-quarters of lone parents were on Income Support (IS; the latest form of means-tested benefit for non-employed people replacing Supplementary Benefit), while its value fell. One-Parent Benefit continued for as long as parents had a child in long-term, non-advanced, education, but it was not inflation proofed, which reduced its real value as the cost of living rose. The additional tax allowance for lone parents was not up-rated in 1991 and 1992.[59] Whether in work or on benefit, life became harder for lone mothers.

WORK AND TRAINING

Another key theme of central government policy was encouraging voluntary action and, where possible, delegating welfare work to voluntary agencies. OPF rose to the demands as far as it could, but, like other organizations, knew its limitations and continued to press for improved government provision as the only means to

---

[53] NC Annual Report 1988, 7–9.   [54] NC Annual Report 1989, 7.   [55] Ibid. 9.

[56] Undersecretary of State at DHSS, *Hansard*, House of Commons, 18 Feb. 1985, col. 397.

[57] Kiernan et al., *Lone Motherhood*, 128.

[58] H. Land, 'Slaying Idleness without Killing Care: A Challenge for the British Welfare State', *Social Policy Review*, 21 (2009).

[59] Kiernan et al., *Lone Motherhood*, 266.

meet the extent of need. It encouraged the formation of local self-help groups, affiliated to OPF, to advise and support families around the country. There were over 260 such groups by 1985 giving advice to 7,500 families.[60] From 1985 OPF ran legal and welfare rights courses for lone parents and community groups.[61] More than 1,300 people attended 51 sessions in the first year.[62] OPF then won a three-year grant from the EEC to run courses in financial management for lone parents,[63] followed by pre-employment courses advising on how to get a job, education and training opportunities, childcare and benefits, which again had very positive responses from parents.[64] All the evidence suggested that lone parents were keen to find ways out of dependence on welfare, given the opportunity that OPF tried hard to provide.

OPF continued to use the media to promote their services. In October 1984 a 30-second announcement on London Weekend Television was shown seven times over one weekend, resulting in 1,000 enquiries to the advice service in the following month.[65] In 1987 they advertised in the popular *Sun* newspaper for lone parents to contact them for information about benefit entitlements.[66] They maintained a high profile. In 1991–2 over 15,000 lone parents, from all parts of England and Wales, contacted them for help.[67]

Particularly after Sue Slipman[68] took over as Director in 1985, OPF focused on helping parents into education, training, or employment as the best means to help them to independence. With help from a philanthropic trust, it gave grants to parents in training or education towards the costs of childcare, books, travel, equipment, and projects.[69] Unmarried parents in higher education suffered discrimination from government regulations because they could not now claim the additional grants for dependants available to married, widowed, divorced, and separated single parents, contrary to the practice when the grant scheme was established in the early 1960s.[70] In 1985 OPF took up the case of Peggy Shaffter, who was studying for a social work qualification at Middlesex Polytechnic and was refused both the additional grant available to other lone parents and the Student Hardship payment administered by the DHSS. OPF helped her challenge the Secretary of State for Education in court, alleging sex discrimination, contrary to the principles enshrined in the EC Directive on equal access for men and women to vocational training. The High Court found that existing grant regulations did result in indirect sex discrimination because four times as many female as male lone parents were ineligible for additional dependents' grants. It ordered removal of those parts of the regulations and awarded Peggy the grant she had been denied.[71]

---

[60] NC Annual Report 1985, 15. [61] NC Annual Report 1986, 5. [62] Ibid. 16.
[63] Ibid. [64] NC Annual Report 1987, 17. [65] NC Annual Report 1985, 1.
[66] NC Annual Report 1988, 10. [67] NC Annual Report 1991–2, 2.
[68] Born 1949, attended Stockwell Manor Comprehensive, South London, and University of Wales, Lampeter; National President, National Union of Students, 1975–6; Area Officer National Union of Public Employees, 1979–85; Director NCOPF, 1985–95.
[69] NC Annual Report 1982, 12.
[70] NC Committee of Management minutes (hereafter CMM), 7 Oct. 1965.
[71] NC Annual Report 1986, 6.

Despairing of effective government policies to help lone parents into work and training, despite the official rhetoric, OPF itself sought to fill the gap. In 1988 they prepared a report, followed by a conference, on *Helping One-Parent Families to Work*, promoting the idea that, to earn a decent family income, parents had to escape from means-tested benefits into paid employment. It emphasized particularly that Government and employers needed to recognize the potential gains from employing lone mothers, such as their reliability. Since recruitment campaigns aimed at women returners often did not take account of the specific problems of lone parents, especially for childcare, it established a Return to Work Strategy in 1988 and developed a specially tailored training programme for parents, with crèches provided. Half the funding came from the EC, the rest from companies, local authorities, and charitable trusts.[72] By 1990 over three-quarters of parents who attended training courses said it had changed their lives for the better. Most moved into paid work or education or training for work. Five per cent became self-employed.[73] The success was sustained. Almost 1,000 parents were trained in the first four years of the programme, though finding work became harder as unemployment increased. Others were helped by OPF into further education and training, for example:

Having been accepted for an A-level course, Jenny Simpson, a lone mother of three, found it hard to meet fares and childcare costs. She received a grant, £75 from us, and wrote: 'It was extremely heart-warming to receive not only the monetary support but also the encouragement and support I felt on reading your letter.'[74]

A continuing major obstacle was shortage of affordable childcare. The Employment Act, 1988, granted lone parents £50 per week for childcare only if they joined the newly created Employment Training Scheme. OPF supported this, but it was available only if parents had been registered as unemployed for at least six months, and even then they were hampered by the shortage of registered childminders and the value of the allowances was eroded in later Budgets. OPF carried on trying hard to encourage the Government, local authorities, and employers to improve childcare, with little effect. With other organizations they campaigned on the issue in the European elections of 1989.[75]

McGregor resigned in 1989 after 14 years as President. He had reservations about OPF's focus on employment. The Council determined to find a successor who represented business and could promote the employment strategy. Their choice was Ian Hay Davidson of Laing and Cruikshank, the investment banker,[76] later described as someone for whom 'cracking heads and being unpopular has been something of a career',[77] rather a contrast with the background and inclinations of previous Presidents, but better suited to the Government in office. And, as we will see, unlike members of the Government, he seemed more inclined to 'crack the heads' of critics of lone parents than of the parents themselves. He remained President until 1995.

[72] NC Annual Report 1989, 18.   [73] NC Annual Report 1990–1, 6.
[74] Macaskill, *From the Workhouse*, 49–50.   [75] NC Annual Report 1989, 11–12.
[76] NC CMM, 9 July 1991.   [77] *Sunday Times*, 26 Jan. 2003.

Slipman worked to persuade the Government to fund training programmes and childcare for lone parents, as positive not punitive means to help them into employment. She had several meetings with the Head of the Government's Policy Unit and submitted a policy paper which the Government welcomed.[78] OPF embodied its proposals in *Helping One Parent Families to Find Work* (1989), which seems to have prompted John Moore, Minister at DHSS, to establish a major policy review on lone parents.[79] Meanwhile, the campaign continued. Representatives of OPF lobbied members of relevant government departments, where necessary using the personal contacts of their Chair, Catherine Porteous.[80]

This time the effort paid off. In 1990, Patrick Nicholls, Parliamentary Undersecretary of State for Employment, attended an OPF Return to Work course and, in 1991, the government granted £1 million to expand the initiative.[81] From 1992 OPF ran 24 training courses a year for two years, nation-wide, while working with large employers, training bodies, the Benefits Agency, and Employment Services to promote the employment prospects of lone mothers. It also helped establish childcare schemes.[82] For those unable to attend courses, it produced a guide to returning to work, including details of tax and benefit implications and training and education initiatives in their area. In 1992, it held meetings with Safeways and Tesco, both potentially large employers of single parents, though not necessarily at higher levels or pay, followed by similar meetings with other large employers, to persuade them of the potential value of lone parents as reliable employees. It produced and sold an Information Manual for Employers, which was a successful revenue raiser.[83] In 1991 Slipman joined a working group established by Gillian Shepherd, Secretary of State for Employment, and lobbied for favourable treatment of lone parents in employment.[84] In 1994 local partnerships were established in six areas to continue training for three more years.[85] In 1994 the Government at last introduced a Childcare Allowance for parents on Family Credit.[86]

However, parents' problems persisted even when they did their best to work full-time. One mother's experience expressed the difficulties of many in the early 1990s:

Janet Osborne is a single parent earning just above the national average income for women. But because of the system's failure to meet lone parents' needs she would be £4–£10 a week better off on Income Support.

From her taxed earnings plus her child and one-parent benefit she pays her childcare and travel to work expenses: this leaves a maximum of £115.21 a week. In a week when she has

---

[78] Tanya Evans, interview with Sue Slipman, 14 July 2005; CMM, 10 Oct. 1987, 11 Jan. 1988.

[79] *One Parent Times* (Spring 1989), 5/OPF/10/2/b.

[80] Chair 1988–93 after membership of the Committee of Management since 1969. Chair of the Friends of OFP and responsible for successful fundraising drives. She was also a magistrate and governor of a comprehensive school. NC CMM, 21 Feb. 1989; 3 Apr. 1989; Tanya Evans, interviews with Sue Slipman and Catherine Porteous, 12 July 2005.

[81] NC CMM, 21 Feb. 1990.

[82] NC Annual Report 1990–1, 'Foreword'; CMM, 24 Oct. 1990.

[83] NC CMM, 5 May 1992, 15 June 1992.   [84] NC CMM, 15 June 1992.

[85] NC Annual Report 1993–4, 9–13.   [86] Ibid. 2.

to buy medicines, visit the dentist, or in very cold weather she would be even better off out of work as income support would cover all of these.

Janet travels 20 miles to work, as there are no jobs nearer home. 'When you've got a job you keep it don't you?' she says. 'If I didn't work I'd go mad—I dread the thought of vegetating. Its good for Thomas: at the weekend we do special things together. If he wasn't happy I'd give up because his happiness is the most important thing to me.'

Janet could earn more if she sat accounting exams. 'I thought about going back to college—that it might be worth living off the state for a while if something good came out of it. But I phoned the college and childcare there is £40 a week...that's more than our food bill.'[87]

FAMILY LAW—THE END OF 'ILLEGITIMACY'

More positively, the Family Law Reform Act, 1987 achieved something OPF had aimed for since its foundation: it removed all legal differences between 'legitimate' and 'illegitimate' children. A Law Commission Working Party on Illegitimacy was set up in the mid-1970s, chaired after the death of Hon Mr Justice Cooke in April 1978 by Stephen Cretney, then a Law Commissioner, later of Bristol then Oxford Universities and a distinguished legal historian whose insights have greatly assisted the writing of this book. The OPF submitted its views and a copy of its publication *Illegitimate*, which described the inequalities arising from the law as it stood.[88] The Working Party reported in 1979 that it favoured 'the principle that the status of illegitimacy should be abolished and that the law applicable to legitimate children should apply to all children without distinction'. Their final report in 1982, in which the input of OPF was acknowledged,[89] reinforced this. The recommendation came about partly because English law had become increasingly difficult to reconcile with international conventions with which the UK had acceded, notably the European Convention on Human Rights and the European Convention on the Legal Status of Children Born out of Wedlock.[90]

The Government responded slowly. OPF kept up the pressure and in 1983 held a seminar, *Women and Children outside Marriage*, debating and supporting the proposals. In 1984 they sent 100 MPs a detailed briefing on the issue, urging them to embody the proposals in a Private Members' Bill. Twenty agreed to do so, but were unsuccessful in the ballot. Members of the House of Lords, including McGregor and Baroness Ewart-Biggs (a Vice-President 1986–90), and MPs including Leo Abse supported their public campaign to Reform Illegitimacy Laws. In 1986 a delegation organized by OPF met the Lord Chancellor to press the point.[91]

Following the change in the law, there was no longer a separate affiliation procedure for unmarried parents, and, for most purposes, children had the same legal

---

[87] NC Annual Report 1992.   [88] NC Annual Reports, 1976–7, 8; 1977–8, 13.

[89] Law Commission, *Illegitimacy*, Report 118 (1982).

[90] Stephen Cretney, *Family Law in the Twentieth Century* (Oxford: Oxford University Press, 2003), 563.

[91] NC Annual Report 1986, 9; CMM, 2 June 1986; 20 Oct. 1986.

rights whether or not their parents were married. Unmarried fathers for the first time gained the right to custody. However, for fear that even a completely unmeritorious father (e.g., one who had raped the mother) might gain this right, this was admissible only after scrutiny by the courts of the rights and interests of the child.[92] A child born to unmarried parents still might not inherit the father's nationality, an issue on which OPF continued to campaign.[93] Nor could they succeed to a hereditary peerage, though, comments Cretney, 'there seems to be no enthusiasm for the removal of this historic disability'.[94] OPF published *Maintenance for Children of Unmarried Parents* explaining the benefits of the change in the law. The availability now of DNA 'finger printing' assisted lone mothers to establish paternity.[95]

THE CHILD SUPPORT ACT

The 1986 Social Security Act failed to cut welfare spending, mainly due to growing unemployment. UK expenditure on social security benefits rose from 12.7 per cent of GDP in 1980, to 15 in 1985, to 17 per cent in 1995.[96] Margaret Thatcher, in particular, was determined to go further and transfer the cost of supporting lone mothers to the fathers of their children. She was not motivated solely by her determination to cut public expenditure. As she recalled in her memoirs, she

was appalled by the way in which men fathered a child and then absconded, leaving the single mothers—and the tax payer—to foot the bill for their irresponsibility.[97]

There is every sign that she meant it. By the late 1980s, only one in three lone mothers received regular maintenance from the fathers of their children, while almost 60 per cent relied on state benefits. In 1981/2, state spending on income-related benefits for lone parents was £1.4b, by 1988/9, £3.2b. It was widely accepted, and social security policy had previously assumed, that if a man formed and lived with a second family, his primary responsibility was to this family. Mrs Thatcher set out to change this and to force fathers to support all their children rather than leaving some of them to the state, partly in the hope of dissuading fathers from forming second families they could not afford. The outcome was the Child Support Act, 1991. The problem, as implementation of the Act was to reveal, as the Finer Committee had shown, and as had long been known, was that many men who already had two families could not afford to support both, and the law was unlikely to deter men from fathering children in future.

The Child Support Act was drafted in a hurry. There was pressure from Mrs Thatcher, whose priority was to punish 'feckless fathers', though she lost power and was replaced by John Major as Prime Minister and Conservative Party leader before

---

[92] Cretney *Family Law*, 564.   [93] NC Annual Report 1987, 1, 9–10; CMM, 15 Dec. 1986.
[94] Cretney, *Family Law*, 564.   [95] NC Annual Report 1989, 7.
[96] CSO, *National Income and Expenditure*, 1961–97; *Economic Trends Annual Supplement 1997*, Table 1.2.
[97] Margaret Thatcher, *The Downing Street Years* (London: Harper Collins, 1995), 630.

the Bill reached the statute book. There was also pressure from the Treasury, which wanted a lower benefit bill, and from the Lord Chancellor's Office which sought to reduce the role of the courts in maintenance cases. The Government was also keen to get the Bill through before the election expected in 1990. A White Paper, *Children Come First*,[98] was published in October 1990, embodying proposals for reform and inviting consultation. Meanwhile, the Social Security Act, 1990, for the first time allowed the DSS to recover the cost of IS from a former spouse, if it could, for the maintenance of the parent caring for the child(ren), or from an unmarried partner if a maintenance order was in force (a rare occurrence). Previously the absent parent had been required to support only the children. The new principle continued into the Child Support Bill.

Ninety responses to the White Paper were received, from OPF among others, but they were not taken into account in the rush to draft the Child Support Bill and get it through Parliament.[99] Also overlooked was the extensive research available on the needs and incomes of families and fathers and the relevant experience of other countries, such as Australia. A skeletal Child Support Bill was rushed through the Commons, where the efforts of OPF failed to arouse much interest— 'a disgrace to the word democracy', a DHSS civil servant of the time later commented on the Commons' performance.[100] McGregor and his allies failed in a valiant attempt to amend it in the Lords. The media showed little interest.

The Bill was prepared on the assumption that the needs of most families were fairly simple and routine and could be dealt with by a fixed formula, while special needs would be covered by regulations drafted by civil servants after its passage, and would not be debated in Parliament. The formula embodied in the Bill established another new principle: that the needs of first families took precedence over the second, even when the father lived with the latter. Also, the Secretary of State gained new powers to initiate a maintenance order even if a claimant wanted no contact with, normally her, partner. Refusal to name the partner 'without good cause' would lead to reduction in benefit, by 20 per cent (in practice later up to 40 per cent). 'Good cause' was defined in the White Paper as 'if the child has been conceived as a result of rape, or where there has been incest', despite the evidence that 1 in 6 divorced and 1 in 10 single or separated women on benefit gave domestic violence as the main reason for leaving their partner.[101] For this reason, the Lords rejected this clause. It was reinstated in the Commons but amended to allow that 'risk to her or any child living with her suffering harm or undue distress' must be considered before insisting upon compliance.

The new system was to be administered not by a civil service department but by a new Child Support Agency (CSA), a 'next steps agency', a new breed of quasi-governmental body, less accountable to voters and to Parliament, invented and

[98] *Children Come First: The Government's Proposals on the Maintenance of Children*, Cm. 1264 (London: HMSO, 1990).
[99] Witness seminar on making of the CSA, discussed in Mavis Maclean with Jacek Kurzewski, *Making Family Law: A Socio-Legal Account of Legislative Process in England and Wales, 1985–2010* (Oxford: Hart, 2011).
[100] Ibid.   [101] Kiernan et al., *Lone Motherhood*, 199.

much favoured by the Conservative Government. It was to open in 1993. Ministers and civil servants later admitted that, as they drafted the Bill and then the regulations, they had no idea of the complexity of many peoples' lives or even how many families might be involved, despite the experience of administering the benefit system. 'Few of us appreciated how complicated some peoples' lives had become,' the Minister responsible later admitted.[102] It is remarkable that they had apparently not tried to find out. The regulations were drafted by a different set of civil servants from those who drafted the Bill, again with insufficient time for consultation, and the Ministers concerned had also moved on.[103] The CSA was staffed by people with no previous experience of administering welfare benefits. The aim was to ensure that old principles and practices did not continue, but the lack of experience and of institutional memory in the CSA proved problematic.

The intended role of the CSA was to ensure that the children of an absent parent and the 'caring parent' (overwhelmingly the mother) had adequate maintenance from the absent parent (overwhelmingly the father), whether or not the mother claimed any form of benefit, though priority was given to assessing the circumstances of claimants. The CSA was to assess and administer both benefits and maintenance payments, whether agreed legally or privately. They took over from the courts full powers to assess, collect, and enforce maintenance payments. IS was reduced by the full amount of any maintenance payment. The needs of first families took absolute precedence over those of later families, which at first were not taken into account at all. When it was belatedly realized that the children of later partnerships were in poverty as a result, at potential cost to the benefits system, complex rules for their support were introduced.

The CSA had been established mainly to reduce the benefits bill by transferring maintenance costs to absent parents. It set out, therefore, to investigate not only new claims for benefit but the incomes of lone parents already receiving benefit. This saddled CSA's too few and inexperienced staff with the impossible task of reviewing 527,000 cases in their first six months. It had also apparently been assumed that most 'cases' would be straightforward to assess. The numerous 'special cases', which had always complicated the benefits system, undermined that hope. A large backlog built up, along with an alarmingly large number of over-hasty, mistaken assessments by inexperienced staff, often due to the fact that parents were rarely interviewed: assessments were made by post and telephone.[104]

The new system was a shock to parents since the retrospective scope of the Agency had not been publicized in advance. It could challenge existing settlements where it was estimated that the father was making inadequate provision. 'Clean-break' divorce settlements where, for example, a father gave up his equity in the family home to the mother and children rather than pay maintenance, or he had borrowed to provide them with a home in return for paying less; or private, voluntary agreements whereby the father paid an amount agreed between the partners,

---

[102] Maclean with Kurzewski, *Making Family Law.*   [103] Ibid.
[104] Kiernan et al., *Lone Motherhood*, 204; *Child Support Agency Annual Report and Account*, HC 596 (London: HMSO, 1994–5).

perhaps including buying food, clothes, or helping with bills, could be challenged and higher payments required. Those who drafted the Act and regulations had not anticipated the numbers of fathers who were not 'feckless' but had done their best to provide for their first families and now felt unfairly persecuted. There was no independent appeal procedure.

The CSA rules infuriated fathers who believed they were making the fairest settlement they could afford, sometimes created conflict in what had been amicable separations and were a disincentive to voluntary settlements. No allowance was made to absent parents for the costs of time spent with their children, or of travelling to see them, leading some to give up access because they could no longer afford it. Not surprisingly these deprived—and some less worthy—fathers protested vociferously. To add to the difficulties, the Inland Revenue was expected to track fathers for payment, but quickly grew tired, as others had before it, of hounding lots of fathers for small sums and the task fell back to the CSA. The centuries-old problem of persuading fathers to pay had not been legislated away, not least because many of them could not afford to pay. The CSA failed to cut costs as required: it was ordered to cut £530m from the benefit bill in the first year and missed the target by £112m, while managing to arrange maintenance in fewer than one-third of eligible applications.[105]

The CSA was arguably the greatest fiasco of the century in British social security policy. Not surprisingly, it immediately faced a mass of complaints from parents and criticism from the media, fuelled by high profile protests by some fathers. Mothers complained more quietly, or were not heard. It was criticized in the Commons and by the House of Commons Select Committee on Social Security.[106] The Chief Executive resigned after a year. There were some amendments to regulations, making allowances for property transfers and travel to work costs, and setting a ceiling on liable partner contributions of 30 per cent of his or her net income.

Further modifications were made in the Child Support Act, 1995. These limited the arrears of maintenance that could accrue from CSA delays, deferred indefinitely any consideration of non-benefit cases, introduced a Child Maintenance Bonus payable when a lone parent returned to work, and compensation for parents eligible for Family Credit or Disability Working Allowance whose maintenance had been cut. It thus removed some of the more glaring, and predictable, weaknesses of the system. But the CSA continued to be a slow, clumsy, often inefficient focus of widespread criticism that failed even to cut benefit costs.

OPF was closely involved with the establishment of the CSA in 1993, and tried to support it in order to ensure that it helped families as much as possible, while closely monitoring its effects on families and pressing for changes.[107] They differed from CPAG and other non-governmental groups who were far more critical and kept their distance from CSA. This caused some tensions in the voluntary sector.

[105] *Guardian*, 5 July 1993; Kiernan et al., *Lone Motherhood*, 201.
[106] Social Security Committee, *The Operation of the Child Support Act*, HC 303 (London: HMSO, 1994/5). Fifth Report of the Social Security Committee, *The Operation of the Child Support Act: Proposals for Change*, HC 470 (London: HMSO, 1993/4).
[107] NC Annual Report 1993–4, 1.

In the first year of the CSA, OPF received over 4,000 requests for help from lone parents arising from its operations.[108] They encouraged parents to tell the Government how the Act was affecting their lives.[109] They were concerned that the press focused almost entirely on the plight of the fathers, who were highly vocal and organized critics of the new arrangements, staging some high profile, dramatic, public protests in central London, and hardly at all on the needs of lone mothers who were too absorbed in the day-to-day struggle for survival to organize protest. They spoke up for mothers and were particularly protective of women who would not reveal the father's name to the CSA due to fear of violence. They reported: 'It has been a real uphill battle to get the voice of lone parents heard in the sometimes virulent campaign of absent parents who remain reluctant to pay their child maintenance.'[110]

BLAMING THE VICTIM 2: 'BACK TO BASICS'

The Child Support Act did not silence the attacks on lone mothers by members of the Government, rather the reverse. In a notorious, widely publicized, speech to the Conservative Party Conference in 1992, Secretary of State for Social Security Peter Lilley intoned, in a long remembered pastiche of Gilbert and Sullivan, that he 'had a little list' of

benefit offenders who I'll soon be rooting out …[including] young ladies who get pregnant just to jump the housing list. And dads who won't support the kids of ladies they have kissed. And I haven't even mentioned all those sponging socialists.

He did not stop there. In an article in the *News of the World* in early 1993 he wrote: 'We have produced a generation of fatherless children. No father to support them, discipline them and set them an example.' He argued that the rise in violent crime since 1950 was largely caused by the absence of fathers from increasing numbers of families.

In July 1993, John Redwood, Secretary for Wales, generated further publicity after visiting an estate in Cardiff, which, he claimed, was 50 per cent populated by lone-parent families. In a speech to a Conservative Political Centre Summer School shortly after, he proposed that benefit be withheld from women not only until fathers paid maintenance but until they moved back in with their families, to provide 'the normal love and support that fathers have offered down the ages'.[111] He claimed that single-parent families were 'one of the biggest social problems of our day' and that on the Cardiff estate

people had begun to accept that babies just happened, and there was no presumption in favour of two adults creating a loving family background for their children…what is more

---

[108] Ibid.; CSA 5/OPF/9/1/1, Memo, 1 Dec. 1993; Policy Team Minutes (PTM) 5/OPF/2/17/c, 2 June 1993.
[109] NC Annual Report 1992–3, 6.
[110] NC Annual Report 1994–5, 10.   [111] *Guardian*, 6 July 1993.

worrying is the trend for young women to have babies with no apparent intention of even trying marriage or a stable relationship with the father.[112]

In fact, only 17 per cent of the 3,500 families on the estate were lone parents and many had been married or in a long-term partnership and 60 per cent of the parents were aged over 24. The Vice-chair of the local social services committee, herself a social worker, responded: 'For the majority of people their aim is to be a family unit with two parents. I don't think there are large numbers of teenagers who are setting out to have families on their own.' A colleague agreed: 'We have some smashing people out there. We have some problem families, but mainly families with problems.'[113] They pointed out that it was an area with few jobs and poor childcare facilities: the families' 'greatest problem was poverty', but it was very hard for mothers to escape from it by finding jobs, as most would prefer. An experienced senior police officer on the estate commented that 'as the police had exclusion orders for violence against half the men involved, the last thing they wanted was to see women and children forced to allow the fathers to return.'[114] The suggestions from members of the Government were criticized in the Commons by Labour for attacking single mothers and by Conservative backbenchers for announcing policy outside Parliament.[115]

Redwood's pronouncements prompted enthusiasm in sections of the media, indeed provoked a storm, including a remarkably vicious cartoon in the *Sunday Times* (Fig. 8.1), a supportive *Times* leader,[116] and a spate of articles in the *Daily Mail*. The latter even-handedly blamed both mothers—'Women must say No'[117]— and fathers—'Feckless, unreliable, that's men says David Willets'.[118] Conservative MP Willetts blamed the rise in single motherhood on the shortage of well-educated, employable men and the welfare state:

The welfare state has taken over the traditional roles of the husband: it provides housing and a steady income. If there are not many reliable men, you can in effect marry the state instead.

None of this is the fault of the single mothers. Indeed it is striking how much responsibility these women, often still only girls in their teens, are taking on. They are leading tough, demanding, tiring lives. I believe that it is the men who are feckless and unreliable.

Particularly unpleasantly, the *Mail*'s regular columnist Keith Waterhouse ranted that, in the 'Single Parent State...the single mum can rake in over £100 a week in state benefits...she can jump the housing queue and raise her family in one of those lovely tower blocks...the majority of unmarried mums seem to regard the father as being as dispensable as the umbilical cord'. He attacked social workers, feminists, even David Willetts, as all encouraging the single mothers' 'gravy train':

Then there is the Unmarried Mothers' Union—the single parents' militant wing where having a baby is not so much a happy event as a political statement. You cradle the little mite to your boiler suit and carry a placard demanding crèche facilities at the bingo hall.[119]

---

[112] *The Times*, 3 July 1993; *Daily Express*, 3 July 1993.
[113] *Community Care*, 5 Aug. 1993, 3.   [114] Ibid.   [115] *Guardian*, 5 July 1993.
[116] *The Times*, 3 July 1993.   [117] Jessica Davies, *Daily Mail*, 6 July 1993, 9.
[118] Ibid.   [119] *Daily Mail*, 5 July 1993.

Fig. 8.1 'Wedded to Welfare: Do They Want to Marry a Man—or the State?', *Sunday Times*, 11 July 1993.

A fantasy unrecognizable as reality. Sue Slipman complained to the Press Complaints Commission and the editor of the *Daily Mail* about the spate of ill-informed articles, especially the 'particularly offensive' piece by Waterhouse. Paul Dacre, the editor, dissented, especially about Waterhouse—'one of Britain's greatest columnists'.[120] The PCC also rejected the complaint on the grounds that 'there was no prima facie breach of the Code. The article complained of was clearly a comment piece.'[121]

The Government, however, seemed a little uncomfortable. A DSS source stated that Redwood's comments did not represent government policy.[122] Peter Lilley felt forced to reassure the public that mothers in need would continue to receive benefit, while adding 'we can give money, but we cannot give love and commitment'.[123] But John Gummer at the Department of the Environment launched an inquiry into assumed discrimination against two-parent families in the allocation of council housing, suggested that lone parents' access to public housing should be

---

[120] Dacre to Slipman, 13 July 1993.
[121] PCC Public Records (Aug./Sept. 1993), Report 20. We are grateful to the Director of Communications at the PCC for this information.
[122] *Independent*, 6 July 1993.
[123] NC Annual Report 1993–4, 2; *Guardian*, 6 July 1993.

restricted[124] and was said to have been asked by Lilley to investigate creating hostels for lone parents.[125] There were rumours that the Government was considering requiring parents to take responsibility for unmarried, pregnant daughters and also tightening the liberal divorce law.[126] A junior health minister, Tom Sackville, was widely quoted as blaming 'the feminist movement' for 'giving encouragement to the concept that it is all right to have a child and bring the child up on your own', ideas that he believed had 'even permeated the Church'.[127]

On the other hand, the Director of the Institute of Housing Policy patiently explained that lone mothers did not receive priority access to council housing,[128] while the *Independent* commented that many homeless single parents were still placed in bed and breakfast accommodation.[129] The *Guardian* pointed out that it was, of course, desirable to reduce the number of teenage single pregnancies, so it was a pity that government cuts had led to the closure of one in four local authority family planning clinics.[130]

Then, a BBC TV *Panorama* programme, 'Babies on Benefit', reinforced the representation of single mothers as feckless scroungers. It opened with the statement:

This woman was sent to prison for neglect, after leaving her two-year-old child at home alone whilst she went out to work. Heidi Colwell did it to avoid living off handouts from the government. But thousands of other single mothers are raising families at the State's expense. Tonight, on *Panorama*, should the taxpayer foot the bill for women who have babies on benefit?

It then introduced another untypical case: a 22-year-old unmarried woman, daughter of a twice divorced lone mother, pregnant for the fifth time by two fathers, neither of whom lived with her and her children. It claimed that 'those women in their early twenties who have never married and for whom men have ceased to have any real role in bringing up their children...is the fastest growing group of lone parents', which it was not. The programme interviewed Redwood and visited the Cardiff estate. There they found that the police had been called because 'a twelve year old boy has gone berserk and is wrecking his home', where he lived with his unmarried mother and her 'three children by two different men'. They talked to 'men at the local disco complaining of being sidelined by the women' who moaned that 'the women are getting more independent' and 'the government make it too easy really, independence, its so easy for them isn't it...before the man used to provide didn't he, at one time, but now they don't need all that'. They were not asked why they were not 'providing'. *Panorama* interviewed Conservative councillors in Wandsworth, London, who wanted to give married couples priority for housing, 'to discourage the irresponsible'. The programme recommended capping benefits to reduce the numbers of lone mothers, a system it, wrongly, claimed had been effective in New Jersey with improbable speed—'in the first month since they became law the number of babies born to single mothers has halved'.[131]

---

[124] *The Times*, 6 July 1993.   [125] *Guardian*, 6 July 1993; *Independent*, 6 July 1993.
[126] *Guardian*, 6 July 1993.   [127] Ibid.   [128] Ibid.
[129] *Independent*, 6 July 1993.   [130] *Guardian*, 7 July 1993.
[131] Quotes from *Panorama* from a transcript lodged with the High Court in 1994, in OPF file.

Sir George Young, former Housing Minister, quoted the programme in Parliament when introducing a housing review prompted by lone parents allegedly jumping the housing queue; and Peter Lilley referred to it favourably.[132] OPF scored a 'major victory' when they referred the programme to the Broadcasting Complaints Commission, who upheld their complaint 'that this programme was unfair and some of its contents irresponsible'.[133] The BBC 'completely refuted' the BCC's finding, while admitting that the New Jersey evidence 'should have been described as provisional'.[134] They were supported by columnist Melanie Phillips in the *Observer*, who, wrongly, claimed that 'young never-marrieds...[are]...only about one-third of the total of lone parents but they're the fastest growing group', while paying Sue Slipman the probably unintended compliment that she was 'a formidable lobbyist who has transformed the image of lone parents from social pariahs to untouchable victims'.[135] Only 16 per cent of unmarried mothers were aged under 24 in 1989–91 and the 25–34 cohort was the fastest growing age-group of lone parents, many of them previously married.[136]

The Conservative Party was in some disarray at this time, over Europe and how to deal with high unemployment, among other things. At their autumn conference in October 1993 John Major strove to pull them together with an appeal to 'get Back to Basics' and unite behind 'commonsense British values', the 'old core values' of 'neighbourliness, decency and courtesy...self-discipline and respect for the law'. He pledged to roll back the 'permissiveness' of the 1960s, crack down on child pornography, and promote 'accepting responsibility for yourself and your family and not shuffling it off on the state'. The speech was enthusiastically received.[137] However, within the next seven months one Minister was revealed to have fathered an illegitimate child, two to have had secret gay relationships, another resigned after his wife committed suicide due to his relationship with another woman, and another after a 'friendship' with a House of Commons researcher.[138] It was later revealed that Major himself had had a four-year extramarital affair with a parliamentary colleague.[139] Thus tainted, along with various non-sexual corruption scandals, the Conservatives found it a little harder thereafter to occupy the moral high ground.[140]

Undaunted, the *Mail on Sunday* sought out a 'typical inner city street' and found King Street, in a run-down area of Liverpool near the docks. They revealed the 'astonishing' news that of the 70 properties, 18 were occupied by single mothers

---

[132] *Hansard*, House of Commons, 26 Jan. 1994, col. 309.

[133] NC Annual Report 1992–3, 1.

[134] BBC News and Current Affairs, Press Release, 13 Sept. 1994.

[135] *Observer*, 12 Sept. 1994.

[136] *Population Trends*, 71 (Spring 1993).

[137] *Independent*, 9 Oct. 1993.

[138] 'UK Politics: The Major Scandal Sheet', 27 Oct. 1998, available at http://news.bbc.co.uk/1/hi/uk_politics/202525.stm, accessed 15 Feb. 2011.

[139] 'Major and Currie Had Four Year Affair', 28 Sept. 2002, available at http://news.bbc.co.uk/1/hi/uk_politics/2286008.stm, accessed 27 Apr. 2011.

[140] Andrew Holden, *Makers and Manners: Politics and Morality in Post-War Britain* (London: Politico's, 2004), 267–309.

and only 17 housed families with a father, whereas in 1962 '50 households were headed by a man'. In fact, their own article showed that of the 50 houses, 6 were empty, 16 residents refused to reveal their status, there were five pensioner households, four containing single younger men and women without children, 6 divorced or separated lone mothers, three widows, twelve married couples, and one cohabiting couple without children. Some of the mothers pointed out that they lived there because it was run-down and cheap, no one else wanted the homes, and they could not afford anything better. The paper reported that, back in 1962, 'it was a thriving community'.[141] It did not point out that poor people, including one-parent families, now lived there because it had declined along with the Liverpool docks. They had not caused the decline. Again, Slipman complained to the Press Complaints Commission, after receiving two letters from mothers in King Street, complaining that the journalist had misled them about the purpose of her article and had not questioned them directly about their family status. Thirty-three of the 48 people named in the article wrote to the editor to complain, including about the publication of their names and addresses. The *Mail* rejected the complaint, claiming that residents had been made aware of the nature of the article and no details had been included of residents who requested their exclusion. The PCC accepted this defence and rejected the complaint, noting that they had received no direct complaint from residents of the street.[142]

In his 'Foreword' to the OPF Annual Report that year, Hay Davidson commented that 'the public debate has been accompanied by some unnecessary and harmful hysteria that risks "blaming the victims"...it has also been notable that the Council has been the major voice of reason within the debate.'[143] He repeated in the following year:

We have been involved in a high profile public debate over the causes of family breakdown; the growth of numbers of one parent families and their increasing reliance on state support. The Council has argued firmly against a punitive approach towards lone parents and their children, and has advocated policies which will help them become finally independent.[144]

OPF followed up with *Child Law: The Government's Policy Proposals for One Parent Families*, arguing that the growing number of lone parents was not an outcome of welfare or housing policies but of social and cultural change: increased public acceptance of cohabitation and the birth of children in stable unmarried relationships, increased marriage breakdown, and divorce. It pointed out, yet again, that most lone mothers were not teenagers, many were considerably older: the structure of the family was changing.[145] In 1994 they publicized research by the Department of the Environment showing that more than 40 per cent of unmarried mothers

[141] *Mail on Sunday*, 14 Nov. 1993.
[142] Press Complaints Commission Report 23 (Jan./Feb. 1994). We are grateful to the Director of Communications at PCC for this information.
[143] NC Annual Report 1992–3, 1.
[144] NC Annual Report 1993–4, 1.
[145] NC CMM, 10 Oct. 1993; NC Annual Report 1993–4, 2–3; 1994–5, 12; Policy Team, Aug. 1993.

under 20 lived in households owned or rented by their parents, not in council housing.[146]

Again, the onslaught on lone parents was not universal, outside government and sections of the media. The co-author of *Crime and the Family*, published by the Family Policy Studies Centre, complained to *The Times* about a columnist

who ascribes to our study precisely the kind of moral judgements that we are at some pains to avoid. We do not say that a tranquil and loving home is 'preferable' to an unhappy family headed by two parents. What we do report is that homes marked by affectionate and effective parenting, whether headed by one parent or two, are less likely to produce young criminals.... Low family income and children's underachievement in primary school are other factors that must not be ignored. Our report suggests that the time has come for a wide-ranging initiative on social crime prevention, addressing multiple family problems with multiple solutions. Stigmatising lone parents has no practical part to play in such a programme.[147]

A national opinion poll found that 53 per cent of people believed that a woman could bring up a child on her own perfectly adequately. As Slipman pointed out:

In reality most families now have a close relative bringing up a child alone and they know from personal experience that lone parents are not a breed apart; that they are doing a very good job in tough circumstances...we have been at pains to point out that far from gleefully milking the state, surveys show that the vast majority of lone parents want to become financially independent by taking a paid job which will increase their family income.[148]

OPF continued to promote a balanced picture of the lives of lone parent families in the face of persistent political and media attacks upon them.[149]

The 1995 CSA Act set off another frenzy among certain politicians and newspapers. In November 1995 the *Independent* leaked a story that the Treasury and Peter Lilley, still Secretary of State at DSS, had agreed a 'drastic package' of cuts, first proposed in the following year but abandoned after the 'back to basics' debacle.[150] These included cuts to housing benefit and 'a tough new clampdown on payments to single parents', abolishing One Parent Benefit for new claimants for IS and freezing it for existing ones. Lilley was said to have resisted demands to cut One Parent Benefit altogether, mainly because he feared that, with the Government's shrinking majority following by-election losses, the necessary legislation would not get through Parliament.[151] The cuts were announced in the 1996 Budget, the Chancellor, Kenneth Clarke, having promised a 'a family-friendly' budget (lone-parent households, as ever, not being regarded as 'families'). It was argued that lone parents should not receive more than two-parent families. As a General Election loomed in 1997 John Redwood returned to the fray, proposing that, for the sake of 'family values', single mothers should give up their children for adoption. There were rumours in the press that the Government proposed to take this up.[152] The election intervened. Labour won a landslide victory.

---

[146] NC Annual Report 1994–5, 3. [147] Letter, *The Times*, 6 July 1993.
[148] NC Annual Report 1993–4, 2. [149] Ibid.
[150] *Daily Telegraph*, 31 Mar. 1995. [151] *Independent*, 8 Nov. 1995.
[152] Single Parent Action Network, *Positive Images: Negative Stereotypes* (Bristol: SPAN, 1998), 31–4.

CONCLUSION

This was an extraordinary time. Never in history had so many children been born outside marriage in England and Wales and never had so many unmarried couples lived together openly, facing little evident disapproval from friends and neighbours but attacked by a government which objected strongly to any transgression of 'family values', which appeared to mean raising children in a lasting marriage. But it seemed unable to stem an apparently unstoppable tide of cultural change. Interestingly, the first female Prime Minister tried to hold fathers responsible, against the established trend of blaming the mothers. But the resulting legislation, establishing the CSA, was put through too fast, with too little attention to evidence and failed comprehensively in its purpose of holding fathers to account. In apparent desperation, prominent Ministers reverted, equally ineffectively, to blaming unmarried mothers for causing this and an array of other social problems, including crime, in particular a mythical tribe of teenagers who chose pregnancy as the route to a council home. All deviants from 'family values', whatever their backgrounds, were criticized in principle, but poorer mothers were butts of the most explicit blame by Ministers and sections of the media, as part of a wider assault on 'welfare dependency', which was assumed to be a voluntary state, chosen by the feckless and work-shy. Yet, the Conservative Government's efforts to force or persuade lone mothers off welfare into work were unsuccessful, despite the evidence demonstrated by OPF of the willingness of very many of them to take employment compatible with their childcare responsibilities when given adequate support. As so often in the past, it was left to voluntary agencies, especially OPF, to help them train and find work and to meet their welfare needs.

The 'permissive' sixties did not banish the stigma of unmarried motherhood. There was no simple path of progress to general greater enlightenment on such issues. Public attitudes remained as divided as ever between tolerance and blame, but Government Ministers led the attack as never before. The Government blamed lone parents and family breakdown for causing social problems and blamed the Welfare State, which it aimed to cut, for causing the family breakdown. It overlooked the possible contribution of pervasive social and economic inequality, which grew markedly through the 1980s and 1990s.[153]

---

[153] A. B. Atkinson, 'Distribution of Income and Wealth', in A. H. Halsey and J. Webb (eds), *Twentieth Century British Social Trends* (London: Macmillan, 2000), 348–84.

9

Into the Twenty-First Century: Progress?

'NEW LABOUR'

The vilification of lone parents by politicians ceased after the 1997 election. The 'New Labour' Government shared its predecessor's commitment to encouraging lone parents to seek work rather than benefits, and quickly cut Lone Parent Premium and One Parent Benefit, as planned by the Conservatives, in keeping with the Chancellor Gordon Brown's promise to keep within stringent Conservative spending plans. This was much criticized, opposed in Parliament by many Labour backbenchers, and supported reluctantly by others. The cut was compensated by increases to other benefits, but gradually, over several years.[1] Between 1999 and 2003 Child Benefit for the first child increased by 25.3 per cent and for subsequent children by 3.1 per cent in real terms.[2] In 1999, a more generous Working Families' Tax Credit was introduced, replacing Family Credit, supplementing the incomes of families with at least one parent in low-paid work. Less positively, in 2004 child benefit was withdrawn from migrants with no 'right to reside', including a number of lone parents, part of a wider policy of deterring immigrants.

In other respects, Labour tried to develop positive, not punitive, means to assist the transition from welfare to work, similar to the pioneering efforts of OPF in the 1980s, with some success. It provided services to advise unemployed parents about work or training, help with childcare, funds for training, and improved benefits for those in training. The Minimum Wage, introduced in 1998, though at a low level, helped some lone-parent households. At least as important for assisting lone parents into work, the Government made a commitment to a national childcare strategy. By 1997, one in three children in Britain was living in poverty, compared with fewer than one in ten twenty years earlier, and Labour aimed to reduce the numbers. Poverty was greatest in households in which no one was employed and Labour recognized that childcare was essential to any strategy to get more parents into work. As part of the welfare-to-work strategy, unemployed lone parents were expected to attend interviews with an adviser on training and work. Stiffer sanctions were applied, requiring single parents of children over age 7 to move from Income Support onto Job Seekers Allowance. The latter had been introduced in

---

[1] K. Stewart, 'Towards an Equal Start? Addressing Childhood Poverty and Deprivation', in J. Hills and K. Stewart (eds), *A More Equal Society? New Labour, Poverty, Inequality and Exclusion* (Bristol: The Policy Press, 2005), 143–65.

[2] Ibid.

1996 and required claimants to take any work on offer. It was now accompanied by the positive support of improved access to advice on work or training, but it still proved too stern for the circumstances of many families. In 2009, the rules were eased to require single mothers to take employment only if it suited school hours and they had adequate childcare.[3]

In 2003 Working Tax Credit (WTC) and Child Tax Credit (CTC) replaced the Working Families' Tax Credit. Support for children was separated from support for workers on low pay. Child Tax Credit replaced allowances for children of unemployed parents, reducing the complications, delays, and interruptions to income when they moved in and out of work, as many low-paid, low-skilled workers frequently did. It benefited all families with children, but was paid at lower levels to those on higher incomes, and lower income families received an additional benefit for each child, which was significantly more generous than previous means-tested support. This additional benefit was increased in line with average earnings. Child Benefit was still paid to all families.

These changes were designed to help all poorer working families and included childcare subsidies. Half the beneficiaries were lone mothers. Their economic activity rates increased from 45 per cent in 1997 to 57 per cent by 2008, due to Labour's measures combined with greater buoyancy in the employment market, though they were still below the employment rates of partnered mothers (70 per cent[4]) and less than Labour hoped.[5]

The White Paper *Raising Expectations and Increasing Support: Reforming Welfare for the Future*, published in December 2008,[6] further promoted Labour's belief that 'work is the best form of welfare'. Gordon Brown, now Prime Minister, explained in the Foreword that the benefit system should help all 'to develop their skills, make the most of their talents and build a better life for themselves, their families and their communities'. The independent Social Security Advisory Committee, which advised the Department of Work and Pensions, had pointed out that by equating 'work' solely with paid employment, the Government 'appears to ignore the important and complex social and economic role of unpaid work by carers in all its many guises'.[7] The White Paper acknowledged the value of full-time caring, for adults as well as children, given the growing population of disabled and frail older people. It also recognized the needs of parents of children with severe disabilities and lone parents of children under age 3, who would not be required to prepare for or actively seek employment. Three was the lowest age since 1948 for a child whose parent was required to take work or training rather than benefits. The change mirrored the growing trend for partnered mothers to take ever briefer periods out of employment to care for children, but it raised concerns about lone

---

[3] P. Toynbee and D. Walker, *The Verdict: Did Labour Change Britain?* (London: Granta, 2010), 203.

[4] ONS, *Social Trends*, no. 38 (London: The Stationery Office (TSO), 2007).

[5] Toynbee and Walker, *Verdict*, 203.

[6] Department of Work and Pensions (DWP), Cm 7506 (London: TSO, 2008).

[7] DWP, *No-One Written Off: Reforming Welfare to Reward Responsibility*, Public consultation, Cm 7363 (London: TSO, 2008).

mothers' loss of choice about how best to meet the needs of young children, given their greater childcare difficulties in the absence of a partner.

The White Paper assumed that children aged 3 to 5 could access part-time nursery education, while their mothers engaged in training or voluntary work, in preparation for paid employment when the child entered full-time schooling. Failure of a parent to make such preparations could lead to a cut in benefit. Employment need not be full-time. Parents caring for a child under 12 could receive tax credit while working 16 hours per week or less. But part-time work was generally low-paid, with less security (despite improvements in job security and benefits for part-time workers introduced by Labour) and fewer opportunities for training and promotion than full-time work. It provided an alternative to benefits but not necessarily a significantly higher standard of living and could severely complicate people's lives and increase stress as they juggled work with caring responsibilities.

The assumptions underlying these policies oversimplified the situation of many mothers.[8] More childcare was available—the number of formal childcare places doubled between 1997 and 2008—but it was not accessible or affordable to all parents, especially those with more than two children. The childcare tax credit paid nothing for third or subsequent children. Care provision for older and disabled children, e.g., after school and in school holidays, was inadequate though improving.[9] Lone mothers were more likely than others to care for a child who was disabled or had severe health problems. An increasing amount of childcare was provided by family and friends, mainly by grandparents (mostly, but not exclusively, grandmothers) often at some cost to themselves. In October 2010, 57 per cent of grandparents who cared for grandchildren had given up paid work or reduced their hours in order to do so, but this was not officially recognized or rewarded. In 2007 almost 40 per cent of mothers in paid employment depended to some extent on informal childcare of this kind.[10]

Lone parents, like other parents, benefited when the right to maternity leave doubled to nine months, then, from April 2010, rose to 12 months. In both cases, the first six weeks were paid at 90 per cent of salary, the remainder at a weekly flat-rate of £123. This was still below the standard recommended by the EU, and below that in Albania and Belarus, but an improvement for the UK.[11] Parents gained the right to ask for flexible hours to suit their caring responsibilities, but employers retained the right to refuse and many exercised it.

Maintenance from the absent parent remained an important, but often problematic, source of income for lone-parent families. The CSA continued to administer it, with 'no discernible improvement' as the National Audit Office reported in

---

[8] M. Brewer and G. Paull, *Newborns and New Schools: Critical Times in Women's Employment*, DWP Research Report 308 (London: TSO, 2007).

[9] Daycare Trust response to *No-One Written Off*, Cm 7363, chapter 8.

[10] *Grandparents Plus*, http://www.grandparentsplus.org.uk, accessed 1 March 2011. Hilary Land, 'Slaying Idleness without Killing Care: A Challenge for the British Welfare State', *Social Policy Review*, 21 (2009).

[11] Toynbee and Walker, *Verdict*, 158.

2001.[12] Labour tried to simplify the assessment formula and spent huge sums trying to clear the backlog of cases and get the inefficient IT system running at last. Some fathers deliberately clogged the system by sending in new records of their income every month, requiring new assessments of what they owed. Still, in 2006, it cost the CSA 70p to collect £1 from an absent parent. The auditors asked why it was so reluctant to use its enforcement powers against non-paying parents.

In 2008 the Government established the Child Maintenance and Enforcement Commission (CMEC) to promote voluntary arrangements between parents, with the CSA keeping the role of stepping in when they could not agree. The aim was to make the CSA more efficient by simplifying its tasks. Thereafter, parents with care of children could keep up to £20 per week of maintenance payments before losing any benefit rights. In 1997 the CSA recouped 58 per cent of benefit payments from absent parents. By 2009 this had crept up to 61 per cent. In that year the CMEC gained stronger enforcement powers, including to confiscate non-paying parents' passports and driving licences without taking them to court.[13]

For all the policy changes of the Labour years, which showed greater sensitivity to the lives of lone parents than their predecessors, popular stereotypes of single parents changed much less. A poll carried out for OPF in 2008 showed that they were generally regarded as teenage, never-married benefit claimants despite the evidence to the contrary.[14] Eighty-three per cent of single parents, from all backgrounds, surveyed by OPF in 2009 felt that the media portrayed them negatively. The number of people who believed that single parents did not work had increased although the numbers employed had gone up. Those who were employed risked blame for neglecting their children. Gingerbread, as OPF had become after merging with its sister organization in 2009, launched a campaign in February 2010—*Let's Lose the Labels*—to challenge stereotypes and stigma. It was formally supported by the leaders of all three leading political parties before the coming election. It raised public awareness of Gingerbread, but the 'labels' persisted.[15]

Labour lost the election of May 2010. Since they came to power in 1997 there had been real, if limited, improvements in the incomes, from work and welfare, of lone parents and support available to them. There were 600,000 fewer children in poverty (defined as living in a household with less than half the median income, adjusted for family size) than in 1997, a fall from 17.4 per cent of children in 1995 to 10.5 per cent in 2005, against an average of 12.7 per cent in OECD countries, a faster decline than in any other of the 34 OECD countries.[16]

[12] Toynbee and Walker, *Verdict*, 158.
[13] Ibid. 158–9.
[14] See ch. 8.
[15] NC Annual Report 2010, 11–12.
[16] OECD, *Doing Better for Families* (Apr. 2011), available at http://www.oecd.org/social/family/doingbetter, accessed 28 Apr. 2011.

NEW 'COMPASSIONATE' CONSERVATISM?

Labour was replaced by a Conservative–Liberal Democrat coalition government, led by David Cameron, who has frequently described his brand of Conservatism as 'compassionate'. The new Government moved quickly to propose reforms to the welfare system which strongly recalled those of the Conservative Governments of 1979–97. Within six months of gaining office it proposed cutting Child Benefit, for higher earners only, but it was frozen for three years for all families, while prices of essential items, including food, rose.

A Welfare Reform Bill was introduced to Parliament in February 2011. It aimed—recalling, consciously or not, the claims of a previous Conservative administration in 1985[17]—to legislate for 'the biggest change to the welfare system for over 60 years' and to simplify an over-complex system. It planned, again reminiscent of the 1980s, to take claimants off welfare into work, as Labour had been doing quite successfully, though they received no credit from the new Government. The claimed objectives were 'to make the benefits and tax credits fairer and simpler' by:

- Creating the right incentives to get more people into work by ensuring work always pays;
- Protecting the most vulnerable in our society; and
- Delivering fairness to those claiming benefit and to the taxpayer.[18]

The Bill included the introduction, from 2013, of a 'Universal Credit to provide a single streamlined benefit that will ensure work always pays', replacing the existing income-related working age benefits and tax credits. The Credit would be provided by a new 'unified delivery agency'. It also promised 'a stronger approach to reducing fraud and error with tougher penalties for the most serious offences' and 'a new system of child support which puts the interest of the child first'.[19] The Secretary of State for Work and Pensions, Iain Duncan Smith, promised that there would be 'no losers' from the changes. However, £18b was to be cut from the cost of benefits. CPAG, the respected Institute for Fiscal Studies, and the equally respected OECD, calculated that the loss or freezing of benefits would bring real income cuts to many poorer families.[20]

Among welfare reforms specifically affecting lone parents, it was proposed to lower further the age of a youngest child when a lone parent could no longer claim Income Support from 7, as set by Labour in 2008, to 5, on the grounds that it was reasonable to expect lone parents to take up paid work once their children were in full-time education. There was no immediate return, at this point, to the explicit demonization of lone-parent families of previous Conservative Governments.

---

[17] See p. 177.
[18] http://www.dwp.gov.uk/policy/welfare-reform/legislation-and-key-documents/, accessed 25 Feb. 2010.
[19] Ibid.
[20] http://www.cpag.org.uk; http://www.ifs.org.uk; OECD, *Doing Better for Families.*

However, prominent (Conservative) members of the coalition, including the Prime Minister, David Cameron, and the Secretary of State for Work and Pensions, Iain Duncan Smith, talked of family breakdown as a fundamental cause of the problems of 'Broken Britain' and suggested tax incentives to encourage marriage. There was little positive support for the needs of lone parents, rather the opposite. There were no signs of increased government investment in childcare to assist more lone parents to enter employment. Instead, childcare credits were cut by 10 per cent, reducing family incomes by £430 p.a. while the costs of day-care rose.[21] Severe cuts to local authority budgets led to the closure of many childcare facilities and after-school and school holiday centres to preserve still more vital services for disabled and frail older people. In 2011 the OECD reported that the exceptionally high costs of childcare in the UK compared with most other OECD countries were a 'barrier to work for parents'.[22]

It was also proposed to overhaul the Child Support system, again. The situation, as set out in documents accompanying the Welfare Reform Bill, was that there were 2.5m lone-parent families in Great Britain, and 1.2m had been assessed through the statutory system (the CSA). Of these 850,000 received child maintenance and 77 per cent of absent fathers paid their dues. As many as 720,000 families had no maintenance arrangement; 550,000 had a private, family-based arrangement, or a court-based arrangement (110,000 families). There were 150,000 cases outstanding that the still problematic computer system could not handle, requiring 'costly clerical handling'.[23] Administration now cost 40p for every £1 collected, rather less than the 70p in 1997 and 2006, before Labour's reforms to CSA.

The principle underlying the latest changes was that 'The Government believes parents have responsibilities to their children whether they live with them or not. . . . Ideally a child should have access to the same resources, principally money and time, when parents separate or do not live together as the child would have if they lived together.' Hence the Department of Work and Pensions (DWP) set out to 'work with other Government Departments and voluntary and community services to support and empower more of those parents who can make their own family-based child maintenance arrangements to do so, while recognizing that for some parents collaboration is not possible or appropriate' and 'to deliver a more efficient statutory child maintenance service for those who need it and to provide greater value for money for the taxpayer'.[24]

The scheme would eventually be administered wholly by the Child Maintenance and Enforcement Commission (CMEC) and the CSA would close. Parents requesting help from CMAC to gain maintenance (i.e., the resident parent) would

[21] Daycare Trust, http://www.daycaretrust.org.uk.

[22] OECD, *Doing Better for Families*.

[23] DWP, 'Welfare Reform Bill, 2011', Impact Assessments: Child Maintenance (new scheme), p. 6, http://www.dwp.gov.uk/policy/welfare-reform/legislation-and-key-documents/, accessed 9 May 2011.

[24] Ibid.

be charged an application fee of £100, in advance (£50 for those on benefits, £20 payable in advance). Seven to 12 per cent of any child maintenance paid would be charged to the non-resident parent, as a 'collection charge'. If CMEC also collected the maintenance payment, the non-resident parent would pay a collection sur-charge of 15–20 per cent, plus a further charge where enforcement action was needed. CMEC would also provide a calculation-only service, for parents negotiat-ing a private agreement, assessing how much the non-resident parent should pay, for a charge of £20–25. Existing CSA users could choose whether to opt into the new scheme, and pay the charges, or make their own arrangements.[25] The charges would, of course, reduce the disposable incomes of lone-parent families.

The government aimed to encourage parents to make private arrangements not involving the state. The rationale for charges was to 'encourage the resident parent to make more effort to collaborate with the other parent and agree their own arrangements instead', since there was evidence that maintenance arrangements worked best when parents could collaborate, whereas the state scheme could be long-drawn-out and add to tensions and uncertainty for parents and children. Victims of domestic violence (only) would be exempt from the CMEC application charge.[26] There was no apparent effort to investigate other circumstances in which it might be difficult for couples to reach amicable arrangements. Parents whose relations with a former partner were tense but not violent stood to suffer most.

OPF kept a close watch on all the changes from 1997, as ever advising parents about them and seeking to advise government. In 2007 it merged with Ginger-bread, with which it had long worked closely, and in 2009 officially took its name. They continued to provide wide-ranging services for single parents, including their successful re-entry to work courses.[27] For these, they gained from Labour long-term government contracts and they worked closely with local authorities. In 2009–10 over 700 parents completed programmes designed to enhance confi-dence, motivation, and awareness of further education and training opportunities and many moved into work, despite the recession.[28] In 2011, Gingerbread feared that the costs attached to the proposed changes to the child support system would deter many lone parents from applying to CMEC if they and the absent parent could not reach a voluntary agreement. As Gingerbread put it:

The charges weaken the bargaining position of the parent with care. A non-resident parent may use them as an excuse to offer less. More parents could end up with little or no main-tenance at all for their children. Yet child maintenance makes the most difference to chil-dren's lives in the lowest income groups, research shows.[29]

---

[25] 'What Is the Government Planning?', *Gingerbread: Single Parents, Equal Families*, available at http://www.gingerbread.org.uk/content.aspx?CategoryID=575, accessed 22 Feb. 2011.

[26] 'Why Charge for a New Child Support Service?', *Gingerbread: Single Parents, Equal Families*, available at http://www.gingerbread.org.uk/content/577/Why-charge-for-a-new-child-support-service, accessed 22 Feb. 2011.

[27] See pp. 179–81.

[28] NC Annual Report 2010, 16–17.

[29] 'What Does Gingerbread Think about New Child Maintenance Proposals?', *Gingerbread: Single Parents, Equal Families*, available at http://www.gingerbread.org.uk/content/578/What-does-Gingerbread-think-about-new-child-maintenance-proposals?, accessed 22 Feb. 2011.

Even if the parents paid the charges, they would be left with smaller net incomes from which to support themselves and their children. Gingerbread campaigned vigorously against the charges.[30]

Gingerbread was wholly in favour of cooperation between separated parents, and indeed had long campaigned 'for more and better services to assist parents to deal practically and emotionally with separation and help them to agree arrangements for their children and cooperate better'. But they were all too aware of potential problems that the Government had apparently overlooked:

even if both parents are prepared to give it a try, such services are patchy, can be hard to find and may be too expensive for parents who really need them. . . . The government has not so far mentioned investment in a network of good quality affordable services—essential if the large numbers of parents who currently use the CSA are to be helped to reach reliable and sustainable private maintenance agreements to support their children.[31]

They pointed out that:

Private arrangements are most likely where separated parents get on OK and both remain involved in their children's lives. Agreements are also more likely to succeed when parents are better off. . . . But the lives of many parents do not fit this picture. The majority live in rented housing. 44% at any one time are not working. There may be hostility, conflict or lack of trust between parents. The other parent may have moved away or be in a new relationship. The parents may never have lived together or had only a brief relationship, or there can be poor or non-existent communication . . . Under the government's proposals, children whose non-resident parents cooperate the least will lose out the most. This is wrong and unfair.[32]

They recognized, unavoidably, that the CSA had problems. Nevertheless, Gingerbread argued, it

provides an essential service, currently used by over a million parents. The CSA can try to trace parents who try to disappear; it can find out a parent's earnings and make deductions if necessary to ensure the correct amount of maintenance is paid; it can act as an intermediary so that parents do not have to argue with each other over money; it collects payments and can intervene at once if a payment is missed; it will pursue arrears. These are all necessary services to ensure parents' responsibilities towards their children are met.[33]

It also provided an incentive for some parents to reach private agreements:

It is precisely because a parent with care can easily go to the state child support service, that non-resident parents are more likely to agree good private arrangements. . . . The charges will lead to many children in low income families receiving no maintenance at all, or lower amounts than at present. That is unfair and will damage their future. And is it really value for the taxpayer that these already vulnerable children lose out?[34]

---

30 'What does Gingerbread Think?'   31 Ibid.
32 Ibid.   33 Ibid.   34 Ibid.

At the same time, the coalition government made similar proposals to compel separating couples to undergo mediation to try to achieve an amicable divorce settlement rather than taking the case to court. As an incentive, legal aid was to be terminated for divorce cases for the first time since its introduction in 1948, except in cases of domestic violence or child protection, whereas it would be paid for the cheaper mediation process. Couples taking a divorce to court would be required to present evidence that they had tried mediation. The aim was both to reduce the number of divorces and the costs of legal aid.

Experienced mediators and lawyers were immediately apprehensive. It was not obvious that there were enough mediators to meet the likely demand. Also, they knew from experience that successful mediation required goodwill between the partners—precisely what was often lacking when a couple decided to part. It already happened that the partner in the stronger financial position—normally the father—refused to cooperate, forcing the other either to accept an inadequate settlement or a costly court case, or to try to represent herself in a complex and confusing legal process. Divorce lawyers pointed out that it was already their normal practice to encourage mediation and their advice at an early stage, currently often funded by legal aid, prevented many cases reaching court by achieving a settlement. If legal aid was withdrawn, this opportunity would be closed to many. Only a minority of the 130,000 divorces each year went to court, usually those that could not be resolved in any other way.[35] The changes were likely to lead to increased numbers of court cases and high public costs.

Early in the consultation process, the Judges' Council, chaired by the head of the judiciary, warned—in a highly unusual criticism of government proposals—that the likely increase in 'litigants in person' without legal advice, would slow down the legal system and increase costs, leading to an 'inevitable' decline in the quality of justice in England and Wales at a time when courts were already facing government-imposed cuts in staff and budgets. As the President of the Family Division of the High Court put it: 'Litigants in person do not understand the process, which has to be explained to them. Cases... inevitably take more time.' If litigants had no access to legal advice at an early stage more unwinnable cases would clog up the courts. At the same time, cuts to local authority budgets were causing the closure or cutting back of free legal advice services provided by local authorities or voluntary agencies such as Citizens' Advice. Winnable cases might be lost due to lack of legal representation or unfair settlements reached.[36] There was a serious risk that divorce would, again, become inaccessible to many poorer people.

By the end of the first year of the coalition government there were widespread fears, shared by Gingerbread, that lone-parent families were suffering from the array of government reforms and cuts. When tax credit cuts were implemented in

---

[35] Afua Hirsch, 'Divorce Is Messy: There Are Times When Mediation Won't Work', *Guardian*, 25 Feb. 2011.

[36] 'Courts Could Grind to a Standstill If Legal Aid Slashed, Say Judges', *Guardian*, 25 Feb. 2011.

April 2011 they estimated that working lone parents would lose an average £500 p.a., while those paying for childcare would lose twice as much in percentage terms as those who did not, due to the reductions in childcare tax credits.[37] One lone mother, Louise, complained to Gingerbread: 'It's infuriating that the Government's encouraging us back to work but then cutting the support that we need to make that possible.'[38] Another, Becky, wrote: 'This will be very, very hard for me. I was going to try to set up a pension but I won't be able to make those payments every month now. I've already cut down on all our non-essential spending.'[39] Caitlin protested:

I am a parent of a 16 year old mildly Autistic son who also has a learning difficulty, up until last year and from the age of nine my son received only £5 a week from my ex-partner it has been a constant battle living from day to day. I fought and got an increase in my son's maintenance last year. My ex partner is extremely angry that he has to pay at all and as I was a victim of domestic violence it has made things so much harder, how the hell can they expect anyone who has survived an appalling abusive relationship to sit down and work this out with such a person fills me with utter fear and dread. I use the csa [*sic*] as I feel slightly protected as I will never be able to reach any kind of agreement with my ex partner.[40]

Nina also posted her story:

The father of my child walked out on me a month before our daughter was due. He decided he just wasn't ready to have a child. We had been together for three years and had what I assumed was a happy relationship, I guess I was wrong. Anyway, I got on with it and moved back to where my family lived, I was fine for about four months and then things got very tight financially. I had to quit my job as my daughter was quite ill so I had to move onto benefits. I got in touch with my daughter's father and he decided that because he had nothing to do with our daughter he didn't have to give anything, I never told him he couldn't be involved with her, he chose not to be involved just shows the amazing logic some men use. Sadly he was a very clever man and he signed all his assets over to his new wife, business included, and now 'doesn't work' but also doesn't claim benefits. His now wife was also pregnant at this time so the CSA told me they couldn't take money from them as she was supporting him and was also going to be supporting a baby. I can't afford a solicitor and I can't afford to pursue it any further with the CSA. I'm not sure what I am meant to do, and the people at the CSA could offer me no advice.... The whole system needs re-evaluating.[41]

Gingerbread was the only source of support for these and many other desperate women whose lives did not fit the tidy patterns on which government policy

[37] Gingerbread, *Working but Losing* (Apr. 2011), available at http://www.gingerbread.org.uk/uploads/media/28/7198.pdf.
[38] 'Tax Credit Cuts Will Hammer Hard-Working Single Parents', *Gingerbread: Single Parents, Equal Families*, available at http://www.gingerbread.org.uk/news/99/Tax-credit-cuts-hammer-single-parents, accessed 24 Apr. 2011.
[39] Ibid.
[40] Comment to 'STOP CSA CHARGES—Don't Make Children Pay', *Gingerbread: Single Parents, Equal Families*, available at http://www.gingerbread.org.uk/content.aspx?CategoryID=574, accessed 24 Apr. 2011.
[41] Ibid.

appeared to be based. Its judgement, and theirs, that their incomes, support services including childcare, and employment opportunities were shrinking was supported by the OECD. It reported in April 2011 that progress in child poverty reduction in the UK had stalled due to the government spending cuts, including in Child Benefit, and that 'cutting back on early years [such as the Sure Start Centres introduced by Labour] services will make it difficult for the UK to achieve its policy of making work pay for all.' They commented in particular on Britain's poor childcare provision compared with other OECD countries.[42] This was corroborated by independent economists who pointed out that, in cash terms, single-parent households were by far the worst hit by cuts in education, the Working Tax Credit, and Child Tax Credit, whereby they would make an average annual loss in income of £248, plus over £300 p.a. in childcare support for those who needed it. Consequently the incentive to work was reduced, most of all for families with more than two children, those using paid childcare, and those working full-time.[43]

The vital support provided for lone parents by Gingerbread and other non-governmental organizations and their knowledge of the realities of their lives seemed to go unnoticed by the Prime Minister, though he had given a keynote lecture at Gingerbread's AGM in 2009, promising single parents that he was 'on their side'.[44] From the time of the election, he promoted the idea of the 'Big Society', a clarion call for more voluntary and community action, based apparently on the belief that it had been throttled by the Big Welfare State, but should be encouraged to grow again and, in its turn, squeeze out the state. The underlying assumption was challenged by official statistics, which showed that from 2001 to 2009 around 40 per cent of adults had volunteered in the past 12 months through formal voluntary organizations, while many more gave informal help to others in their neighbourhoods and communities.[45] We have seen the indispensable non-stop role of NCUMC, then OPF, then Gingerbread, through the whole history of the Welfare State, advising lone parents on entry to work, training, and access to benefits and legal advice, giving practical help and campaigning on their behalf, always working closely with public bodies. There was no sign that this activity was flagging, not least because the need for it had not gone away.[46]

BLAME AGAIN

Then in August 2011 came four days of riots, mainly by young men, in London and other English towns and cities. Again, Conservative politicians and some

[42] OECD, *Doing Better for Families*.

[43] T. Hortin and H. Reed, 'Analysis of the Impact of Tax Credit Changes on Working, Single Parents' (London: Gingerbread, 2011).

[44] NC Annual Report 2010, 13.

[45] *Citizenship Survey 2009–10, England* (22 July 2010), available at http://www.communities.gov.uk/publications/corporate/statistics/citizenshipsurveyq4200910.

[46] *Gingerbread: Single Parents, Equal Families*, http://gingerbread.org.uk.

media commentators rushed to blame the usual culprits—family breakdown, teen-age motherhood, welfare dependency—and to deny that poverty, inequality, or cuts to public benefits and services might have played a part. Before any evidence emerged about the backgrounds of the rioters, the Prime Minister claimed that 'many' of them came from 'families with no fathers at home', announcing: 'This is not about poverty, this is about culture' and that British society had been undergo-ing a 'slow-motion moral collapse over several generations'.[47]

However, like Margaret Thatcher, and perhaps trying to distance himself from the disrepute still attached to his party for the attacks on lone mothers in the 1990s, he focused blame on absent fathers, rather than mothers. Shortly before, on Father's Day 2011, he had attacked 'runaway dads' for 'leaving single mothers, who do a heroic job against all odds, to fend for themselves'.[48] Not everyone agreed. Melanie Phillips, in the *Daily Mail*, responded:

In line with politically correct thinking Mr Cameron presents such girls or women as the hapless victims of predatory males. But that is just plain wrong. For at the most fundamen-tal level, this whole process is driven by women and girls.

In those far-off days before the sexual revolution, relations between the sexes were based on a kind of unspoken bargain.

Women needed the father of their children to stick around while they grew up, in return for which a woman gave a solemn undertaking to be faithful to this one man.

For his part, the father's interests were served by being offered not just a permanent sex-ual relationship but a guarantee from the trust placed in his wife that the children were, indeed, his.

This idyllic—imagined—past had been undermined by 'the combination of the sexual revolution, the Pill and the welfare state'. Women in all classes were guilty, for 'Among upper-middle class trendies, marriage became an irksome anachronism and "living together" became fashionable', but the effects were most disastrous 'at the bottom of the social scale'.[49]

After the riots, Phillips returned to the assault:

At the very heart of these problems lies the breakdown of the family.

For most of these children [involved in the riots] come from lone-mother house-holds...Of course there are many lone parents who do a tremendous job. But we're talking here about widespread social collapse...successive generations are being brought up by mothers, through whose houses pass transitory males by whom these women have yet more children—and who inevitably repeat the pattern of lone and dysfunctional parenting.

For which she blamed the previous Labour Government, 'ultra-feminist wreckers', and the 'Welfare State, which conceives of need solely in terms of an absence of money, and which accordingly subsidized lone parenthood and the destructive

---

[47] *Daily Telegraph*, 11 Aug 2011.
[48] *Daily Telegraph*, 18 June 2011.
[49] Melanie Phillips, 'It's Not Just Absent Fathers, Mr Cameron. Family Breakdown Is Driven by Single Mothers on Benefits', *MailOnline*, 20 June 2011, available at http://www.dailymail.co.uk/debate/article-2005677/Family-breakdown-driven-single-mothers-benefits-absent-fathers.html.

behaviour that fatherlessness brings in its train'.[50] All this before any analysis was available of the actual social backgrounds, or motivations, of the rioters.

Gingerbread soberly pointed out some facts about single parents, as up to date as official statistics allowed, in place of the 'myths and labels'.[51] Almost a quarter—23 per cent—of households with dependent children were lone-parent families, including three million children, 24 per cent of all dependent children.[52] A few thousand people at most had been involved in the riots. Contrary to another stereotype, 90 per cent of single parents were white, 5 per cent black, 2 per cent Asian, and 3 per cent from other categories.[53] Only 2 per cent of single parents were teenagers. The median age for a single parent was 36.9. Fifty-five per cent had their children within marriage, a figure that had been stable for 10 years. Only 6 per cent of births were registered by the mother alone and 9 per cent by parents who lived apart.[54] As many as 56.7 per cent of lone parents were in work compared with 71 per cent of mothers in couples.[55] Once children were aged 12 or over the employment rate of lone mothers equalled that of partnered mothers,[56] but still 21 per cent of lone parents who worked full-time were in poverty.[57] Thirty-six per cent of unemployed single parents had a disability or long-standing illness and 30 per cent had a disabled child.[58] Such realities had little apparent impact on the dominant discourse around the riots.

CONCLUSION

Since 1918 so much had changed, yet so much had stayed the same. It was a kind of triumph that the National Council for the Unmarried Mother and Her Child, established with minimal voluntary funds to support a distinctly unpopular cause, survived for almost a century, becoming and remaining highly influential and, above all, giving essential support to generations of parents and their children. Its survival and adaptation to successive profound social, cultural, political, and

---

[50] Melanie Phillips, 'Britain's Liberal Intelligentsia Has Smashed Virtually Every Social Value', *MailOnline*, 11 Aug. 2011, available at http://www.dailymail.co.uk/debate/article-2024690/UK-riots-2011-Britains-liberal-intelligentsia-smashed-virtually-social-value.html.

[51] 'Gingerbread—Statistics—Facts and Figures', available at http://www.gingerbread.org.uk/content.aspx?CategoryID=365, accessed 21 Aug. 2011.

[52] General Household Survey 2007, table 3.7. Office for National Statistics (ONS), Labour Force Survey 2009, *Social Trends*, 40, ch. 2.

[53] *Families with Children in Britain*: findings from the 2007 Families and Children Study. DWP Research Report 578.

[54] ONS Statistical Bulletin, Dec. 2009.

[55] ONS Statistical Bulletin, Labour Market Statistics, June 2009, available at http://www.ons.gov.uk/ons/rel/lms/labour-market-statistics/june-2009/labour-market-statistics.pdf

[56] Analysis of Labour Force Survey data from April–June 2009, produced for Gingerbread, in V. Peacey, *Signing ON and Stepping Up? Single Parents' Experience of Welfare Reform* (London: Gingerbread, 2009).

[57] *Households Below Average Income: An Analysis of the Income Distribution 1994/5–2008–9*, (London: DWP, 2010), table 4.11ts.

[58] *Families with Children in Britain*.

economic changes is an impressive testimony to the indispensable role of voluntary action in British society alongside the emergence and growth of the Welfare State.

Yet its very survival testified to its failure to eradicate prejudice against single-parent families and their persistent disadvantage. These remain, as they were in 1918, among the poorest social groups whilst their numbers have grown. They also remain objects of prejudice and stereotyping, often blamed, not pitied, for their poverty and for a variety of socials ills and given little credit if they pulled out of poverty and brought up model children. This book has shown that prejudice was never universal. There have always been many open-minded people of all social groups who were tolerant of close relatives and others who did not attain contented marriage and family life, often for reasons beyond their control. Many people felt no inconsistency between accepting successful families headed by married parents as an ideal and recognizing that circumstances created other family forms that could, though not invariably, be highly successful, just as married partnerships could fail. For a long time, such views guided the everyday action of many people but were rarely expressed in public. From the later 1960s diverse family forms became pub-licly acceptable and unprecedented numbers of people lived in families with single parents, step-parents, and gay parents. But the old prejudices and stereotypes sur-vived in sections of the population, including parts of the political class, indeed were reinforced by their perception of these changes as 'family breakdown'.

A common justification for such views was that children growing up in one-parent families were more likely than others to fail at school, face trouble with the law, and suffer alcohol or drug addiction and unemployment. Even if this were so, it was never clear what could be done about it. Nowhere has any government succeeded in design-ing policies to persuade people to establish successful two-parent families. It also undervalues the strength and success of many less conventional families and misreads the evidence. Unmarried parenthood and partnership breakdown is and has always been most frequent among those on lowest incomes who experience most stress asso-ciated with deprivation, though it is by no means exclusive to them. Those born into the poorest families have the poorest outcomes in terms of education, employment, and a stable adult life, whether they live with two married parents or not. Measures to minimize inequality, starting from birth—such as Sure Start—are more likely to improve their life chances than attempts to promote marriage as a norm.[59]

The Welfare State failed to eliminate the serious inequalities that contributed to the difficulties of unmarried mothers and other single parents and their children, though they narrowed between 1945 and the 1970s. Throughout its history, the National Council, now Gingerbread, has drawn attention and when possible filled the gaps in state provision, working with the state (both local and central), not in competition with it. Without the hard and persistent work of this non-governmental organization, very many unmarried mothers and their children would have had even harder lives over the past century. Sadly, they remain desperately hard for all too many people.

[59] *Social Science and Family Polices* (London: British Academy, 2010).

Bibliography

ARCHIVAL SOURCES

The Women's Library, London Metropolitan University
Archive of National Council for the Unmarried Mother and Her Child/One Parent Families. The Women's Library, London Metropolitan University.
Papers of Helena Normanton.

Mass Observation Archive, University of Sussex
Mass Observation diarist 5245, Mass Observation Diaries 1939–45

The British Library of Political and Economic Science, London School of Economics
Minutes of the Finer Committee on One Parent Families, 1969–74
Richard Titmuss Papers

University of Lancaster Library
Elizabeth Roberts, interviews Lancaster and Barrow, 1890–1940

The National Archive
For details of documents consulted see chapter footnotes.

Parliamentary papers
Child Support Agency Annual Report and Account, HC 596 (1994–5).
Children Come First: The Government's Proposals on the Maintenance of Children, Cmd. 1264 (1990).
Department for Communities and Local Government, *Citizenship Survey 2009–10, England* (22 July 2010).
Department for Work and Pensions, *No-One Written Off: Reforming Welfare to Reward Responsibility*, Public consultation, Cm 7363 (2008).
Department of Health and Social Security, *Report of the Committee on One-Parent Families*, Cmnd 5629 (Finer Report, 1974).
Departments of State and Official Bodies, *Separation Allowances for Dependants of Unmarried Soldiers (or Widowers) during the War* (17 November 1914).
Department Office of National Statistics, *Families with Children in Britain*: Findings from the 2007 Families and Children Study *Statistical Bulletin* (December 2009).
Departmental Committee on Adoption Societies and Agencies, *First Annual Report: Ministry of Health, Parliamentary Papers*, 1920, vol. xvii, Cmd.5499 (1936–7).
Fifth Report of the Social Security Committee, *The Operation of the Child Support Act: Proposals for Change*, HC 470, 1993/4.
HM Treasury, *Taxation of Husband and Wife*, Cmnd 8093 (1980).
House of Commons Social Services Committee, *Perinatal and Neonatal Mortality* (1980).
Ministry of Social Security, *Circumstances of Families* (1967).
Office of National Statistics, *Birth Statistics*, 2002 series, FM1 31.
Papers of the Royal Commission on Population, vol. II: *Reports and Selected Papers of the Statistics Committee* (1950).

Registrar General's Statistical Review of England and Wales for the Six Years 1940–1945, Text, vol II: *Civil.*

Registrar General's Statistical Review of England and Wales for the year 1964, Part III: Commentary.

Report on the Administration of the National Relief Fund up to 31st March 1915, Cd 7756, Parliamentary Papers, 1914–16.

Report of the Committee on Amenities and Welfare Conditions in the Three Women's Services, Cmd 6384 (1942).

Report of Committee on Local Authority and Allied Personal Services, Cmnd 3703 (The Seebohm Report) (London: HMSO, 1968).

Report of the Inter-Departmental Committee on Abortion (1939).

Report of the Ministry of Health for the year ended 31 March 1948, Cmd 7734.

Report of the National Assistance Board for the year ended December 1949, Ministry of National Insurance, Cmd 8030 (1950).

Report of the Royal Commission on Divorce and Matrimonial Causes, Cd. 6478 (1912), Parliamentary Papers, Vol. 18.

Report of the Royal Commission on Marriage and Divorce, Cmd 9678 (1956).

Report of the Supplementary Benefit Commission for the year ended 1979 (1980).

Second Annual Report of the Ministry of Pensions, 1918/19, House of Commons Papers 39 (1920).

Social Insurance and Allied Services, report by Sir William Beveridge, Cmd 6404 (1942).

Social Security Committee, *The Operation of the Child Support Act,* HC 303 (1994/5).

Summary Report of the Ministry of Health for the year ended 31st March 1943, Cmd 6468.

INTERVIEWS

Pat Thane, interview with Richard Balfe (April 2008).

Tanya Evans, interview with Mary Bennett, daughter of H. A. L. and Lettice Fisher, Principal of St Hilda's College, Oxford, 1965–80 (5 February 2005).

Tanya Evans, Interview with Sue Slipman (14 July 2005).

Tanya Evans, interview with Catherine Porteous (July 2005).

Tanya Evans, interview with Rodney Bickerstaffe (27 June 2006).

Tanya Evans, interview with Balfe (July 2006).

WEBSITES

BBC, http://www.bbc.co.uk

Communities and Local Government, http://www.communities.gov.uk

Child Poverty Action Group, http://www.cpag.org.uk

Daycare Trust, http://www.daycaretrust.org.uk

Department for Work and Pensions, http://www.dwp.gov.uk

Institute for Fiscal Studies, http://www.ifs.org.uk

Gingerbread, http://www.gingerbread.org.uk

Grandparents Plus, http://www.grandparentsplus.org.uk

NEWSPAPERS AND PERIODICALS

Community Care
Daily Express

Daily Mail
Daily Mirror
Daily Telegraph
Guardian
Mail on Sunday
Manchester Guardian
New Statesman
News of the World
Star
Sunday Chronicle
Sunday Pictorial
The Independent
The Lancet
The Observer
The Times

THESES

Debenham, Marian Clare, 'Grassroots feminism: a study of the campaign of the Society for the Provision of Birth Control Clinics, 1934–1938', PhD thesis, University of Manchester (2010).

Glew, Helen, 'Women Workers in the Post Office, 1914–1939', PhD thesis, Institute of Historical Research, University of London (2010).

Moyse, Cordelia, 'Reform of Marriage and Divorce Law in England and Wales 1909–1937', PhD thesis, University of Cambridge (1996).

DISSERTATIONS

O'Brien, Daisy, 'In No Man's Land', MA Dissertation, Oxford University (2009).

Yelloly, M., 'Social Casework with Unmarried Parents', MA thesis, University of Liverpool (1964).

BOOKS AND BOOK CHAPTERS

Abel-Smith, Brian, and Peter Townsend, *The Poor and the Poorest* (London: George Bell, 1964).

Adams, Sally, 'Adams [*née* Campin], Mary Grace Agnes (1898–1984)', *Oxford Dictionary of National Biography* (Oxford: Oxford University Press, 2004).

Andrews, Maggie, *The Acceptable Face of Feminism: The Women's Institute as a Social Movement* (London: Lawrence and Wishart, 1997).

Atkinson, A. B., 'Distribution of Income and Wealth', in A. H. Halsey and J. Webb (eds), *Twentieth Century British Social Trends* (London: Macmillan, 2000), 348–84.

Baird, Julia, *Imagine This: Growing Up with My Brother John Lennon* (London: Hodder and Stoughton, 2007).

Barnes, Helen, Patricia Day, and Natalie Cronin, *Trial and Error: A Review of UK Child Support Policy* (London: Family Policy Studies Centre, 1998).

Behlmer, George K., *Child Abuse and Moral Reform in England, 1870–1908* (Stanford, CA: Stanford University Press, 1982).

—— 'Artificial Families: The Politics of Adoption', in *Friends of the Family: The English Home and its Guardians, 1850–1940* (Stanford: Stanford University Press, 1998), 272–316.

Bingham, Adrian, *Family Newspapers? Sex, Private Lives and the Popular Press, 1918–1979* (Oxford: Oxford University Press, 2009).

Black, Lawrence, 'There Was Something about Mary: The National Viewers' and Listeners' Association and Social Movement History', in N. Crowson, M. Hilton, and J. McKay (eds), *NGOs in Contemporary Britain: Non-state Actors in Society and Politics since 1945* (London: Palgrave, 2009), 182–200.

Booth, C., *Life and Labour of the People of London*, Final Volume: *Notes on Social Influences* (London: Macmillan, 1903).

Bourne, Joan, *Pregnant and Alone: The Unmarried Mother and her Child* (Royston: Priory Care and Welfare Library, 1971).

Bowlby, J., *Maternal Care and Mental Health*, 2nd edn (Geneva: World Health Organization, 1952).

Braybon, Gail, and Penny Summerfield, *Out of the Cage: Women's Experiences of Two World Wars* (London: Pandora, 1987).

Brewer, M., and G. Paull, *Newborns and New Schools: Critical Times in Women's Employment*, DWP Research Report 308 (London: TSO, 2007).

Caine, Barbara, *English Feminism 1780–1980* (Oxford: Oxford University Press, 1997).

Carey, Jane, '"Women's Objective—A Perfect Race": Whiteness, Eugenics and the Articulation of Race', in L. Boucher, J. Carey, and K. Elinnghaus (eds), *Re-Orientating Whiteness: Transnational Perspectives on the History of an Identity* (London: Palgrave, 2009).

Castle, Barbara, *Fighting All the Way* (London: Macmillan, 1993).

Clapton, Eric, *The Autobiography* (London: Broadway Books, 2007).

Cook, Hera, *The Long Sexual Revolution: English Women, Sex and Contraception, 1800–1975* (Oxford: Oxford University Press, 2004).

Corley, T. A. B., 'Wakefield, Charles Cheers, first Viscount Wakefield (1869–1941)', *Oxford Dictionary of National Biography* (Oxford: Oxford University Press, 2004).

Crafts, N., I. Gazeley, and A. Newell (eds), *Work and Pay in 20th Century Britain* (Oxford: Oxford University Press, 2007).

Crellin, E., M. Kellmer Pringle, and P. West, for National Children's Bureau, *Born Illegitimate* (London: National Foundation for Educational Research, 1971).

Cretney, Stephen, '"What Will the Women Want Next?" The Struggle for Power within the Family, 1925–1975', in *Law, Law Reform and the Family* (Oxford: Oxford University Press, 1998), 155–83.

—— *Family Law in the Twentieth Century: A History* (Oxford: Oxford University Press, 2003).

—— 'Finer, Sir Morris (1917–74)', *Oxford Dictionary of National Biography* (Oxford: Oxford University Press, 2004).

Crick, Bernard, *George Orwell: A Life* (London: Secker and Warburg, 1980).

Crowson, N., M. Hilton, and J. McKay (eds), *NGOs in Contemporary Britain: Non-state Actors in Society and Politics since 1945* (London: Palgrave, 2009).

Crozier, Andrew J., 'Chamberlain, (Arthur) Neville (1869–1940)', *Oxford Dictionary of National Biography* (Oxford: Oxford University Press, 2004–10).

Davidoff, L., M. Doolittle, J. Fink, and K. Holden, *The Family Story: Blood Contract and Intimacy, 1830–1960* (London: Longman, 1999).

De Montmorency, J. E. G., rev. Hugh Mooney, 'Barnes, John Gorell, first Baron Gorell (1848–1913)', *Oxford Dictionary of National Biography* (Oxford: Oxford University Press, 2004–9).

Dwork, D., *War Is Good for Babies and Other Young Children: A History of the Infant and Child Welfare Movement in England, 1898–1918* (London: Routledge, 1987).

Evans, Tanya, *'Unfortunate Objects': Lone Mothers in Eighteenth Century London* (London: Palgrave 2005).

—— 'Stopping the Poor Getting Poorer: The Establishment and Professionalization of Poverty NGOs, 1945–1995', in N. Crowson, M. Hilton, and J. McKay (eds), *NGOs in Contemporary Britain: Non-state Actors in Society and Politics since 1945* (London: Palgrave, 2009), 147–63.

Eyler, John M., 'Newsholme, Sir Arthur (1857–1943)', *Oxford Dictionary of National Biography* (Oxford: Oxford University Press, 2004).

Fairbairn, J. S., revised June Hannam, 'Champneys, Sir Francis Henry (1848–1930)', *Oxford Dictionary of National Biography* (Oxford: Oxford University Press, 2004).

Faithful, Lucy, 'Younghusband, Dame Eileen Louise (1902–81)', *Oxford Dictionary of National Biography* (Oxford: Oxford University Press, 2004).

Ferguson, S. M., and H. Fitzgerald, *History of the Second World War*, Studies in the Social Services (London: HMSO/Longmans, 1954).

Fisher, Mrs H. A. L., *Twenty-One Years* (London: NCUMotherHC, 1939).

Forster, Margaret, *Hidden Lives: A Family Memoir* (London: Penguin, 1996).

Frost, Ginger, *Living in Sin: Cohabiting as Husband and Wife in Nineteenth Century England* (Manchester: Manchester University Press, 2008).

Gillis, John, *For Better for Worse: British Marriages, 1600 to the Present* (Oxford: Oxford University Press, 1988).

Gingerbread, *Working but Losing* (April 2011), available at http://www.gingerbread.org.uk/uploads/media/28/7198.pdf.

—— 'Why Charge for a New Child Support Service?', *Gingerbread: Single Parents, Equal Families*, available at http://www.gingerbread.org.uk/content/577/Why-charge-for-a-new-child-support-service, accessed 22 Feb. 2011.

—— 'Gingerbread—Statistics—Facts and Figures', available at http://www.gingerbread.org.uk/content.aspx?CategoryID=365, accessed 21 Aug. 2011.

Glennerster, Howard, *British Social Policy since 1945* (Oxford: Blackwell, 1995).

Gorer, G., *Exploring English Character* (New York: Criterion Books, 1955).

Graham-Dixon, Sue, *Never Darken My Doorstep: Working for Single Parents and Their Children, 1918–1978* (London: NCOPF, 1981).

Hall, Lesley, *Sex, Gender and Social Change in Britain since 1880* (London: Macmillan, 2000).

Halsey, A. H. (ed.), *Trends in British Society since 1900* (London: Macmillan, 1972).

——'Titmuss, Richard, Morris (1907–73)',*Oxford Dictionary of National Biography* (Oxford:Oxford University Press,2004–11).

—— and J. Webb (eds), *Twentieth Century British Social Trends* (London: Macmillan, 2000).

Hannam, June, 'Pankhurst, (Estelle) Sylvia (1882–1960)', *Oxford Dictionary of National Biography* (Oxford: Oxford University Press, 2007).

Harris, Jose, *William Beveridge: A Biography*, 2nd edn (Oxford: Oxford University Press, 1997).

Hart, Jenifer, 'Ashby, Dame Margery Irene Corbett, 1882–1981', *Oxford Dictionary of National Biography* (Oxford: Oxford University Press, 2004–10).

Heron, Liz (ed.),*Truth, Dare or Promise? Girls Growing up in the 1950s.* (London: Virago, 1985).

Higginbotham, Anne R., 'Respectable Sinners: Salvation Army Rescue Work with Unmarried Mothers, 1884–1914', in Gail Malmgreen (ed.), *Religion in the Lives of English Women, 1760–1930* (London: Croom Helm, 1986).

Holden, Andrew, *Makers and Manners: Politics and Morality in Post-War Britain* (London: Politico's, 2004).

Holden, Katherine, *The Shadow of Marriage. Singleness in England, 1914–60* (Manchester: Manchester University Press, 2007).

Hortin, T., and H. Reed, 'Analysis of the Impact of Tax Credit Changes on Working, Single Parents' (London: Gingerbread, 2011).

Howe, A. C., 'Sanderson, (Julia Sarah) Anne Cobden- (1853–1926)', *Oxford Dictionary of National Biography* (Oxford: Oxford University Press, 2004–10).

Humphreys, Margaret, *Empty Cradles* (London: Doubleday, 1994), reissued as *Oranges and Sunshine: Empty Cradles* (2001).

Jones, Greta, 'Scharlieb, Mary Ann Dacomb (1845–1930)', *Oxford Dictionary of National Biography* (Oxford: Oxford University Press, 2004).

Jones, Helen (ed.), *Duty and Citizenship: The Correspondence and Papers of Violet Markham, 1896–1953* (London: The Historians' Press, 1994).

—— 'Markham, Violet Rosa (1872–1959)', *Oxford Dictionary of National Biography* (Oxford: Oxford University Press, 2004–9).

Jones, Kathleen, *Catherine Cookson* (London: Time Warner, 1999).

—— 'Cookson, Dame Catherine (1906–98)', *Oxford Dictionary of National Biography* (Oxford: Oxford University Press, 2004–9).

Keating, Jenny, *A Child for Keeps: The History of Adoption in England, 1918–45* (London: Palgrave, 2009).

Kenney, Catherine, 'Sayers, Dorothy Leigh (1893–1957)', *Oxford Dictionary of National Biography* (Oxford: Oxford University Press, 2004).

Kiernan, K., H. Land, and J. Lewis, *Lone Motherhood in Twentieth-Century Britain* (Oxford: Oxford University Press, 1998).

Kime, Bonnie Scott Andrews, 'Isabel, Dame Cicily [Rebecca West] (1892–1983)', *Oxford Dictionary of National Biography* (Oxford: Oxford University Press, 2008).

Labour Party, *National Superannuation: Labour's Policy for Security in Old Age* (London: The Labour Party, 1957).

Laslett, Peter, *Family Life and Illicit Love in Earlier Generations* (Cambridge: Cambridge University Press, 1978).

Last, Nella, *Nella Last's War: A Mother's Diary, 1939–1945* (London: Sphere Books, 1983).

Law, Cheryl, *Suffrage and Power: The Women's Movement, 1918–28* (London: I. B.Tauris, 1997).

Law Commission, *Illegitimacy*, Report 118 (1982).

Leneman, Leah, 'Phillips, Mary Elizabeth (1880–1969)', *Oxford Dictionary of National Biography* (Oxford: Oxford University Press, 2004–10).

Lewis, Jane, *The End of Marriage? Individualism and Intimate Relations* (Cheltenham: Edward Elgar, 2001).

—— 'Marriage', in Ina Zweiniger-Bargielowska (ed.), *Women in Twentieth-Century Britain* (Harlow: Pearson Education, 2001), 69–85.

Llewelyn Davies, Margaret (ed.), *Life as We Have Known It, by Co-operative Working Women* (London: Hogarth Press 1931, repr. London: Virago, 1977).

Logan, Anne, *Feminism and Criminal Justice: A Historical Perspective* (London: Palgrave, 2008).

Macaskill, Hilary, *From the Workhouse to the Workplace: 75 Years of One-Parent Family Life, 1918–1993* (London: NCOPF, 1993).

McGregor, O. R., *Divorce in England* (London: Heinemann, 1957).

—— L. Blom-Cooper, and C. Gibson, *Separated Spouses: A Study of the Matrimonial Jurisdiction of Magistrates Courts* (London: Duckworth, 1970).

McKay, J., and M. Hilton, 'Introduction', in N. Crowson, M. Hilton, and J. McKay (eds), *NGOs in Contemporary Britain: Non-state Actors in Society and Politics since 1945* (London: Palgrave, 2009), 1–20.

Maclean, Mavis, with Jacek Kurzewski, *Making Family Law: A Socio-Legal Account of Legislative Process in England and Wales, 1985–2010* (Oxford: Hart, 2011).

Marris, Peter, *Widows and Their Families* (London: Routledge and Kegan Paul, 1958).

Marsden, Dennis, *Mothers Alone: Poverty and the Fatherless Family* (London: Allen Lane 1969; 2nd edn, 1971).

Meehan, Elizabeth, 'British Feminism from the 1960s to the 1980s', in H. L. Smith (ed.), *British Feminism in the Twentieth Century* (Aldershot: Edward Elgar, 1990), 189–204.

Morley, Sheridan, 'Cooper, Dame Gladys Constance, 1888–1971', *Oxford Dictionary of National Biography* (Oxford: Oxford University Press, 2004–10).

Mort, Frank, *Capital Affairs. London and the Making of the Permissive Society* (New Haven, CT: Yale University Press, 2010).

Moyse, Cordelia, 'Fisher, Lettice (1875–1956)', *Oxford Dictionary of National Biography* (Oxford: Oxford University Press, 2004).

National Birth-Rate Commission, *The Declining Birth-Rate: Its Causes and Effects* (London: Chapman and Hall, 1916).

National Council for the Unmarried Mother and Her Child (NCUMC), *Homes and Hostels of the Future: Report of a Conference arranged by the NCUMC* (London: NCUMC, 1945).

—— *Forward for the Fatherless* (London: NCUMC, 1971).

Neville-Rolfe, Sybil, *Social Biology and Welfare* (London: George Allen and Unwin, 1949).

Nicolson, Jill, *Mother and Baby Homes* (London: Allen and Unwin, 1968).

OECD, *Doing Better for Families* (April 2011) http://www.oecd.org/social/family/doing-better, accessed 28 April 2011.

Oldfield, Sybil, 'Macmillan, (Jessie) Chrystal, 1872–1937', *Oxford Dictionary of National Biography* (Oxford: Oxford University Press, 2004–10).

Pankhurst, Richard, *Sylvia Pankhurst, Artist and Crusader: An Intimate Portrait* (London/New York: Paddington Press/Virago, 1979).

Parr, Joy, *Labouring Children: British Immigrant Apprentices to Canada, 1869–1924* (London: Croom Helm, 1980).

Parrinder, Patrick, 'Wells, Herbert George (1866–1946)', *Oxford Dictionary of National Biography* (Oxford: Oxford University Press, 2008).

Parry, Colin J., 'Lambert, Dame Florence Barraclough (1871–1957)', *Oxford Dictionary of National Biography* (Oxford: Oxford University Press, 2004–10).

Peacey, V., *Signing On and Stepping Up? Single Parents' Experience of Welfare Reform* (London: Gingerbread, 2009).

Phillips, Roderick, *Putting Asunder: A History of Divorce In Western Society* (Cambridge: Cambridge University Press 1988).

Pick, D., *Faces of Degeneration: A European Disorder, c.1848-c.1918* (Cambridge: Cambridge University Press, 1998).

Pinker, Robert, 'McGregor, Oliver Ross, Baron McGregor of Durris (1921–97)', *Oxford Dictionary of National Biography* (Oxford: Oxford University Press, 2004).

Pizzey, Erin, *Scream Quietly or the Neighbours Will Hear You* (1974; repub. London: Enslow, 1978).

Prescott, P., *Smile Though Your Heart is Breaking* (London: Harper Collins, 2010).

Pugh, Martin, *Women and the Women's Movement in Britain*, 2nd edn (London: Macmillan, 2000).

Reynolds, Barbara, *Dorothy Sayers: Her Life and Soul* (London: Hodder & Stoughton, 1993).

Reynolds, David, *Rich Relations: the American Occupation of Britain, 1942–1945* (New York: Random House, 1995).

Richardson, Angelique, 'Neville-Rolfe, Sybil Katherine (1885–1955)', *Oxford Dictionary of National Biography* (Oxford: Oxford University Press, 2004).

Riley, Denise, *War in the Nursery: Theories of the Child and the Mother* (London: Virago, 1983).

Roberts, Elizabeth, *A Woman's Place: An Oral History of Working Class Women, 1890–1940* (Oxford: Blackwell, 1995).

—— *Women and Families: An Oral History 1940–1970* (Oxford: Blackwell, 1995).

Roberts, Robert, *The Classic Slum: Salford Life in the First Quarter of the Century* (Manchester: Manchester University Press, 1971).

Rose, Sonya O., *Which People's War? National Identity and Citizenship in Wartime Britain, 1939–1945* (Oxford: Oxford University Press, 2003).

Ross, E., *Love and Toil: Motherhood in Outcast London, 1870–1918* (Oxford: Oxford University Press, 1993).

Ryan, Alan, 'Fisher, Herbert Albert Laurens (1865–1940)', *Oxford Dictionary of National Biography* (Oxford: Oxford University Press, 2004).

Sage, Lorna, *Bad Blood* (London: Fourth Estate, 2001).

Scharlieb, Mary, *Reminiscences* (London: Williams and Norgate, 1924).

Searle, G., *The Quest for National Efficiency* (Oxford: Blackwell, 1971).

—— *Eugenics and Politics in Britain, 1900–1914* (Leyden: Noordhoff International, 1976).

Searle. G. R., 'Saleeby, Caleb Williams Elijah (1878–1940)', *Oxford Dictionary of National Biography* (Oxford: Oxford University Press, 2004).

Single Parent Action Network, *Positive Images Negative Stereotypes* (Bristol: SPAN, 1998).

Spence, Sir James, et al., *A Thousand Families in Newcastle-upon-Tyne* (Oxford: Oxford University Press, 1954).

Steedman, Carolyn, *Landscape for a Good Woman: A Story of Two Lives* (London: Virago, 1986).

Stern, G. B., *Trumpet Voluntary* (London: Cassell, 1944).

Stewart, K., 'Towards an Equal Start? Addressing Childhood Poverty and Deprivation', in J. Hills and K. Stewart (eds), *A More Equal Society? New Labour, Poverty, Inequality and Exclusion* (Bristol: Policy Press, 2005), 143–65.

Sturdy, Steve, 'Robertson, Sir John (1862–1936)', *Oxford Dictionary of National Biography* (Oxford: Oxford University Press, 2004–10).

Szreter, S., and K. Fisher, *Sex before the Sexual Revolution: Intimate Life in England, 1918–1963* (Cambridge: Cambridge University Press, 2010).

Thane, Pat, 'Labour and Welfare', in D. Tanner, P. Thane, and N. Tiratsoo (eds), *Labour's First Century* (Cambridge: Cambridge University Press, 2000), 80–118.

—— 'What Difference Did the Vote Make ?', in Amanda Vickery (ed.), *Women, Privilege and Power: British Politics 1750 to the Present* (Stanford, CA: Stanford University Press, 2001), 253–88.

—— *Happy Families? History and Family Policy* (London: British Academy, 2010).

—— (ed.), *Unequal Britain: Equalities in Britain since 1945* (London: Continuum, 2010).

Thatcher, Margaret, *The Downing Street Years* (London: Harper Collins, 1995).

Thomson, Matthew, *The Problem of Mental Deficiency: Eugenics, Democracy and Social Policy in Britain 1870–1959* (Oxford: Oxford University Press, 1998).

Timmins, Nicolas, *The Five Giants: A Biography of the Welfare State* (London: Fontana, 1996).

Tomlinson, Jim, 'Labour and the Economy', in D. Tanner, P. Thane, and N. Tiratsoo (eds), *Labour's First Century* (Cambridge: Cambridge University Press, 2000), 46–79.

Townsend, P., *Poverty in the United Kingdom* (Harmondsworth: Penguin, 1979).

Townsend, Peter, 'Smith, Brian Abel- (1926–96)', *Oxford Dictionary of National Biography* (Oxford: Oxford University Press, 2004–11).

Toynbee, P., and D. Walker, *The Verdict: Did Labour Change Britain?* (London: Granta, 2010).

Weale, A., B. Bradshaw, A. Maynard, and D. Piachaud, *Lone Mothers, Paid Work and Social Security* (London: Bedford Square Press, 1984).

West, Anthony, 'Introduction', in *Heritage*, 2nd edn (London: Coronet, 1984).

——*H. G. Wells: Aspects of a Life* (New York: Random House, 1984).

Willetts, D., *The Pinch* (London: Atlantic, 2010).

Wilson, Elizabeth, *Women and the Welfare State* (London: Tavistock, 1977).

Wimperis, V., *The Unmarried Mother and Her Child* (London: George Allen and Unwin, 1960).

Wrigley, Chris, 'Bevin, Ernest (1891–1951)', *Oxford Dictionary of National Biography* (Oxford: Oxford University Press, 2004–9).

Wynn, Margaret, *Fatherless Families* (London: Michael Joseph, 1964).

Younghusband, E. L., *Social Work and Social Change* (London: Allen and Unwin, 1964).

ARTICLES

Cassie, Ethel, 'The Care of Illegitimate Children', *Public Health*, 57 (February 1944).

Cobbe, F. P., 'Wife-Torture in England', *Contemporary Review*, 32 (1878), 55–87.

Evans, Tanya, and Pat Thane, 'Secondary Analysis of Dennis Marsden's *Mothers Alone*', *Methodological Innovations Online*, 1:2 (2006).

Field, Frank, 'How Good a Model is FIS for a Means-Tested GMA?', *Poverty*, 31 (1975), 17–22.

Fink, Janet, 'For Better or For Worse? The Dilemmas of Unmarried Motherhood in Mid-Twentieth Century Popular British Film and Fiction', *Women's History Review*, 20:1 (February 2011), 145–60.

Frost, Ginger, ' "The Black Lamb of the Black Sheep": Illegitimacy in the English Working Class, 1850–1939', *Journal of Social History*, 37 (2003), 293–322.

—— ' "Revolting to Humanity": Oversights, Limitations and Complications of the English Legitimacy Act of 1926', *Women's History Review*, 20:1 (February 2011), 31–46.

Greenland, C., 'Unmarried Parenthood: Ecological Aspects', *Lancet* (19 January 1957), 148–51.

—— 'Unmarried Parenthood: I—Unmarried Mothers', *Medical Officer*, 99 (1958), 265–72.

—— 'Unmarried Parenthood: II—Putative Fathers', *Medical Officer*, 99 (1958), 281–6.

Grey, Daniel J. R., 'Women's Policy Networks and the Infanticide Act, 1922', *Twentieth Century British History*, 21:40 (2010), 441–63.

Klein, Joanne, 'Irregular Marriages: Unorthodox Working Class Domestic Life in Liverpool, Birmingham and Manchester, 1900–1939', *Journal of Family History*, 2 (2005), 210–29.

Land, H., 'Slaying Idleness without Killing Care: A Challenge for the British Welfare State', *Social Policy Review*, 21 (2009).

Langhamer, Claire, 'Adultery in Post-war England', *History Workshop Journal*, 62 (Autumn 2006), 86–115.

Lewis, Jane, and John Welshman, 'The Issue of Never-Married Motherhood in Britain, 1920–70', *Social History of Medicine*, 10:3 (December 1997), 401–18.

Lowe, Rodney, 'The Rediscovery of Poverty and the Creation of the Child Poverty Action Group, 1962–68', *Contemporary Record*, 9:3 (Winter 1995), 602–11.

Lowe R., and P. Nicolson (eds), 'The Formation of the Child Poverty Action Group', Witness Seminar, *Contemporary Record*, 9:3 (Winter 1995), 612–37.

Luddy, M., 'Unmarried Mothers in Ireland, 1880–1973', *Women's History Review*, 20:1 (February 2011), 109–26.

McCarthy, Helen, and Pat Thane, 'The Politics of Association in Industrial Society', *Twentieth Century British History*, 22:2 (2011), 217–29.

Macdonald, E. K., 'Follow-up of Illegitimate Children', *Medical Officer*, 196 (1956), 361–5.

Morgan, R. I. 'The Introduction of Civil Legal Aid in England and Wales', *Twentieth Century British History*, 5 (1994), 38–86.

Political and Economic Planning (PEP), 'The Unmarried Mother', *Planning*, no. 255 (1946).

Probert, R., 'Cohabitation in Twentieth Century England and Wales: Law and Policy', *Law and Policy*, 26 (2004), 273–88.

Savage, Gail, 'Erotic Stories and Public Decency: Newspaper Reporting of Divorce Proceedings in England', *Historical Journal*, 41 (1998), 511–28.

Thompson, B., 'Social Study of Illegitimate Maternities', *British Journal of Preventive and Social Medicine*, 10 (1956), 75–87.

Thompson, Derek, 'Courtship and Marriage between the Wars', *Oral History*, 3:2 (1975), 42–3.

Townsend, Peter, 'Measuring Poverty', *British Journal of Sociology* (June 1954), 130–7.

—— 'Problem of Introducing a Guaranteed Maintenance Allowance for One Parent Families', *Poverty*, 31 (1975), 21–39.

Index

abandoned mothers 94–5, 98, 116, 133
Abbot, D. C. H. 142–3
Abel-Smith, Brian 123–4, 129–30, 162
abortion 39, 83
  illegal 23, 64, 74
  legalization 3, 86, 128, 135
Abortion Law Reform Association 23
abuse *see* domestic violence
Adams, Mary 113
adoption 23, 37, 60, 62, 69, 79–81, 96, 193
  Adoption Acts 43, 64, 79, 98
  agencies 65
  informal 26
  law 79–81, 96–100
  legalization 16, 27, 49
  numbers 43, 88, 103, 134
  orders 43, 51–2, 97
  overseas 77
adultery 8, 29, 34, 49–50, 85–6, 95–6
advice 15, 66, 70, 97, 99, 177, 179
  financial 176
  legal 68, 144, 203, 205
  newspaper columns 114, 119, 175
affiliation orders 78, 110–11, 114, 123
alcoholism 7, 27, 208
armed forces
  Armed Women's Social Services Section 26
  Auxiliary Territorial Service (ATS) 65, 68, 73
  Women's Army Auxiliary Corps (WAAC) 66
  Women's Auxiliary Air Force (WAAF) 65, 67–8
  Women's Royal Naval Service (WRNS) 68
Astor, Nancy 23, 51
August riots 205

baby farmers 25, 27
'back to basics' 164, 187–93
Barnardos 26, 44, 143, 176
Barraclough Lambert, Florence 21
Bastardy Acts 15, 22, 29, 31, 47, 49–50
Bates, Doreen 71–3
BBC 43, 91, 98, 113, 117, 136, 190–1
bedsits 138
Bennett, Mary 18 n. 66, 19 n. 67
Beveridge, William 78–9, 106–7, 110, 123, 128
Bevin, Ernest 33
Bickerstaffe, Rodney 94–5
'Big Society' 205
Birmingham 14, 20–1, 57–8, 61–2, 81, 90
birth certificate 6–7, 51, 54, 108–9
birth control 22–3, 39–40, 87
blackmail 48, 99
blood tests 30, 49, 111, 165
Bottomley, Virginia 105

Bowlby, John 1, 3, 82, 85, 92–5, 97, 143
Bowyer, Captain 50
Boyson, Rhodes 171
Bramall, Margaret 144, 167
'broken Britain' 1, 200
Brown, Gordon 195–6

Cameron, David 199–200, 206
Cardiff 187, 190
Castle, Barbara 162–7
Chamberlain, Neville 21, 31, 43, 47–50, 52, 61
charity 16, 32–3, 63, 106, 114, 137
Charity Organisation Society 80
Chesser, Eustace 86
child and maternal welfare services 25, 32,
    58–9, 66–7, 70, 98, 109, 156
Child Benefit 164, 167, 175, 195–6, 199, 205
  Child Benefit Act 1975 164
  Save Child Benefit campaign 176
Child Poverty Action Group (CPAG) 124, 161,
    167, 175–6, 186, 199
Child Support Acts 183–7
Child Support Agency 184–7, 193–4, 197–8,
    200–2, 204
Child Tax Credit 197, 204
Child Welfare Council (CWC) 15
childbirth 12, 23–5, 57, 107, 147
childcare 194–5, 197, 200
  allowance 153, 181, 196
  availability 58, 95, 102, 112, 155, 180,
    188, 197
  costs 177–9
  employment 26, 33, 150–1
children
  adopted 26–7, 81, 99
  Children Acts 33, 100, 168
  numbers of illegitimate children 6, 12, 62,
    170, 207
  poverty 128, 205
  protection 34, 203
Church of England Moral Welfare Council 59,
    60, 62, 80, 91, 109
churches 14, 21, 40, 44, 49–50, 56, 60–1, 85,
    98, 104, 113, 177
Circular 2866 60–3, 107
citizenship 19, 53, 99
civil service 34, 71–3, 134–5, 155
Clapton, Eric 75, 93
Clarke, Kenneth 193
class
  middle 25, 39–43, 71, 73, 87, 104, 127,
    136, 206
  upper 39, 86

class (*cont.*)
  working 33, 37–9, 42–3, 49, 75, 83, 87, 194, 126
Cobden-Sanderson, Anne 20
cohabitation 8–13, 34–5, 51, 85, 88, 90–2, 127, 153–65, 192
  and NAB/SBC 110, 129–30, 141, 149–50
  numbers 88–9, 170
conception 54, 55, 132
Conservative Party 144, 183, 187, 191
Cookson, Catherine 7–8, 35, 39, 75, 93
Cretney, Stephen 168, 182–3
Crossman, Richard 130, 140, 142, 162
custody 92, 98, 183

desertion 8, 11, 34, 130
Department of Health and Social Security 140, 143–6, 148, 150, 152, 154, 162, 167, 177–9, 181, 184
Department of Social Security 184, 189, 193
Department for Work and Pensions 200
Devlin, Bernadette 137
divorce 8, 11, 85, 90, 95, 104, 132, 142, 147, 192, 203
  numbers 120–1, 146, 150
divorce law 8, 10, 11, 34, 49, 41, 113, 141, 146, 190
Divorce Law Reform Union 10, 20, 34
domestic service 26, 36, 69, 122
domestic violence 7, 10, 26–7, 84, 101, 160, 184, 201, 203–4
Domestic Violence and Matrimonial Proceedings Act, 1976 166
Duncan Smith, Iain 199–200

European Court of Human Rights (ECHR) 182
European Economic Community (ECC) 175, 179
emigration 26, 46
employers 32, 45, 69, 137, 159–60, 175, 180–1, 197
employment 82, 112, 138
  Employment Act 1988 180
  Employment Protection Act, 1975 166
  employment rates of lone parents 175, 178, 196, 207
  opportunities 87, 169, 174, 205
  part-time 118, 147, 150, 160, 178, 197
  unemployment 13, 161, 164
Equal Pay Act, 1970 147, 155, 180
equality 8, 10–11, 46, 124, 147, 155–6, 169, 194, 206, 208
eugenics 15, 19–20

Family Credit 181, 186, 195
Family Income Supplement 131, 177
family law 141, 158, 165–6, 168, 182–3
Family Planning Act, 1967 120

Family Planning Association 120
'family values' 193–4
fathers
  absent 30, 187, 206
  'feckless' 183, 188
  financial responsibility 47–8, 128, 142, 151, 194
  foreign 30, 50, 115
  protests against the CSA 186–7, 198
  rights 92, 183
feminism 15, 23
Ferguson and Fitzgerald 56, 63, 70–1, 107
Field, Frank 161, 167
filius nullius 27
Finer Joint Action Committee (FJAC) 165
Finer, Morris 130, 140
Finer Report
  committee 141–3
  conclusions 158–60
  NCOPF evidence 143–6
  responses to 161–7
First World War 11, 13–14, 26, 42, 91
Fisher, H. A. L. 18, 50
Fisher, Lettice 14, 18–19, 43
Forster, Margaret 87
Forward for the Fatherless 140, 157
fostering 25–7, 33, 38, 61, 64, 102, 113
  effects on children 95
  foster parents 14, 33, 42, 58, 61–2, 68–9, 76, 95, 111, 116, 173
Fothergill, Tess 136
Fowler, Norman 176
fraud 130, 199

Germany 115
Gingerbread 136–7, 144, 146, 162, 165, 167
  merger with OPF 198, 201–8
Gorell of Brampton, 1st Baron Gorell (John Gorell Barnes) 11
Gorell of Brampton, 2nd Baron Gorell (Henry Gorell Barnes) 11
Gorell of Brampton, 3rd Baron Gorell (Ronald Gorell Barnes) 113
Gorer, Geoffrey 86
gossip 6, 38, 54, 139
Gowing, Warden 47
grandparents 7, 27, 35–9, 61–2, 75, 88, 92–5, 135, 197
Granger, Isabelle 115
Greenland, Cyril 89–90
Greenwood, Margaret 47
Gummer, John 189

Hay Davidson, Ian 180, 192
Hayman, Helene 164–5
Home, Evelyn (real name Peggy Makins) 87, 113
Home Office 23, 48, 80
Homelessness (government circular 1974) 154
Horsbrugh, Florence 64

housing
  council housing 112, 126–7, 138, 159, 166,
    171–2, 189–90, 193
  Housing (Homeless Act) 1977 166
  landlord hostility 33, 111, 126

Income Support 178, 181–2, 195, 199
infant mortality 14–15, 19, 25, 46, 54, 61, 107
infanticide 25, 51
inheritance 27, 41, 48, 50, 96, 99, 165
Inland Revenue 111, 123, 152, 186
internationalism 23, 45
Ireland/Irish unmarried mothers 30, 45, 94,
    136, 173

Job Seeker's Allowance 195
juvenile delinquency 123, 170

Labour Party 22, 49, 52, 143, 147
Lawson, Nigel 171
legal aid 11, 144, 203
legitimacy 50–1, 92, 95–6
Leicester 51, 88
Lennon, John 79
'Let's lose the labels' 198
Levin, Jenny 167
Lilley, Peter 187, 189, 191, 193
Litvin, Ray 42
Liverpool 191–2
Lloyd, Stephan 144
local authorities 63–5, 79, 81, 95
  co-operation with voluntary
    organizations 60–3, 109
  services 21, 46, 52, 107–9, 120, 156–7
London County Council 21, 32, 100
Long, Pauline 73
Lord Chancellor's Office 91, 182, 184

Macmillan, Chrystal 20, 47
magistrates 10, 29–30, 48, 52, 97, 100, 165
maintenance 141, 144, 146, 150–3, 183–7,
    200–5
  benefit system 110–11, 131, 149, 184
  Child Maintenance and Enforcement
    Commission (CMEC) 198, 200
  Guaranteed Maintenance Allowance 152–3,
    159, 161, 164, 166
  numbers receiving 174, 183, 200
  see also Child Support Agency; separation orders
Major, John 143, 183, 191
Markham, Violet 66, 77
Marsden, Dennis 125–8, 131, 144–5, 167
Mass Observation 71, 73–4
maternity benefits 107, 110, 159, 177
maternity leave 156, 160, 166, 197
Mathieson, Hilda 43
Matrimonial Causes Acts 10, 34
McEwan, Ian 79
McGregor, Oliver Ross 141–3, 145–6, 149,
    154, 171, 180, 182, 183

media 16, 49, 60, 80, 98, 102, 125, 136, 179,
    188–9, 193
medical profession 18, 59, 63, 80, 86, 98, 114,
    126, 143
Mental Deficiency Act 24
Ministry of Health 19–21, 36, 45, 57, 59,
    62–6, 68, 70, 76, 79, 80, 88, 107, 109,
    113, 122, 128, 157
Ministry of Health and Social Security 128
Ministry of Labour 63, 69
Moore, John 181
moral panic 54–81, 83–6, 191, 132, 147
mother and baby homes 60–2, 66, 68–9, 92,
    97, 99, 107, 117, 156–60
Mothers in Action 143, 146

National Assistance Board (NAB) 108, 125,
    110–11, 129–30, 132, 142, 145, 149,
    150, 162
National Children's Bureau 121
National Council for Maternity and Child
    Welfare 17
National Council for the Unmarried Mother
    and her Child (NC) /National Council for
    One Parent Families (NCOPF) /One
    Parent Families (OPF)
  aims and founding 14–16
  assistance to parents 25, 32, 36, 45, 76, 95,
    97, 172, 174–80, 187
  campaigns 16, 21, 31, 46–53, 76, 96–7,
    108, 111–12, 131–2, 138, 140, 165, 171,
    175–6, 180–3, 198, 202–5
  co-operation with state 60, 62–4, 66–8
  finances and fundraising 43–4, 109, 112,
    114, 117, 162
  leadership 18–20, 171
  OPF/Gingerbread merger 198, 201–8
  political support 21, 67
  publicity 43–4, 47, 98, 100, 113–14,
    136–17, 125, 165
  renaming as NCOPF 164
  research 89–90, 141, 157, 172
National Council of Women 21, 51, 143
National Society for the Prevention of Cruelty
    to Children 27
National Union of Societies for Equal
    Citizenship 17, 20, 22–3, 49, 51
nationality 45–6, 50, 67, 96, 115, 183
Neville Rolfe, Sybil 15, 19
Nevitt, Della 144
Newcastle 88–9
Newsholme, Arthur 20
nurseries 58, 60–3, 64, 69, 87, 123, 138, 175

orphanages 26
Orwell, George 81

Pankhurst, Sylvia 41–2
Panorama programme, 'Babies on Benefit' 190
Parker, John 96

paternity 29, 31, 48, 76, 89, 111, 165, 183
'permissive society' 120–39, 147–8
Phillips, Mary 20
pill 120, 139, 206; *see also* birth control
Poor Law 20–1, 27, 52, 61, 153, 176
    institutions 32, 59, 66, 68, 71
    relief 31, 106, 108
Poor Persons Procedure 11
pregnancy 13, 23, 35, 39, 72, 110, 194
prejudice 72, 76, 131–2, 137, 171, 208
    from public officials 155
premarital sex 2
Prescott, John 102
Prescott, Pauline (Tilston) 101–2, 115
Proops, Marjorie 143, 175
prostitution 86, 176
Public Assistance 59, 61, 70, 78
public attitudes 87, 133–4, 168, 171, 194
putative father 29, 95, 99, 153, 159
Puxley, Zoe 60, 63, 112–13

race 45, 76–7, 104, 116–17, 126, 158
rape 8, 13, 27, 39, 45, 51, 56, 84, 184
Redwood, John 187, 190, 193
Registrar General 14, 54–6, 73, 132–3, 148
religious organizations 33, 156
Roberts, Elizabeth 35, 68
Robertson, John 20, 61, 74
Royal Commission on Divorce and Matrimonial
    Causes (Gorell Commission), 1910–12 11
Royal Commission on Marriage and Divorce
    (Morton Commission), 1952–4 95–6
Royal Family 44, 77
rural 6, 59, 83, 75, 104

Sage, Lorna 104–5
Salvation Army 7, 21, 25–6, 44, 51, 62
Saleeby, C. W. 19–20
Sayers, Dorothy L. 41
Scharlieb, Mary 20–1
schoolgirls 83, 133, 141, 160, 175; *see also*
    teenagers
Scotland 6 n. 1, 8, 26, 47–8, 76, 89, 108, 155,
    157, 170
    Scottish National Council for the Unmarried
        Mother and her Child 76
scroungers 169, 190
Second World War 11, 13, 18, 54–82, 147, 177
separation 16, 31, 39, 57, 96, 122, 142, 147,
    150, 186, 202
    allowances 12, 91
    orders 10, 12, 123, 146
servicemen 12–13, 56–7, 76–8, 114
servicewomen 58, 65–70
Sex Discrimination Act 1975 160
Sex Disqualification Act 1919 52
sex education 20
sexual behaviour 13, 56, 133, 147
shame 9, 22, 27, 37, 39, 48, 51, 53, 71, 101,
    122, 126, 128, 133, 136, 145, 148

Shepherd, Gillian 181
Short, Claire 103–5
sickness benefit 64, 107–8, 151
Six Point Group 20, 22, 49, 51
Slipman, Sue 179, 181, 189, 191, 192, 193
Social Fund 177
social research 82, 87, 91, 93–5, 127
Social Security Acts 130, 149, 165, 175,
    183, 184
social stigma 6–8, 75, 79, 85, 122, 128–9, 156,
    171, 173, 193, 194, 198
social surveys
    Family Expenditure Survey 123–4, 150
    General Household Survey 145
social workers 60–1, 64, 69, 82, 91–2, 95, 97,
    100, 107, 114, 115–16, 121, 122, 138,
    149, 155–8, 166, 188
Soldiers', Sailors' and Airmen's Help Society
    (SSAHS) 66, 68
Steedman, Carolyn 90–1
Stross, Lady 144
students 43, 89, 103, 105
suicide 43
Summerskill, Edith 128
Supplementary Benefits Commission 129,
    135–6, 141, 144–5, 159, 166,
    174–5, 178

teenagers 56, 83–4, 93, 101, 132–3, 148, 169,
    172, 188, 190, 192, 194, 198, 207
Thatcher, Margaret 165, 167, 169, 172,
    183, 206
Titmuss, Richard 123, 129–30, 142–4, 146,
    149, 152–4, 162
tolerance 34, 37–9, 86, 103, 121–34, 169, 194
Townsend, Peter 123–5, 129–30, 161
trade unions
    National Union of Women Teachers 51
    Trades Union Congress 143
training/re-training for employment 46,
    59, 69, 99, 117–18, 123, 128, 138,
    155, 160, 175, 179–81, 195–7,
    201, 205
    Employment Training Schemes 178–80
Treasury 63, 64, 66, 72, 163, 164, 184, 193
TV programme, *Women Alone* 114

Unmarried (documentary film) 44
'unmarried wives' 12, 91

victimization 40
Victorian values 169
voluntary action 18, 109–14, 118, 146, 178
voluntary organisations 14, 18, 47, 60–3, 65,
    68, 70, 79, 94, 109, 112, 122, 125, 136,
    157, 160, 175, 205

war workers 58, 63–6, 79
Ward, Irene 67, 80
wartime separation 54–8, 71, 74, 96

Waterhouse, Keith 188–9
welfare state 78, 106–9, 114, 117, 119, 123, 177, 188, 194, 205–6, 208
West, Rebecca 41
Whitehouse, Mary 136
widows 12–13, 16, 33, 85, 88, 105, 11, 121–3, 126, 128–9, 131, 146, 150–2, 163, 170, 179, 192
Willetts, David 188
Wolfenden Committee on prostitution 86

Woman Power Committee 80
Women's Citizens Association 46
Women's Cooperative Guild 16, 22, 51
Women's Freedom League 51–2
Women's Liberation Movement 147, 160
women's magazines 45, 87, 99, 119
workhouse 24–7, 31, 74, 107
Wynn, Margaret 122–3, 125–6, 144, 150, 152

Younghusband, Eileen 122

Printed and bound by CPI Group (UK) Ltd, Croydon, CR0 4YY